Ramsay MacMullen

Why Do We Do What We Do? Motivation in History and the Social Sciences

Ramsay MacMullen

Why Do We Do What We Do?

Motivation in History and the Social Sciences

Managing Editor: Anna Michalska

DE GRUYTER
OPEN

Published by De Gruyter Open Ltd, Warsaw/Berlin
Part of Walter de Gruyter GmbH, Berlin/Munich/Boston

ISBN: 978-3-11-041758-6
e-ISBN: 978-3-11-041759-3

Bibliographic information published by the Deutsche Nationalbibliothek. The Deutsche Nationalbibliothek lists this publication in the Deutsche Nationalbibliografie; detailed bibliographic data are available in the Internet at http://dnb.dnb.de.

Managing Editor: Anna Michalska

www.degruyteropen.com

Cover illustration: © Thinkstock/Evgeny Sergeev

Ramsay MacMullen writes with courage, authority and effect. Few have had the nerve to ask the large question, few could have approached it with the breadth of a distinguished historian who has reflected at length on the social sciences, few can write with his openness and independence of mind, and few have arrived at such an interesting answer. It does MacMullen scant justice to say that he connects what people think with what they feel; relates each to the irreducibly social nature of their lives, and with telling examples, suggests how the cultures created by these facts serve also to frame and direct what they do. All who have thought about his question will be in turn informed, assured, and provoked and those who have not before done so could not have a better guide.

Geoffrey Hawthorn, Professor of International Politics and Social and Political Theory at Cambridge, Faculty of Social and Political Sciences; ex-Syndic of Cambridge University Press and fellow of Clare College, author most recently of *Thucydides on Politics.*

A wonderful, readable panorama of psychological, materialist, and culturalist theories from a tested master in the History of Antiquity, who has read far and wide well beyond the Ancient World, and always proven himself an original thinker. MacMullen's question is, what motivates various humans to act as they do? He discusses and evaluates the answers given by disciplines neighboring that of History, with constant attention, though, to the different agendas of these disciplines, and therefore, to the contours and limits of what they can provide to historians.

Philippe Buc, Professor, University of Vienna, Institute for History, author most recently of *Dangers of Ritual: Between Early Medieval Texts and Social Scientific Theory.*

When we read history or social science, we want to know why people, and peoples, acted in the way they did. Why did they start a war, why did they move to a new land, why did they choose to right a state of oppression? These are fascinating questions, and they are not always asked. In this book, Ramsey MacMullen tackles them head on.

Keith Oatley, Professor,University of Toronto,Department of Human Development and Applied Psychology, author most recently of *Emotions. A Brief History.*

Contents

Preface — 1

1 Psychology and Individuals — 13

2 Anthropology and Small Populations — 34

3 Reason and Decision-making — 57
3.1 Economic reason — **57**
3.2 Common reason — **64**
3.3 Scientific reason — **75**
3.4 Moral reason — **82**
3.5 Moral culture — **91**

4 Culture as Cause — 99

5 Conclusions — 123

Bibliography — 135
Indexes — 159

Preface[1]

Why do we do what we do? How should one describe the mental process that leads from inaction to action in response to some stimulus? And in addressing so huge a question, how and where on earth should one begin?

I address it as a historian, imagining a shelf of a hundred modern history books to see what they have to say. They won't have time for trivial things. They are concerned with flows of impulse strong enough to determine what people actually *do* and on a scale to affect behavior in groups, not just little personal decisions. Such larger decision-making we would commonly call social.[2]

My sample of books over the decades will also show causal analysis to have had less and less room for people's emotions, more and more room for people's calculations and logic. It is an interpretive tendency not so obvious in popular biographies, but it becomes clearer when specialists offer their analysis to their fellows rather than to the casual reader. Regardless of the intended audience, the whole truth should take account of both operations of our minds, the affective as well as the cognitive. It should take account, too, of the past as much as of the future, not simply to oblige historians like myself but in recognition of a quite obvious fact – that the affective and cognitive in combination have somehow shaped and re-shaped the routines of human life for many thousands of years.

The interplay of these two elements has often occupied me in historiographical experiments, but clearly they needed theoretical justification.[3] It was with this aim in mind that I set to trawling for help in the relevant social research disciplines: psychology, anthropology, behavioral economics, and sociology.

As an illustration of what is useful, in behavioral economics I find at the very center our common faith, our conviction of the plain good sense in *getting*, and then getting more, and then holding on to what one has gotten. Call this "capitalism" for short, a determinant in decision-making millions of times in every day. It is supported as the most reasonable of reasons for common actions, so declared by economists in general or, in the United States, by the Federal Reserve Board and their presiding officer in particular, a sort of priesthood. The truth propounded hardly needs to be defined, only paraphrased, or perhaps defined with no more than trifling if interesting qualifications. Is not this "reason" of ours in fact essential to our species? Thus,

---

1 I take this opportunity to extend sincere thanks to Peter Kiernan, David Brion Davis, Jonathan Dull, Henk Versnel, David Montgomery+, Keith Oatley, and Gerard Saucier, for helping me along the way.

2 As to "social" motivation, I should explain that I do not mean what Geen (1995) 40f. intends, that is, effort increased or diminished by the presence of other people of one's society.

3 My interest from the 1970s I first tried out in *Past and Present* 88 (1980) reprinted in MacMullen (1990) chap. 2; later, in MacMullen (2001a), preface; in (2003) chap. 3 and (2003a); in (2011), the book as a whole and especially 115f.; and in (2014).

inbred? Are there not economic *instincts*? For example, acquisitiveness? Yes, it will be answered – acquisitiveness among other determining traits.[4]

But the belief is false. Such rationality can be shown to be rather a cultural construct. An entire civilization, that of the Roman empire over the course of many centuries, rested in fact on the contradiction of getting: a contradiction, an imperative, inducing the wealthy to pave their cities' streets and plazas as a great gift, to line them with colonnades, to build public places for worship, for ball-games, diversions and festivities of every sort; to pay for public rites and spectacles and the supply of good things to eat; to supply water for baths and fountains, and facilities for the marketing of perishables, all as a gift. At the end, the academic lexicon had even to accept a brand new word: "euergetism". There was need for it at least in learned discussions because the thing it described seemed to the modern world so utterly strange that no term for it in any language had been needed.[5] In those ancient times the rewards sought by the Haves were evidently affective not material.

Equally striking, an area of many millions of square kilometers, an entire continent, was once made happily habitable for centuries (as it is no longer) by a people living and moving on, and returning, and never acquiring more than they could carry. Such was the genius of their way of life, a remarkable fact, undeniable. That genius under sympathetic study turned out to be a great skill in environmental control, so as to maximize the land's carrying capacity. Control was possible as observations of detail about flora and fauna accumulated and were transmitted from one generation to another through rote, song and religion, all at the behest of the divine forces that over-arch the earth.[6] By belief in these forces, one's everyday observations of natural life took on special meaning. They were felt as sacred; they were remembered; and they were acted upon. The result was history on a very grand scale.

Ancient Australia, however, just like ancient Rome, cannot be understood as we understand modern economics, by our own logic. Way of life, learnt in the family, the clan, the tribe, at one's mother's knee with all the attendant loyalties, is seen to have prevailed over material calculation. It is only by historical accident that it may

---

4 Though not in such a condensed form, the ideas I outline constitute a fundamental consensus, a given. See, e.g., John Coates (below, chap. 3 n. 60), or in Demsetz (1996) 485, 490, 491–95 ("we are an acquisitive species" though we should leave room in our thoughts for the odd ascetic); or Greenspan (2013) in a chapter on "animal sprits", by which he means what is "inbred" or instinctual and (14) as found in the standard economic textbooks (though to be "modified" by recognizing faults in our cognitive processes). Yet he finds "all of us", that is, human nature, to be uniform (18), governed, e.g., by "the inbred propensity to save" (with other proposals about humans as a species, 16–30). For the "qualifications", see my chap. 3 on Kahneman et al., below, on whom Greenspan depends.

5 The word "evergetism"/"euergetism", recalling an infinitely lesser cousin, *noblesse oblige*, is established now in many languages. For a good introduction to its meaning, see Veyne (1976).

6 See Gammage (2011), where chapter 4 is crucial for anyone interested in the question addressed by my book; and other anthropological evidence below, in chap. 3 n. 9.

attain a material success; for, to that success, there are many paths. To bring the argument into our own age and Western world, consider how Asian traditions, including the religious, under even the most up-to-date lens of social analysis, are seen to be quite as effective as the Western in a capitalist sense (chapter 1). Modern cultures have given different shapes to motivation, through the union of calculation with affect, as Antonio Damasio and others have shown (chapter 3). They point the way to a better historiographical method (chapter 5).

But should it be the "new cultural" history, as it is called, with Clifford Geertz as guru? The mission of this approach has been to explore the realities that typically occupy such anthropologists as he. Its most admired practitioners have included Robert Darnton, Natalie Davis, and Carlo Ginzburg, along with many others.[7] Their materials for study are popular beliefs, wisdom, folklore; collective ceremonies and associations; familial routines and customs; generally, the ordinary doings of ordinary individuals whose significance lies in their aggregate and who often receive quite minute study in what is termed "microhistory".

There have of course been changes in this approach over the last generation or so, as its older champions have been gently corrected, older applications and devices have been discarded, and the original ties to ethnography have been severed or weakened. Still, the "new" history in its larger sense including the "new cultural" has made a place for itself.[8] Indeed, a veteran of the historical discipline, a very wide reader, was distressed to find the "old" largely displaced by the mid-1980s. Twenty years later things had gone from bad to worse, ever more favoring "the cultural turn in history, and the radical neohistoricism it has helped foster as the profession's methodological dogma".[9]

To show this novel style in its most extreme form, in microhistory, I instance the big killing-off of the neighborhood's cats by a company of teenage employees in eighteenth-century Paris, for a joke, and with much mock ceremonial. One of the lads in his latter years wrote it up. In our own times Robert Darnton told the story once again,

---

7 For these three, see some recent bibliography in MacMullen (2003) 162, and Himmelfarb (2004) 238 with other prominent names; naming the three plus Geertz, Calaresu et al. (2010) 7f.; on the "new cultural history" and, on its inspiration in Geertz (1973), see Hunt (1989) 12; McMillan (1994) passim and 758, "most fashionable of all is the 'thick description' method of Clifford Geertz"; and Himmelfarb (2004) 127, "guru", and all of her chap. 7.

8 Correction of Lynn Hunt, in Beik (2007) 95 or Munslow (2010) 25f., or of Natalie Davis, in Holt (2012) 57f.; on impatience with the founding attachment to anthropology, cf. Sider (2005) 168f., "the conjunction of history and anthropology... became a fad that is fortunately coming to an end", along with "such vacuous concepts as 'thick description'"; further, Buc (2001) passim, pushing back against *ritual* as a heuristic concept; dismissive reference to "folkloric" interpretations, in Beik (2007) 76f., 94f.; and the place of the "new" in the discipline as a whole, Himmelfarb (2004) chap. 1 (of 1984) and chap. 7, no longer "cutting edge" as it claims but mainstream.

9 Himmelfarb (1987) 5 and passim; (2004) 2 ("post-postmodern"), 28f., 129; and Baldwin (2004) 7, quoted.

finding the whole thing utterly baffling. Could anyone today really understand what lay behind it? What was the boys' motivation? Did they perhaps resent their hard work and bad lodgings?

Yet we have a character in *The Brothers Karamazov* (Bk. 3 chap. 6) who "as a child had loved to string up cats and then bury them with full ceremony. He would dress up in a sheet, to represent a chasuble, and chant while swinging some imagined censer over the dead cat". And what of tying a tin can to a dog's tail and watching it run off, and run itself to death, terrified by the clanking – a moment of fun of a certain sort for idle youngsters in Mark Twain's world not all that long ago? Are such pastimes *important*? In that same Paris shop, when Darnton describes the "tormenting" of a junior employee, "mocking" him, making him "the butt of jokes... sending him on wild goose chases", and in sum quite as baffling to Darnton as the cat episode, the same conduct can be seen in modern work-shops; and I recall such treatment on my own first job, just turned seventeen, with a boat crew.[10] The understanding of shared humanity, both good and bad, may be lost as well as found in the library.

Darnton need not puzzle over the question of motivation, anyway, because whatever the reason behind the Paris idea of a joke, it could only be of interest to micro-history as a certain form, as a ritual, illustrative of a bygone culture in an intriguing way. The kind of things an anthropologist would take notes on should interest historians as well, so it was proposed: for example, odd religious practices in out-of-the-way places. Thus the "new cultural" sees the past in snapshots, closely examined, rather than across time in a video-form, with cause and effect, tracing change through decisions, their outcome, and their explanation. In the Paris evidence, as there was no outcome, historians have nothing to learn except perhaps that boys enjoy their moments of cruelty and invention, and may be given a hard time at work.

In a second instance of micro-history, the "new-cultural" addressed a trial in Toulouse in 1560. A certain Martin Guerre, absent and never heard from for many years, at last returned to his little French village only to discover an impostor in his place, master of his house, his lands and his very wife. When she reluctantly joined the charges against the impostor, and after full judicial inquiry among her neighbors and family, the man was found guilty of adultery and the wrongful handling of her property. He was hanged. Today it would make a tabloid headline, "NOT HER MAN!" Like the cat-massacre it was certainly bizarre. Who had ever heard the like? The judge afterwards wrote it up in detail, interspersing his own magisterial ruminations. From a "new-cultural" historian, Natalie Davis, it drew a scholarly monograph, subsequent scholarly articles, a postgraduate seminar at a host uni-

---

10 Darnton (1985) 83 on mistreatment of animals as a form of fun, and (262) insistent on its "otherness", repeating that he doesn't "get it"; 77 and 88, on cruelty to new boys on the job; and Lüdtke (1986) 78f., 91, German work-shop customs ca. 1900.

versity, a movie script, and other elaborations, all exemplary of what Geertz called "thick description". Thus, we are told, to understand the Martin-Guerre imposture, one should understand "nicknaming and carnival masking", marriage law and customs, and so forth. Davis might call the court case "fateful" but, like the cat-massacre, it had the most limited significance: in fact, fateful significance for only one person, the accused, unless one chose to count all three utterly obscure persons, the wife and two husbands residing in an utterly obscure village. So long as there were no repercussions and the imposture could not be shown to be representative of anything bigger than itself, there was little profit in studying it as a train of cause and effect, motivation and action, horizontally.[11] The observer, whether anthropologist or micro-historian, couldn't pretend to say why a people at some point developed characteristic beliefs or forms of action; it was presented as interesting simply because of its "otherness" (favored term) – meaning, at home in settings remote in class or time from the Western scholar.

At a more consequential level than micro-history, consider the violent behavior of crowds. Here we have scenes more usually found in traditional history books. Can they be treated in new-cultural fashion as a matter of a people's traditions so habitual that they have become almost irrational? Or are they not better seen as the expression of class antipathy and material interests, as would have been proposed in the 1950s and 1960s?[12] Should we not see in the crowd's violence a straight-forward acting out of moral values in didactic or retributive fashion rather than as a sort of reflex?[13] Asked also in recent years, "What was behind the feelings of the bourgeoisie?" "What can we learn of the goals of popular religious violence? What were crowds intending to do and why did they think they must do it?" "How do we explain... the visceral emotions that produced such vitriolic rhetoric and collective violence...?"[14] Such challenges to

---

11 Regarding Davis (1983) on Martin Guerre, I agree with the criticism implied by Calaresu et al. (2010) 15, in praising another new cultural historian for "moving anthropology, so to speak, from the periphery to the centre of history, shifting the focus away from the microhiostory of marginal individuals to... cities... and events". Further on Davis, it is worth pointing out that our U. S. appellate courts do not presume to disregard the conclusions jurors arrive at from having the witnesses physically before them. Nevertheless, Davis proposed an elaborate re-telling of the Martin-Guerre story to recast its causes, prompting criticism from Finlay (1988). He found her re-write of the case "unsubstantiated" (559, and passim) to which Davis (1988) could only respond by pointing to a great deal of historical knowledge that was not relevant to the particular case, while admitting her re-write was "conjectural" (574). For "nicknaming", see Davis (1988) 590; for "fateful", ibid. 581.

12 Irrational, cf. Beik (2007) 100. The most often cited writers on crowd behavior in this context are Rudé (1959) 40–43, 195f., and passim, and Thompson (1964), e.g., 672, 689, with typical remarks on motivation, and in more recent decades Holt (2012) 54.

13 Beik (2007) 78.

14 Wolff (1971) 18 and 55 (both, quoted) and discussion of intelligible motive among different groups and interests, Bercé (1990) 30; on emotions, Keith Luria quoted in Holt (2012) 57, and Beik (2007) 80, 84, and 86 on the fierce anger, sense of betrayal, and indignation underlying crowd behavior.

the new history indicate a weakness that even its practitioners seem to be aware of, regarding motivation.

Still, the old-fashioned mostly political narrative is certainly open to challenge. At least in the common mind, there is all too much truth in H. A. L. Fisher's famous dictum, that history is just "one damned thing after another". Let "men wiser and more learned than I", said he, try to find a "plot" or "pattern". There could be no science to it at all, social or other; "there can be no generalizations", only "the play of the contingent and the unforeseen". He despaired of explaining cause and effect in any way that could be trusted, while himself, in the most learned fashion, nevertheless tracing the whole long story of our Western past.[15] One thing just follows upon another, yes, that can be shown. The narrative does seem to play out all on a plane, one might say *horizontally*, dwelling on particulars, just as one standing domino strikes another in a table-top parade. The toppling and the direction of it may have twists and turns diverting to observe.

Human beings, however, are not really dominoes. They are thinking creatures who act out of some urge, some motivation. Where their numbers involved are great enough to lend historical significance to their actions and therefore arouse our rational interest – and this is a crucial consideration – they have inevitably converged from many points of interest, many impulses and objectives. The whole great tangle is rendered too complicated for clear understanding. It is plain chaos and we have to be content with nothing better than half-random choices of what best to describe, and how. Fisher knew this but was nevertheless willing to go ahead with his work – without deceiving himself about its qualifications as a science.

Whether history is or can ever become some sort of science by any accepted definition, and what that claim and title would amount to, was of course a debate that Fisher in the 1930s neither initiated nor resolved, by any means. His words only serve conveniently to show what lies at the center of that debate: the need for "patterns" and "generalizations", to be glossed as "universals", "laws", "consistencies", "regularity" and "predictability". All these characterize sciences at least in the common mind.

Naturally, even in the most exact of sciences there are deficiencies. We can't say in advance which electron in an external ring will be pulled away from one atom by another, any more than we can explain asymmetries in the outline of galaxies or the arrangement of the stars. If we thus tolerate unpredictability on both a nano- and macro-scale, we should hardly expect anything better from that narrative of the horizontal dominoes-variety against which H. A. L. Fisher protested – but which he had to

15 Fisher's dictum, Hill (1961) 3; its more dignified, fuller statement in Fisher (1936) v, in the preface to his three-volume survey of European history; his views often referred to thanks to his prominence, e.g., by Toynbee (1947) 1.445f., recognizing only "the omnipotence of Chance", or K. R. Popper (1962) 2.366.

work with. Its champions, careless of academic jousts and fashions, still work with it, and carry off Pulitzer prizes in biography and history.[16]

If accepted, however, can this *horizontal* approach be improved to bring it closer to science through *vertical* analysis? And might this perhaps open the way to the affect aspect of motivation, as modern social sciences suggest?

To explain: imagine a moment of back-and-forth where I might say, "Here's someone who wants a hundred dollars – but why?" And the historian replies, "Suppose he needs money to buy a suit." "Why a suit?" "Silly, to look good." "Why look good?" "Silly, everybody wants to look good." "But why?" "So everyone else will think well of him, so as to get a job or fit in. He wants approval." At the very end, explanation has thus to reach beneath circumstantial particulars to levels of feeling, to impulses and ultimately to an instinct that will be found in any social animal; and instinct is as far as the search for motivation can go, a mystery to this day.[17]

It is toward such deeper points in the complicated workings of social motivation that I would like to reach. No one doubts they do exist and can be found. We learn about them from the social scientific study of motivational agents such as reciprocity and aggression, taboos or kin-groups, cognition and affect, intuition and reflex. Surely history, too, may learn from its various sister disciplines, or cousins, if you will, or in any case, ways of thinking about humankind that are undeniably rich, even if the truths it arrives at conform only to the discipline's own distinct standards.

It was that confidence in profit that initially inspired my trawling (as I called it, above) in the social sciences. I hoped for help with my question, *Why do we do what we do*? In the end, the yield seems to form itself into a flow of explanatory ideas. I may call it a unified definition since it grows out of and draws on a variety of social-scientific findings reported in the chapters that follow. At many points, to show how it can be justified within some particular context of research, I recall it whether or not in exactly the same words. Spelt out, now: *Social motivation is a flow of mental activity instinctual, affective, and expressive of what most actors hold dear or see as decent and meritorious; it expresses both the impulses thus generated and the collective sense of self that pervades an entire people, shaping the behavior of each individual through time in narratives that can be seen as their collective history*. I do no more than summarize, here, what will be found and is supported in the chapters that follow, so far as it may prove useful in historical study.[18]

---

16 I instance the awards to the admirable work of Robert Caro in 2003 and David Halberstam in 2008, neither of them professional historians in the academic sense, as illustrations of the "old" style of historiography (in the term of Himmelfarb 2004).

17 In a letter to the *New York Review of Books*, May 23, 2013, 51, the neuroscientist J. Herbert confesses, "I cannot tell you what happens in your brain to make you feel hungry, or angry, or recognize your friends, or plan your future".

18 See below, pp. 31, 49, 52, 54f., 83, 91, and 98.

Granted, the definition is all too complex and blurry where I would like it to be parsimonious and crisp; but I long ago learnt from my teachers to tolerate mere probabilities (on which, more in a few pages) and to distrust realist theorizing (so I needn't agonize over what history *is*).[19] I may add, too, that some of the received ideas in the social sciences that I will touch on later can be seen yielding to others that looked better, reminding me that the historians' discipline offers examples of the same come-and-go of fashion. In the great welter of their work over the past century and more, methodological approaches have succeeded one another, to be modified, digested into the larger practice, or abandoned: positivist, Marxist, feminist, or post- or semi-comically titled "post-post-" to signify their coming after and (it is claimed) improving on some earlier "-ism". Truths for all time don't seem to be within reach. Nothing is perfect or for ever.

A single point of consensus, however, did emerge some generations ago and still holds good, as I believe: that the Fisher model of historiography inadequately represented the whole of life that was important. It privileged the elite, the most obvious shapers of change, unmindful of ordinary people and of the role they play in the general narrative. To correct this error, whether as a matter of accurate reportage or of moral obligation, historians needed to focus attention also on the mass of any population large or small. They needed to work around the problem of inadequate sources – inadequate at least as compared with the record left by the elite – using whatever they could learn from the social sciences. Since description of the externals of life was the easy part, economics was earliest and most prominently drawn on. Explanation that would reach further into change and therefore into motivation proved much more difficult to get at; but psychology helped, and sociology and then, from the late '70s, anthropology.

The "new cultural" approach nevertheless involved a weakness having nothing to do with the micro-historical approach criticized above. It derived rather from the choice of the non-elite as subject matter – a class little occupied with long letters, memoirs, litigation, account-books, tracts, chronicles, and all such personal records. Explanation of *why they did what they did* must therefore depend to a great extent on the aggregation of indirect testimony about them: data on life expectancy, fertility rates, price of staples, social mobility, frequency of occurrences of one sort or another, all quantifiable and all evaluated in terms of material benefit. The social sciences

19 From the late Stanley Wheeler I gained an answer to my asking how "reasonable" is defined in our law, cf. MacMullen (2003) 151, (2011) 115f., and below, n. 20 and chap. 3 at nn. 29f. From one of Willard Quine's courses I gained acquaintance with Alexander B. Johnson's *Treatise on Language* (1828, 1836, 1947) and the problem in mistaking words for things, as, for instance, where everyone argues about the nature of what they call "history" (*histoire*, *storia*, *Geschichte*, etc.), and what the reality of it is. For access to the prodigious flood of ink given to this question, see, e.g., Munslow (2007), (2010). For the reception or non-reception of it all, see, e.g., below, chap 5 n. 17 or Kousser (1993) 17 on "the murky vaporings of recent relativists", naming a few in a list all too easily extended.

most often looked to for help will thus be economics, with sociology helping on interpretation.

The resulting emphasis on the more superficial, problem-solving, instrumental levels of motivation – levels in the upper range of *vertical* analysis, in my metaphor – has been essentially strategic. The point is supported by psychologists, anthropologists, and behavioral economists, as I show in a later chapter. They all agree in finding that, when we explain ourselves to others and even to ourselves, it is our rational considerations that we push forward, where rationality means conscious thought supported by calculations of utility, especially regarding whatever is quantifiable. Such too-reasonable self-representation, amounting to misrepresentation, is the everyday practice in our own and many other societies, including the preliterate, and in many settings.[20]

One setting, the courts, was usefully studied many years ago by Lawrence Tribe, professor of law. He noted the marked favor enjoyed by quantifiable argument in American legal cases, where he saw more and more frequent resort to numerical demonstration of all sorts in shaping how evidence is understood and respected. The tendency he noticed has only become more pronounced in recent years. Given our general worship of science founded on numbers, anyone wanting to convince others will take advantage of "the overbearing impressiveness of numbers" and "the dwarfing of soft variables" in making an argument, as Tribe explains.[21]

But such legal arguments as these, as they are actually explored and picked apart and documented, and doubted or defended by advocates on the two sides of every aspect of a problem in the search for truth and justice before a panel of judges – these sound like nothing but works of history in miniature. The analogy seems to me intriguing, well worth a closer look in the pages that follow; for, by reason of scale, cases at law are more easily handled than historical narratives, and they have been often studied for other reasons than mine, with input from the social sciences.

Lawrence Tribe, then, continuing in his analysis, proposes that,

> matters that are objectively verifiable in the world outside the courtroom lend themselves more readily to mathematical treatment than such issues as intent... One consequence of mathematical proof, then, may be to shift the focus away from such elements as volition, knowledge, and intent,... for the same reason that the hard variables tend to swamp the soft. It is by no means clear that such marginal gains, if any, as we make by finding somewhat more precise answers would not be offset by a tendency to emphasize the wrong questions.[22]

20 See below, chap. 3 n. 50 and, in historiography of the U.S., France, and Germany, in chap. 4 at nn. 4f., 26ff.; on the prestige of numeric proofs, see chap. 4 at nn. 44f. and elsewhere; and chap. 5 at nn. 11ff.

21 Tribe (1971) 1361; cf. 1360, "the problem of the overpowering number" which is at the heart of his entire sixty-page article. The increasing use of statistics in trials is noted by Zabell (1993) 268, along with its difficulties; see also Devine (2012) 145, 151.

22 Tribe (1971) 1366; Hastie (1993) 5, 13f.

The preference noted by Tribe has been confirmed by a historian of the next generation, J. Morgan Kousser, who adds, "It is much more difficult to resolve disagreements based on impressionistic evidence, since it is much harder to exchange *Verständnisse* – one's empathetic insights – than computer tapes."[23]

Quite true. The legal community long ago recognized "the impossibility of penetrating into the hearts of men and ascertaining the truth" (it was a justice of the Supreme Court who spoke, in 1884).[24] The warning was wise, the problem and its study falling between psychology and epistemology; and from the social-scientific community, the yield of research since then has been very little and late in coming, even in the study of single individuals – still less, regarding motivation in groups except by inference and the assumption of rationality.[25] The subject is resistant to science for the reason that Lawrence Tribe points to in his choice of the word, "soft"; soft evidence is hard to accept.[26]

Kousser, however, has served as expert witness in a score of civil rights cases where motivation has been, since the 1960s, a central issue. Plaintiffs have protested that a governing body of some sort had meant to deny them their due; so, to settle the matter, both sides to the litigation had to agree on what that intent was – that is, on the "soft" evidence, in Tribe's definition or "deeper" in my own terms. Agreement

---

23 Kousser (1980) 447, where the translation of the German word is my own addition. For the defense of empathy as an absolutely necessary tool of analysis across cultures, see Clifford Geertz quoted in MacMullen (2003a) 29, at note 8, saying, "What happens to *Verstehen* when *Einfühlen* disappears?"

24 Kousser (1999) 320 quoting the Justice of 1884, cf. still a century later in the drafting stage of a law, the admission that proving intent was "inordinately difficult", Kousser (1999) 342; review of the evidence (345) that courts in recent decades have had insurmountable trouble in handling, or even acknowledging, intent at a level of demonstration that constitutes evidence; and (361) the objection by a Justice, 1977, that "Discriminatory intent is simply not amenable to calibration," and thus even the smallest indication of intent makes it real, see also (363) on "mixed motive". On the variety of our basic drives, Pink (2009) considers how to harness them to get more and better work out people, whether children in school or employees, and he reminds readers of the uses of freely flowing thought. To this, the familiar brainstorming, a form of mental play, I would add unfocused play of other kinds shared with other animal species, both among the young and the mature, evidently with survival value; also, what we can learn about ourselves from raccoons or crows that exhibit curiosity, that is, the uneasiness that must be relieved by the inspection and understanding of some novelty; and further, the need for independence in maturing, which continues in humans into adulthood. Beyond all these widely shared drives, it seems to me unnecessary to posit a new one: the sheer joy found in "the performance of the task" (Pink, p. 3), which is "genuine" or "intrinsic motivation" (56, 65). This is proposed to explain such behavior as unrewarded problem-solving, or indifference to rewards, where of course "tasks" are by definition assigned or required by someone else.

25 Little research on intensity, see Verduyn et al. (2009) 1428f.; regarding that of groups, Inbar et al. (2009) 714 refer only to Haidt et al. (1993), and the demonstration there of "the correlation" of "moral disgust" with "more conservative attitudes on a range of political issues". See below, chap. 3 at nn. 92f.

26 Some acceptance of impressionistic conclusions in other disciplines is seen above, n. 25, in Appleby et al., quoted, and again canvassed in chap. 3, below, at n. 139 and in chap. 5 at nn. 17ff. and 23.

in fact could often be arrived at. A successful approach could be found through the open discussion and evaluation of all possible inferences from all sides, pro or con, each taken apart and critically examined. The procedure is exactly what historians depend on. Even so, Kousser asks, "can we announce that we have discovered a truth that can never be overturned, that no rational person can disagree with? Is this what objectivity amounts to? I think not."[27] He doesn't look for that perfection of truth of which the philosophers dream; he will insist only on "the best warranted explanation of any that one can think of", by which lawyers and judges alike, including those of the highest judiciary, have thought it possible to address "such elements as volition, knowledge, and intent" (I quote Tribe's words once more).

In his assumption that adversaries in court can be brought to a common view, and so reconciled, Kousser counts on both sides being reasonable. So he tells us, without saying how exactly he would define a "rational person."[28] Still, it is clear that he brings forward and finds agreement on the basis of those general ideas about human behavior with which the courts – his clients – are all equipped through accumulated experience.[29] These are the probabilities people have in their heads – call them certainties. To these, argument appeals. Within its terms we can be sure, or we think we can be sure, that a person doing X and being in a situation Y is almost certain to have Z in mind. Rational interpretation is key. In adversarial challenge, if our understanding is doubted, then alternatives will be weighed and disposed of as they appear the less likely, the less reasonable; and similarly, variant details in the nature of the persons and the situation involved.

Historians would like to explain the longer stories they tell in exactly the same way that court cases trace their own shorter narratives, reasonably among reasoning actors. But of course everything depends on knowing the values that surround and energize whatever decision is being discussed – knowledge such as jurors ordinarily command. To match it, the historian who reaches further back into the past must give close study to the cultural setting, just as the social scientist does who deals

27 Quoted, Kousser (1993) 26. To illustrate the problems in handling the subject, see Appleby et al. (1994) 263: "to deny the writing of history objective validity because of the historian's essential creative effort is to remain attached to a nineteenth-century understanding" (which is understood to be mistaken); instead (281), "the social approach…, the system of peer review" and other consensual tests "makes objective knowledge possible"; "Telling the truth takes a collective effort", nothing more (309); but at the same time (305), "causal explanations [of things like the French Revolution or the Cold War] can never be wholly satisfying"; and the authors never offer a standard by which to judge if any explanation is in fact "The Truth about History".

28 "Reasonable" invoked in the argument of 1884, and generally, see Kousser (1999) 320, and (340) recommending "careful hypothesis testing of causal explanations [which] was just what political historians had been doing for years"; adding (347f.) that "models of human behavior" and "generalizations" are the top factors to be considered.

29 On the totality of "givens" in a society, see below, chap. 3 at nn. 55.

with some preliterate society or one that has very different values half-way across the globe. Moreover, the surrounding affect must be properly understood. Enter, doubt. It is arises from that very love of quantification that Lawrence Tribe discovered. Social science likes numbers; historians want to be scientific; but the affect surrounding and giving force to values cannot be quantified in past settings as they can in the laboratory. How then can any historical reconstruction prove its claims?

Perhaps there can't be any proof in the full meaning of that word, any more than for a courtroom verdict; but the fact may be no very bad thing. As Lawrence Tribe pointed out, speaking of courtroom reasoning, "It is by no means clear that such marginal gains, if any, as we make by finding somewhat more precise answers would not be offset by a tendency to emphasize the wrong questions". Surely that is true: we risk getting precise answers about things that have little meaning. The best medical diagnosticians are credited with *flair*, which we concede lies somewhere beyond the reach of logical analysis; so also, our interpretations of why people did what they did. We evidently believe in intuitive rightness, for, in our everyday assessments of motivation in the people around us, we don't hesitate to carry our guesswork beyond the problem-solving level of mental activity, down to the levels where action originates. Let rigorists in the courts or the academy dismiss our conjectures, yet still we will insist, "That's just how it *feels*". We will defend our empathetic insights even in serious settings, as for instance, in a jury chamber and on a capital charge. Such *Verständnisse* – granted, they do not prove, but better, they explain; and this is what the social sciences seem now to say.[30]

30 Some acceptance of impressionistic conclusions in other disciplines is seen above, n. 25, in Appleby et al., quoted, and again canvassed in chap. 3, below, at n. 139 and in chap. 5 at nn. 17ff. and 23.

1 Psychology and Individuals

My Preface declared my target for study: collectivities and social behavior. What can psychology, given its ordinary focus on the individual, tell us about population groups of one kind or another? My aim in this first chapter is to identify points of similarity between the individual and the collectivity, with the hope of transferring psychology's insights about the former to the latter. This we commonly do in discussing national character or stereotypes of a class, ethnicity, occupation, or the like.

The difficulties are obvious. To begin with, the psychologist can look inside individuals in ways not available to historians, simply because historians' subjects are all beyond the reach of questionnaires, focus groups, and assorted laboratory tricks. Yet if a record of group action remains, of course inferences can be drawn about tendencies and character. Psychology may suggest rules of prediction to guide such inferences, if something discoverable about individuals can be shown always or generally to have certain results – in short, if there are behavioral consistencies about which the discipline is agreed. In this way not only single individuals can be better understood but a number of individuals together, constituting a body of a size sufficient to have made a difference.

As to consistencies, these must depend on the raising of the psychological discipline to the level of a science, able to discern and define the invariant aspects of personality and fit them together in general statements. Hopes of attaining this goal have animated discussion from well back in the history of the social sciences but, to consider only recent times, we have the recollection of Hazel Markus and Shinobu Kitayama, that "the social psychology of the 1980s was very inclined to universals. Universalism was a sign of commitment to science, and the goal of science was to pursue the universal laws of human nature".[1]

Within psychology, no specialty would appear to be more relevant to my purposes than the study of values, where Robert Hinde is well known for his research. "Some norms, beliefs, and values," he tells us,

> may be shared by most or all members of a society. It is to the latter that the term 'culture' is usually applied. Briefly, 'culture' refers here to the ways in which human groups or subgroups differ that are communicated between individuals, with special reference to beliefs, values, and behaviour. 'Culture' is thus best viewed as existing in the minds (separately or collectively) of the individuals in a group. There is thus a continuum between the culture of a given society and the beliefs and values of the component individuals. It is unfortunate that the former has become the province of sociologists and anthropologists, the latter of social and developmental psychologists

1 Quoted, Markus and Kitayama (2003) 280.

– and he continues with remarks about cross-cultural studies of upbringing and acculturation which bring out the differences from one society to another.[2] The reminder here, that the boundaries between individual and collectivity are almost meaningless, serves me in reviewing the relevant lines of research in recent generations.

The results have not been so helpful as might be expected. How the beliefs and traits of communities play out across time and thereby shape the story of a population is of course endlessly analyzed in the service of educational, penal, economic, public health, or other categories of public policy. The object of study may be a caste, a profession, a class or income level (all, of course, contemporary). In contrast, long-term predictions about individuals, so common in high-school yearbooks and a thing we all take for granted, have run into research problems that invite an explanation.

Where, as it seemed, the approach had been loose and intuitive a century ago, something more scientific was surely possible. One improvement might be found in convincingly large groups of subjects and the translation of test-findings into numbers. Working with groups diminished the risk of conclusions based on exceptional or unrepresentative subjects, and numerical measurement allowed for closer argument and comparison.

A well-known study was Lewis Terman's sampling of some 1500 brighter-than-average children from 1922 on to his death in 1956 and, by continuation under others in research, for decades thereafter. The result could be regarded as a great cluster of tiny histories, however narrowly focused. Terman began with only human intelligence as his target; but in the search for the origin and nature of that advantage, he cast a very wide net. Parents and teachers were invited to describe children under headings like carefulness, anxiousness, sociability, and dozens of other qualities. These could in time be correlated with life-outcomes. Better perhaps than brainy, the chosen children proved also happier and more successful than the average, in the long run.[3]

Alternatively, the focus could be further narrowed to yield more exactitude. "Aggressiveness" in little children could be described by peers, teachers, or parents and measured in various tests. It might show up in many sorts of antisocial behavior, even criminal, twenty years later; and this could be verified. Or "neuroticism" could

---

2 Hinde (1996) 369; (2002) 20, "the basic psychological characteristics to which I refer are at the individual or near-individual level"; and repeated, "culture is best viewed as existing in the minds of individuals". Compare Hofstede (2002) in an interview, "you have to realize that culture is a construct. When I have intelligent students in my class, I tell them, 'One thing we have to agree on: culture does not exist.' Culture is a concept that we made up which helps us understand a complex world, but it is not something tangible like a table or a human being. What it is depends on the way in which we define it".

3 On the need to consider both cognitive and non-cognitive factors in individuals' life development, including both their material success and their personality traits, see, e.g., Jackson (2006), Hall and Farkas (2011), or Friedman and Martin (2011) 7ff., 68.

be rated in a sample of young couples before their marriage and, decades later, it corresponded with the likelihood of success in their marriage.[4] The effects of conscientiousness, measuring how you perform a task even when no one is checking up on you, could be traced in a representative sample of many thousands of American children across many decades, to see what its consequences were (and they were good, of course); similarly, responsiveness to authority in the late teens and early twenties was found to correspond significantly with much later feelings of career satisfaction and contentment in life; and there are many other examples of traits that affect the whole course of life.[5]

The studies just instanced belong to the 1980s and later. They represent more or less current practice. Before that date, however, over a period beginning in the 1960s, such research confronted serious criticism. The problem lay in the prevailing ambition to make psychology not only scientific but rigorously so – like physics, the ideal. The discipline should aim at unified statements holding true over masses of data, the bigger the better; it should aim at laws of Newtonian purview, at theories of Einsteinian compression and parsimony.[6] It should employ only sharply defined terms and exact measurements to allow verification and replication.

By 1964, however, criticism of even the most generally accepted trait- and personality-studies dismissed them all as "a dead end". They had no statistical validity.[7] A further assault of book length was delivered by Walter Mischel a little later (1968). This work was a very careful and forbiddingly technical evaluation of personality research to date. At the end, the author thought it "not surprising that large-scale applied efforts to predict behavior from personality inferences have been strikingly and consistently unsuccessful." Predictions about what a person would do, if asked, in a variety of imagined situations that would reveal character traits, he judged entirely unreliable. Correlations across them all fell below a level of any significance, leading him "to clear conclusions. With the possible exception of intelligence, highly generalized behavioral consistencies have not been demonstrated, and the concept

4 Magnusson (1988) 92, 109, 119–30, tracking early aggressiveness and later criminal problems, and 156, consensus on the correlation between "early aggressiveness and adult criminality"; Bergman and Magnusson (1990) 5f.; and Brody (1994) 420f.

5 On conscientiousness, see Segal (2012) 1438f., 1442, 1453; and other studies, e.g., Winter et al. (1981) 48, 95 or Vaillant (1983) passim, on "maturity of ego defenses" measured across decades.

6 E.g., Tooby et al. (1992) 30 on parsimony ("The goal, as in physics, is for as few principles as possible to account for as much as possible"); also, aim at reduction of variables through taxonomies, Malle and Dickert (2007) 1012; and the declared purpose is "to build a science of the person," "a metadiscipline", working off "meta-theories", as proposed by Mischel (2004) 1, 13, 18.

7 "Dead end," the verdict of Philip Vernon, a student of Gordon Allport, recalled by Mischel (1968) 146, 296; and the "dead end" sensed in sociology in the 1980s as a consequence of logical positivism, cf. Mommsen (1989) 121.

of personality traits as broad response dispositions is thus untenable."[8] The verdict amounted to the dismissal of "personology" and its research literature, wholesale.

Personality-study had been given essential form and standing by Gordon Allport in the generation prior to Mischel. Now to take it on in this all-out fashion as Mischel did was bound to attract attention. At first his work was received with alarm; its impact was said to have produced "a crisis" in the research community.[9] As its argument sank in, Seymour Epstein saw the consequences: "The charge that personality traits do not exist clearly strikes at the very heart of personality theory. One could well argue that if individuals do not have relatively stable behavioral dispositions that differentiate them from other individuals, then the concept of individuality itself can be dispensed with."[10]

Epstein in two articles written as a pair under the title, "The stability of behavior: on predicting most of the people much of the time" (1979–80), went on to make clear one point. This he pressed home with overwhelming statistical support: an individual's traits, detected in response to a variety of situations, scenes, and descriptive phrases, might vary from one to another but not across the board. If the data were aggregated, as aggregation rose, so did over-all consistency.

In challenging Mischel's verdict, what Epstein argued on a theoretical or even philosophical level could only seem self-evident to a layman.[11] We simply cannot imagine that people we think we know will do something they've never done before, tomorrow, and will try something else equally strange to their routines, the day after. What we have observed them to do is what they *are*; their tendencies direct and define them; they are no more likely to change in some radical way than their body to grow a third arm; and while personality may allow an occasional "departure", something "quirky", nevertheless our choice of such descriptive terms testifies to our belief in a stable identity at each person's core.

In one of his articles Epstein made reference to a huge trait-study (on honesty, undertaken in the 1920s) that looked at many thousands of children across many years. The researchers had explained that a lack of correlation indeed showed up in tests, just such as Mischel was to point to much later; but the reliability of these

---

8 Mischel (1968) 146.

9 On Allport's role, see, e.g., Caspi (1998) 312 or Hogan (2009) 249. Mischel's book "strikes at the very heart of personality theory," so, Epstein (1979) 1098; but, while its impact is "an incredible achievement", it has constituted "a major impediment" to progress in the field, so, Roberts (2009) 137f. "The most daring challenge," in the words of Caspi (1998) 313, it "dealt a heavy blow to the trait approach," Schütz and Vater (2007) 995; thanks to Mischel and another researcher, "trait psychology continues to be marginalized," Costa and McCrae (2009) 299; and the field is pronounced in "crisis", Epstein (1980) 790 and still in Costa and McCrae (2008) 179.

10 Epstein (1979) 1098.

11 As Allport insisted, quoted in Caspi (1998) 312f. On animal individuality, a lively field, see, e.g., Bergmüller and Taborsky (2010) or Cote et al. (2012) 1472ff. on the western mosquitofish.

tests would be increased to a probative level if they were multiplied. "Just as one test is an insufficient and unreliable measure in the case of intelligence, so one test of deception is quite incapable of measuring a subject's tendency to deceive. That is, we cannot predict from what a pupil does on one test what he will do on another."[12] It was in line with this dictum by a predecessor that Epstein and others thus recommended a "cross-situational" approach, as it could be termed. It offered distinct advantages over the deceptively precise laboratory measurement of single moments or stimuli.[13]

Epstein's views seem to me doubly interesting. Not only had Mischel been quite mistaken but beyond that, prediction about most but not all people, and about most but not all of the time, was something to be taken seriously even though it might be proposed only in words not numbers. That possibility would have been approved by William Cameron, reminding students of sociology long ago, "Not everything that can be counted counts, and not everything counts that can be counted."[14] Human behavior may be just too complicated for numerical treatment, of which the aims are so easily lost among variables and terms of measurement irremediably subjective. "Science", that ennobling term, may hold out ideals of exactitude that simply do not fit the problems.

On the other hand, there was no need to abandon two essentials. These were the existence of the individual personality and its most usual but not complete or invariable stability. Longitudinal studies that took these essentials for granted, implicitly if not explicitly, could go right on; and in fact, so they did.[15] Their total in fact now reaches into the hundreds.

Mischel himself contributed in a most unpredictable way. He, like his great predecessors in the discipline, William James and Sigmund Freud, had developed an interest in our powers of self-control. Self-control involves two or more psychological attributes in distinct, even antagonistic roles, inside our heads. This invited investigation. Mischel had published a dozen more or less relevant studies when, in 1968,

---

12 Epstein (1979) 1101 on the 1920s study, and the general reminder (1102) that "a trait is a generalized tendency" which "does not imply… trait-relevant behavior in all situations or even on all occasions in the same situation"; further (1980), amplifying his arguments and pointing out the mismatch between the possibility of exact replication in the hard sciences that sets a standard unattainable in the social sciences.

13 Epstein (1984) 210 recalls the reception of his views; further, Magnusson (1988) 4.

14 Quoted, Cameron (1963) 13 (he had proposed a part of the same witty doctrine years earlier; the two-part whole has often been misattributed to other persons).

15 Young et al. (1991) list 213 studies, at a rising rate of increase (pre-1950, only 19). For the continued or revived belief in the (not perfect) stability of personality, see the positions taken, e.g., by Magnusson (1988) 55, 65, Mischel et al. (1989) 933, Aken and Asendorpf (1996) 205–08, Caspi (1998) 312, or Friedman and Martin (2011) 6. Berry et al. (2002) 98 defend Mischel's 1968 dismissal of stable personality while ignoring all of Epstein's work; disregarding the probative value of the longitudinal studies of self-control; and supposing that assessments of stability in traits by one's self are the only sort possible, and may be discounted, without mention of assessments by knowledgeable other parties.

he subjected to irresistible temptation a large sample of four-year-olds in the nursery attached to Stanford University. Singly, the children were offered a reward, a marshmallow, but told they could have two if they could wait a little bit and then ring a bell to call back the research-person. Being left alone in the test-room but observed behind a one-way window, they could be watched and the minutes, even the seconds, could be counted before they made their choice. They did delay and the effort of self-control could be exactly calibrated; but after a few minutes most of them surrendered to the irresistible presence of the single reward.[16] It was a neat, intriguing experiment. It could be described by its author (2011) as "now classic", and similar longitudinal self-control studies continue to date.[17]

Forty years post-facto Mischel recalls how idle conversation with his own children over the kitchen table had once made him wonder, What ever became of those test-children as they grew up? This excellent question occurred in the wake of Epstein's articles, which had perhaps not gone unnoticed. So, beginning in 1981, Mischel got in touch with his test-subjects of 1968 to conduct follow-up outcome-studies. Did children's ability to resist instant gratification indicate, as surely it must, a trait of character, willpower, which as they grew up would register in desirable successes? Did it make for a planful person, a prudent one, with good results?[18] Such questions, taking for granted a notion of personality very different from that proposed in Mischel's 1968 book, led rather to the traditional view of a "basic structure of personality," which, as he said, "underlies the individual's uniqueness" and persists across time.[19] It could be profitably examined through "situationist" questions, just as had been pointed out in the 1920s. The author, in a very abundant flow of publication citing and refining his own past work, gradually edged toward acceptance of the new, or not so new, situational orthodoxy. In the end he seemed to claim it for his own and even earned a tribute of relevant papers in a research journal's honorific volume (2009).[20]

16 Bandura and Mischel (1965) 698 and passim for previous articles by Mischel and many also by the senior researcher, Bandura; acknowledgement of studies by William James and Freud, 704, and Mischel et al. (1989) 934. The test itself has been often described, e.g., by Metcalf and Mischel (1999) 3f., Lehrer (2009) 26, or Mischel et al. (2011) 252, and is a standard one (not with marshmallows) among biologists using rats, cf. chap. 3 at n. 84.

17 Closely similar measurement of delay before cheating, among other things, in Mischel and Gilligan (1964) 412ff. or Nunner-Winkler (1999) 262; "classic," Mischel et al. (2011) 252; Moffit et al. (2011) 2695ff., >1000 New Zealand children tested for self-control and its consequences over three decades.

18 On Mischel's recollections, and testing for planning habits and care, see Mischel et al. (1988) 687 and Lehrer (2009) 27.

19 Quoted, Mischel and Shoda (1995) 254; 246, on "the invariance of personality" in the face of "variability across situations"; Mischel et al. (1988) 693, on "enduring personal qualities", and Mischel (2004) 3, on "stable overall individual differences".

20 "Cross-situational", e.g., Brody (1994) 420; Hogan (2011) 249, recalling Allport's acknowledgement of the flexibility of the personality, as opposed to the "situationists criticizing a non-existent claim" that personality was utterly inflexible; Mischel (1968) 295f., rejecting Allport's misleading doctrines in

Trait-defining before measuring trait-effect might look like this, for "conscientiousness":[21]

Adjectives	Adult Q-Sort Items	Child Q-Sort Items
Organized	Dependable, responsible	Persistent in activities, does not give up easily
Planful	Able to delay gratification	Attentive and able to concentrate
Reliable	Not self-indulgent	Planful; thinks ahead
Responsible	Behaves ethically	Reflective; thinks and deliberates before speaking or acting

Subsequent evaluation of subjects under such headings could claim a degree of uniformity if the definitions were well fixed. Descriptive phrases could support single words, most often adjectives; these latter could be clustered together in turn to make up the meaning of a trait-word. Specifically and under controlled lab conditions, the child who did well on the marshmallow test could plainly think ahead and thus possessed, or demonstrated, or fitted under, "conscientiousness". Illustrated in such ways, a science of personality allowing reliable prediction of outcomes would have great practical use.

Could the science tell us about *Homo sapiens* everywhere and across all time? We would certainly like to know. It was a point of weakness in the claim, however, that terminology can show only what people say they understand when they hear such a word as "conscientiousness", defined by descriptive phrases generated in a given, living speech community. The truth is as old as Protagoras, declaring "Man is the measure of all things" but going on to explain that "things are to you such as they appear to you, and to me such as they appear to me."[22] To bring such relativism up to date, we have only to ask whether a "conscientious" person would turn up for appoint-

this regard; acceptance of the need to mix situation and tendency, often by Mischel, or Shiner (2011) 270 or Hill and Lapsley (2009) 245; so also, for acknowledgment of "aggregation" and credit but also some misperception of Epstein, and the citing of Mischel's own position of 1982, see Mischel (1984) 285, Mischel and Shoda (1995) 246, Mischel (2004) 3f., and Mischel (2007) 267; Mendoza-Denton and Mischel (2007) 176, now explaining Mischel's 1968 work on the "personality paradox" in terms of situations, dismissing Epstein and aggregation; Epstein and his citing of the 1928 Newcomb longitudinal survey, credited in Mischel (2004) 2f.; and Mischel's retreat noted, Schütz and Vater (2007) 995. Beyond the celebratory volume, there were other Festschriften, cf. Donnellan (2009) 117.

21 Caspi (1998) 317, part of Table 6.1, "Examples of Trait Adjectives... defining the Big Five Factors"; for "conscientiousness" among the Big Five see Pervin (1994) 103f., 108, or Löckenhoff and Costa (2007) 115; in longitudinal studies, conscientiousness is a prime agent in longevity, see Friedman and Martin (2011) 9, and in economic success, see Segal (2012) 1439.

22 Plato, *Theaetetus* 152A, trans. Jowett.

ments on time – and not ten minutes late? Certainly not a full half-hour?[23] Or will that person pay bills on time? Does that mean within a week? A month? Two months? And will the conscientious person also care for a ne'er do well second cousin for a week, or over the course of an indefinite illness? Or can't one count on that? Answers will be specific to the respondents' particular culture, each with its own descriptive words and values, whether in New Haven or New York, or in Tangiers or Amman – to say nothing of bygone times and places in which historians are interested.

And as a further difficulty, "trait testers appear to assume that whatever they *name* has objective reality; many need not so much to improve the measures but to improve or change their thought regarding traits."[24] Indeed "conscientiousness" has never been seen or heard or touched – only moments of behavior that might among Anglophones be tagged with that particular phoneme. In reply to this objection on the logical plane, against what philosophers call "realist" interpretations, it could be pointed out that quite similar studies have been made of the lexicon of colors, recognizing that each of the terms represents a semantic pause not a physical one along the spectrum. The pauses differ in number and position in different languages but the resulting terminological ambiguities can be controlled through spectroscopy and wavelength-nanometers. These are quantifiable realities out there for all to see. But alas, no such science can be applied to the lexicon of traits. They remain both subjective and culture-specific, even where the research-objective is the description of human behavior in general.

If the logical problems have not really been addressed, though occasionally noted, at least ethnocentrism can be reduced or corrected.

Cross-cultural studies have been most conveniently directed at ethnic sub-groups within the United States (Asian, African, or other); but also in other countries, overwhelmingly in the West (Iceland, Sweden, the Netherlands, Germany).[25] Even in this limited region results have shown differences not reducible to uniformity. Study could be extended to East Asia, for example, through a test to determine if shyness in a child

---

23 "Large differences" in ideas of punctuality comparing Estonians, Moroccans, and Americans, noted in White et al. (2011) 486; Brody (1994) 420, on punctuality as a subset of conscientiousness, in Mischel's treatment.

24 Lehman and Witty (1946) 490, or Harré (1986) 4, making the same point against realism, where psychologists misrepresent emotions through supposing "there is something *there*" that is the phenomenon, rather than "angry people, grieving families", etc. What we mistake for the object of study is only a word, which in the language of each culture designates something particular to that culture. "We reify and abstract from that concreteness at our peril." Further, below, n. 48.

25 U.S. sub-groups, Asian- or African-Americans in Caspi (1998) 318; Oishi et al. (2008) 307 and passim; Okazaki et al. (2009) 378; German children, Asendorpf and Aken (1999) 817, 831, "predictive of important developmental outcomes in both the cognitive and social domain"; Asendorpf (1999) 227; Bergman et al. (2003) 136f.; and New Zealanders, above, n. 17. In all of these studies the entirety of the population is not well sampled.

turns into a general inability to handle relations with others, amounting to "social incompetence", by which marital and occupational success will be later jeopardized. On this score, in Japan, a style of upbringing would be approved which by American standards would likely handicap a child in adult years. The definition of the trait and the word for it turns out not to be universal. Or consider whether a child, seen by peers, parents, teachers or trained observers as prone to quarrel and bully, would likely get into trouble of some form during the teens and early adulthood.[26] Yet there are worlds where anything else would count as a costly, undesirable weakness. Illustrations of this can be found in the next chapter.

How then could trait research lead to "a *generalizable* and comprehensive representation of personality trait structure", true of all our species?[27] An answer might be sought through a lexical approach – through English, that gigantic conglomerate, so widely spoken. From Gordon Allport's days in the 1930s, people competent to explore it began to pull out words that designate traits, at first identifying close to twenty thousand and reducing this total by amalgamating synonyms so far as these could be agreed on (though anyone acquainted with language history can see how approximate this business must necessarily be). Thus by repeated efforts in successive publications the twenty thousand could be reduced to less than five thousand and then to a mere thirty and at last, in recent decades, still further. The resulting "Big Five" seem now well established. They include neuroticism, extraversion, openness, agreeableness, and conscientiousness, as some say; or the first three of these and culture as a fourth, and several other possibilities for a fifth. Or in preference, the Five should really be Six or Three or Two; or Thirteen.[28] Some limited number of these have been

26 Asendorpf and Weinert (1990) 194f.; Aken and Asendorpf (1996) 206ff., 214.

27 "Trait psychology has been a long quest for a universal taxonomy of traits," so, Mischel (1968) 43; quoted, Caspi (1998) 318 (with my italics), cf. 320, and passim.

28 On Allport's work, see, e.g. Saucier and Goldberg (2006) 268, in the best general account of trait-lexical studies; on the origins of the Big Five, see Smith et al. (2006) 130f.; dependence of the Big Five on English, Zhou et al. (2009) 364; Mischel (1968) 45 ("Culture" included), 58 (traits "involve broad categories with vague semantic referants"); Pervin (1994) 103f.; Ozer and Benet-Martínez (2006) 404 (culture); Löckenhoff and Costa (2007) 115; Schütz and Vater (2007) 994; Caspi (1998) 316 (reduction in numbers of traits, to three); three, six, or seven traits, perhaps, say Winter et al. (1998) 233; lack of the fifth factor in various languages, or variants of all five, Smith et al. (2006) 131; reduction to two, Zhou et al. (2009) 367; and Saucier and Goldberg (2006) 274 and Zhou et al. (2009) 365, on the Six proposed. For Thirteen, to accommodate marked differences in Mexican and Israeli sampling-results, see Diaz-Guerrero and Diaz-Loving (1994) 134; 130, noting the "fascinating" (indeed!) acceptance of U.S. ethnocentrism; an overview minimizing any weaknesses in the Big Five model, in Berry et al. (2002) 92–98, while acknowledging that the Big Five model, formed solely in the USA, needs another superfactor (Asian) to fit test data; and this seems to me equally "fascinating". On the IBM model and Hofstede, Nohria et al. (2008), by questionnaire among many hundreds of very big business employees, finds [only] a 60% fit in "overall motivation" with four "drives" recalling the Big Five; and these are "hardwired" and explain "everything we do" as a species. The study illustrates how much in fashion are such studies; and, oblivious of all the above, Terraciano et al. (2005) 96 find "most

called "superfactors" (and with equal truth, also "psycholexical artifacts"), proposed as the essential elements in human personality.[29] Granted, they do not explain anything, as has often been pointed out. They only describe.[30]

For their study and definition, the lexicon was English. Here lay the likelihood of error. "The danger of universalism," meaning what it is that all cultures share, "is that it can enshrine as universal understandings those that are in themselves culturally limited."[31] Gerard Saucier, long a leader in personality factor analysis, saw the need to expand the search to include other languages. A number of these in recent years had been subjected to analysis (Polish, Croatian, and others), to which Saucier with colleagues added Turkish, Greek, and Chinese.[32] The Chinese team found that a personality model in which Seven factors were imagined seemed to fit the evidence best – better than Five, and consisting of Conscientiousness/Diligence, Extraversion (these two posited in the Big Five model), Unselfishness, Negative Valence, Emotional Volatility, Intellect/Positive Valence, and Dependency/Fragility. The Seven are listed here to give an idea of the highly elastic quality of such hypothesized elements in personality, being no different in this regard from other proposed "Big" traits, all as inclusive as possible and, to that extent, imprecise.[33]

Another ambitious recent survey enlisted the cooperation of psychologists and their students in no less than fifty nations across six continents. The college students used as raters were asked to provide a profile of someone they knew well, under many descriptive headings, and their answers were analyzed to see how well these fitted with the Big Five model. A notable approximation to uniformity was asserted, although in the face of very substantial differences in gender issues and perceptions reflecting "a host of culture-level variables that differentiate Europe from Asia and Africa." At the end, claims that "the data largely confirm recent findings of universality in trait psychology" and "the biological basis of personality traits", do seem excessive.[34]

---

personality psychologists today agree that the dimensions of the five factor model (FFM)... account for the covariation of most personality traits".

29 On these quoted words, see Caspi (1998) 316.

30 For the Big Five model as descriptive not explanatory, see, e.g., Pervin (1994) 109 or Costa and McCrae (2009) 299; and the Five have "no theoretical base", so, Saucier and Goldberg (2006) 278.

31 Kapferer (2002) 4.

32 Saucier and Goldberg (2005) 271 and Zhou et al. (2009) 364f., where a number of discrepancies between the non-English and Big Five results turned up; and 366 (Filipino, Hebrew) and passim (Chinese).

33 Zhou et al. (2009) 363; a preference for a Nine-factor model, not Five, in Diaz-Guerrero and Diaz-Loving (1994) 137.

34 McCrae and Terracciano (2005) 548, the non-Western raters generally "Westernized"; 550, raters choosing generally to profile their peer group, cf. Tables 1–2 showing two-fifths of the site-list in Europe and 89% of persons profiled of age 18–25, 94% of age 18–30; 554f., an enormous range of gender contrasts, from Nigeria to England; 553, deviations in Africa suggesting "some distinctive African

A weakness in this particular survey as more generally, too, was the narrowness of the data-base. Psychologists, not only in the United States, have always been heavily dependent on the enrollments in their very own lecture courses, even though "college students are not, in general, representative of their national populations". The fact is acknowledged (though rarely).[35] College students in the United States have represented only a luckier or more determined quartile, and in numbers further tilted in this or that direction by economic class and ethnicity; by their very age-group they are only themselves, not an entire population.[36] A degree of myopia that tolerates dependence on this test-sample and largely dispenses with history and anthropology seems to pervade the discipline even in discussions about our species generally.[37]

---

personality structure that differs appreciably from [that] found elsewhere in the world"; 559, quoted, "confirm... biological"; further, Optimism not Openness; and Terraciano et al. (2005) passim, condensing McRae and Terraciano without change. Ozer and Benet-Martínez (2006) 404 show that links between two of the Five (Neuroticism and Extraversion) are moderated by culture, while Lehman et al. (2004) 698 show optimism itself, and pessimism, differing in East Asian and American samples; and Okazaki et al. (2009) 382 on comparison of the American Big Five bipolar factors with those of a Chinese version, show a match under only one of the Five (which was not among the three most widely accepted members of that Five).

35 Perhaps needlessly to show the pervasiveness of college students as samples, I instance D'Andrade's study of 1965 in Mischell (1968) 46; Winter et al. (1981) 95; Winter et al. (1998) 239, referring to studies of the 1950s to 1970s; Kahneman and Tversky (1982) 167f.; Vaillant (1983) 344f.; Epstein (1984) 223; Triandis (1989) 512; Miller et al. (1990) 35; Mischel and Shoda (1995) 250; Triandis (1995) 122, 202, and passim; Guimelli (1999) 14; Mischel (2004) 12; McRae and Terracciano (2005) 548; Terraciano et al. (2005) 98; Rohan (2007) 1010f.; Liem et al. (2009) 223; White et al. (2011) 483f.; Kahneman (2011) 403; or Keith (2011) 24f., 27. Seeing the sampling as a weakness are Markus and Hamedani (2007) 9; Oishi et al. (2008) 309, 312, or Shweder and Sullivan (1993) 498 to the same effect, on "one particular population (e.g., the contemporary secularized Western urban white middle class)"; more conclusive, Haidt et al. (1993) 625 and passim. In the social sciences generally, for students as approximately 80 per cent of respondents, see below, chap. 2 n. 64; to be noted is the caution of Stanovich and West (2000) 664, note 2, explaining their use (648) of a range of standard tests of cognitive capacity: "All the work cited here was conducted in Western cultures which match the context of the tests. Of course, we recognize the inapplicability of such measures as indicators of cognitive ability in cultures other than those in which the tests were conducted;" and more plainly, Higgins et al. (2008) 175, "the participants in our studies are college students. Thus, the bad news is that no claim can be made that our samples are representative of the general population of each nation" (Australia, China, Israel, Italy Japan, United States). For the quoted words in my text, "students not, in general, representative of their national populations," see McCrae and Terracciano (2005) 548; similarly Okazaki et al. (2009) 386 on personality assessments cross-culturally, warning of "a critical shortcoming... [samplings] primarily in university settings", see also 378, or McSweeney (2002) 94, or Smith et al. (2006) 267, "university students... hardly representative".

36 Indication of the importance of age-group is clearer among non-Westernized populations than among U.S. students, see Mishra (1994) 225, 235f.

37 Farr (1984) 126, "psychologists are ignorant as they only rarely read the literature of social sciences other than psychology".

As an alternative, however, and to reach out more widely, a kind of participant quite different from American college students could be studied. In the 1970s and subsequently Geert Hofstede turned to the results of a very long questionnaire imposed not long prior on more than a hundred thousand of its employees by the International Business Machine company. The object of this device had been improvement in management policies all over the world: essentially to understand and increase job-satisfaction. It amounted to a gigantic data-base, any use of which for statistical evaluation of personality types was bound to be taken seriously. Hofstede thought he could discern in the data a small number, at first four and then five, of "dimensions" such as "collectivism-individualism" and "masculinity-femininity", in terms of which the whole of any person's behavior and inclinations could be summed up. Differences across countries could be perceived, yielding profiles of national character in quantifiable degree; and the same "dimensions" could be looked for and studied in all sorts of other, smaller samplings, by other researchers, following on his success. A favorite target of research has been the contrast at the center of the dimension "individualism-collectivism" and its expression in the way the typical American, and the typical Asian, act and see themselves.[38]

To illustrate the kind of project inspired by Hofstede, one of some scores of questions in a survey will serve, asking respondents:

You're starting a new business, and you are looking for a partner. Which is the most important factor in choosing a partner?

A. Someone with the same business interests
B. Someone who has been successful in previous business ventures
C. A close friend
D. A senior, successful, experienced member of the community

Answers were interpreted as showing, (A) so-called horizontal individualism, HI; (B) vertical individualism, VI; (C) horizontal collectivism, HC; and (D) vertical collectivism, VC; and these were in turn believed to show what Hofstede had explained as societies in which the individual floats free, so to speak, and looks around for help among his peers or others according to the needs of the moment, or instead, feels himself or herself from birth a member of a group to which loyalty and respect are owed, either at the peer level or in the hierarchy.[39]

Hofstede's books have been much admired and described by their author himself as producing "a paradigmatic shift in cross-cultural studies". His results nevertheless have come in for scattered criticisms which Brendan McSweeney capped off in 2002

---

38 See below, chap. 3 at nn. 135ff, and chap. 4 at nn. 58ff.

39 For the question, see Triandis (1995) 210; for the meaning underlying the four answers, see a convenient condensation of Hofstede on individualism-collectivism in Kim et al. (1994) 2.

with a full-scale appraisal.[40] In brief, the whole edifice of interpretations could be brought down by a careful look at its various parts, of which those that seem weakest to a historian are the quite inadequate nature of the sampling, and the "stories" that Hofstede proposed to illustrate his ideas. The choice of respondents was really no more representative of the larger surrounding communities than an equal number of college students would have been (and in many countries, too, the number of respondents was very small). The illustrative stories raised further problems: for example, showing how only the Austrian national character, and by itself alone (if it could be known in the relevant period), could have produced Freud and his theories – an idea no historian would agree to.[41]

Attempts continue to discern some governing pattern in human behavior. They extend from the way individuals are commonly observed to act (and so are judged to have some certain "trait"), to their motivating "values", "beliefs", or "principles". These last three terms are quite conventionally treated as synonymous by Shalom Schwartz in recent studies.

It was Schwartz' aim "to identify the structure of value relations", those "guiding principles" by which individuals in dozens of different countries direct their behavior, and are moved to act in certain culture-specific ways.[42] Respondents gave ratings to over fifty words and phrases like "humble", "moderate", "clean", "national security", "reciprocation of favors", "devout"', "respect for tradition". These, Schwartz arranged under three headings responsive to "universal requirements": that is, answering to our human needs as individual organisms; second, governing our successful relations with our fellows; and, thirdly, enabling the group or society to function as a whole. Under these three, he arranged Ten values (e.g., "power", or "stimulation") displayed in a pie-chart so as to bring out their relation to each other, adjacent values being nearly similar (and so judged by the scaling technique, "Smallest Space Analysis"). On the pie chart were arranged all fifty-six values which respondents were asked to rate, itself divided into ten sections, and these grouped into four "higher order value systems" (e.g., "self-transcendence", "self-enhancement"). The four were determined to be "nearly universal," while even in the Ten "many people across contemporary societies recognize value types". "The basic structure... points to the broad

---

40 Quoted, Hofstede (2002a) 1355, again in (2002); (1994) ix, seeing himself as "spiritual parent" to such studies; a survey of his reception in Berry et al. (2002) 399–401; Smith et al. (2006) 37; and McSweeney (2002) and (2002a).

41 McSweeney (2002a) 1366f. (where in my opinion national character does not permit the prediction of individuals' behavior, only the likelihood of group behavior); further, 1369, destruction of Hofstede's treatment of patterns of labor unrest in several countries.

42 Schwartz (1994) 20ff.; for a slightly fuller definition of "values" see Schwartz (2007) 170f., in a chapter extending his 1994 article into Europe's recent survey; for the history of the term, which most often uses the term or synonyms for "normative" and "belief", see Parsons and Shils (1962) 390, 395.

underlying motivations that may constitute a universal principle that organises value systems."[43]

As has been true of other assessments of foreign cultures beyond that of the prime investigator, respondents to questions have had to be found in the most convenient quarters; so, for Schwartz' work, about four-fifths were university students and school teachers (the remainder, without further description, being simply "general adults"). In Britain, they were 158 students; in Italy, 200 teachers and 350 students all from Rome; in Indonesia, 263 students (eleven ten-thousandths of one per cent); in India, 200 students (in a population of more than a billion); and so forth. How inadequate the samples were to represent their respective populations is all too clear; and more needs to be said on this point (chap. 3 §4). Nevertheless, the publication has been described as "the most influential and respected in the field".[44]

This same assessment of Schwartz' work goes on to add that it is notable principally in its "assumption (which is supported by research) that all people, everywhere, have the same values but differ in terms of the relative importance they place on each value". To say this is to concede an infinite variety in ways of life, such as historians indeed discover; for among every people can be found, no doubt, some minority who hold as a value one of the proposed Ten "motivational values" that everyone else repudiates: for example, "Hedonism... pleasure and sensuous gratification for oneself" as "a goal... that serves the interests of some social entity".[45] It is no more odd to include this, describing (let us say) the Puritan Colonies of the seventeenth century, than to exclude "God-fearing" as a value, which would figure in the favored list of any number of populations today, not to mention the company on the Mayflower. Its absence in fact inclined Schwartz to invent an Eleventh value, of a rather watery consistency ("spiritual life, inner harmony") which might or might not be added.[46] A Twelfth would be the personal and societal goal of leaving behind a large progeny: therefore "Reproduction" which is found everywhere and across all time. There must be room, too, for the personal and societal goal of renown beyond mere acceptance: therefore, "Approval" or enjoyment of general good repute as a Thirteenth.[47] I return to "Approval" a little later.

In the end, research into "personology" seems to me to have been fairly described by Seymour Epstein, quoted above. It is capable only of "predicting most of the people much of the time". Limitations on understanding pervade the field. Nothing better than Epstein's dictum appears possible in the absence of any such rules as those that

43 Schwartz (2007) 176.
44 Rohan (2007) 1009f.; criticisms in Smith et al. (2006) 39f., 46, 77.
45 Quoted, Schwartz (1994) 21f.
46 Schwartz (1994) 23.
47 Among his Ten, Schwartz includes "Achievement: Personal success through demonstrating competence according to social standards" – which may indeed help in the attainment of fame, but is different.

Newton discovered in the universe. Indeed, "structure", the very term in English or other languages in which personality is normally described in realist fashion, betrays in the observer's mind a mental image of a more or less simple, comprehensible design – an inanimate thing; but nothing of the sort has so far been discovered.[48] If instead personality were thought of not as a Rubik's cube but as a well-populated Petri dish, the mental image would allow life itself to control understanding, and with life, change. This, of course, historians would prefer; this is what they work with. There are consequences in modes of thinking.

The labors of Terman, Hofstede, Schwartz and many others in search of universals, using ever-grander samples and more elaborate quantification, have produced at least one clear finding. They have revealed (and it is very striking) an increasing homogeneity of values and behavior in the developed world of telecommunication, university education, desk-jobs, business attire, and associated features of modern life on which research commonly reports. They are all contemporary since psychology with any pretense of being a science can operate only on the living. There are, however, societies like fossils still alive but properly belonging only to the past, which allow a kind of time travel. A hint of what can be learned from them may be found through trait-analysis of Maasai, spoken by the people of that name in East Africa. This lexical study by Gerard Saucier "indicates a high degree of generalizability in the single-factor structure of a highly traditional culture." That is, personality is more easily subsumed under a very small number of traits, to the extent it is "tighter (more strict)"; and this can be demonstrated in the range and number of words describing "character/virtue", "competence/status".[49] Although at the moment Saucier's choice of subject appears to be unique,[50] it allows the conjecture that in long-past centuries such a phenomenon was more the rule than the exception. The number of detectible personality "superfactors" is thus not fixed but varies at different points in time and complexity of civilization.

For this possibility there is in fact some support. Psychologists using other methods have shown how qualities seen in a given society simply as socially desirable or the opposite can, by researchers, be bundled together notionally to yield a one-factor model of personality.[51] This fits with what Harry Triandis and others

---

48 As a reminder, no doubt needless, that psychologists think about the mind and its operations in a misleading way, as "structure" and "constructed", see, e.g., Cosmides et al. (1992) 91 ("architecture", "structure"), Mischel and Shoda (1995) 253, Caspi (1998) 312, 316f., 323, and passim, Löckenhoff and Costa (2007) 115, Schütz and Vater (2007) 994, or Roberts (2009) 139; also above, n. 24.

49 Personal communication (2011) from Saucier, by permission.

50 The Maasai study in Saucier and Goldberg (2006) 272, referring to Saucier's unpublished paper of 2006 and instancing a number of studies or proposals of a Big One structure. McRae and Terracciano (2005) 548 believe "no preliterate cultures have been examined" (ever).

51 Notice the item "Negative Valence", NV, i.e., simply a general and unexplained disapproval, counted among the Big Seven cited above at n. 26 and in Zhou et al. (2009) 378.

found in forager or hunter-gatherer groups – populations exhibiting a far narrower range of relationships for members to choose from, therefore a limited range of roles and expectations, therefore far simpler value systems and correspondingly effective group-pressures.[52] The !Kung of the Kalahari serve to illustrate this at one end of a spectrum, at the other end of which lies our modern city life. In contemporary cultures, simple means poor, complex means rich; rich means able to look around and create one's own life's situation – as is easier to do in the United States, Canada, and Western European countries than in the "collectivist" world of Asia, Africa, and Latin America.[53] Something of history is implied; the industrial revolution and the development of capitalism are implied; a fourth dimension is rendered in three.[54]

Richard Shweder and Maria Sullivan may serve to conclude my sketch on psychologists' search for rules and universals. The two not only find many and undeniable differences among living societies, they even extend the impact of those differences into the individual personality.

> While researchers in cultural psychology are still alert to the possible existence of cross-cultural empirical generalities, which might be derived from comparative research, new presumptions have emerged, e.g. that cultural and institutional factors particular to a population may have a major impact on the processes of psychological functioning and human development, and that local factors of a particular environment typically interact with more widely distributed factors to produce diverse outcomes.[55]

In this opinion may be seen a return to the question put by Auguste Comte in 1852 and asked again by Gordon Allport a century later:

> How can the individual be both a cause and a consequence of society? That is to say: How can his nature depend indisputably upon the prior existence of cultural designs and upon his role in a predetermined social structure, while at the same time he is clearly a unique person, both selecting and rejecting influences from his cultural surroundings, and in turn creating new cultural forms for the guidance of future generations?[56]

And the assumption here is just what Robert Hinde proposed, quoted at the beginning of this chapter: everything that constitutes the individual as such is derived from the surrounding community ("norms, beliefs, and values", as he says, to which other psychologists and anthropologists would add artifacts and everything that makes up a "shared way of life"). The community, so far as it is shared and has boundaries to

---

52 Triandis (1989) 508ff.

53 Newson et al. (2007) 462; Hofstede (1994) xii; or Triandis (1995) 25 ("affluence leads to individualism"); Kim et al. (1994) 1.

54 Recognized by Kashima and Kashima (2003) 125, while (127) pointing out problems in the idea.

55 Shweder and Sullivan (1993) 501.

56 Allport (1954) 9.

define it, is in turn the sum-total of the individuals within it. And as they behave, so is their community constituted. "Psyche and culture make each other up."[57]

To explain the origins of personality a little further: let it be said first that historians – except in biography, and then, with reserve – cannot follow psychologists very far. They cannot profit from the discussions in which Comte and Hinde were engaged, or join in, simply from lack of evidence in such depth as personality studies assume. They cannot be concerned with the debate between the so-called "constructionists" who magnify the culture-added parts of personality, and seem to have the better of the argument, versus "geneticists" who focus on inherited tendencies.[58] Geneticists in fact, beyond basic or hard-wired urges, instincts, or drives governing reproduction, hunger, social relations, and so forth, can point to our latent capacities, the linguistic being the most obvious; and still further, in newborns, and therefore individually innate, personality asserts itself to make a child easily cared for, or alertly responsive, or otherwise unique at birth.[59] Thereafter successive stages of maturation have been distinguished by (among others) Piaget and Kohlberg. These stages, at least in part and in sequence, are also innate.[60] The balance, then, between constructionist and geneticist is hard to strike; the questions are too detailed and complicated for clear answers. They can't be applied, anyway, as models in the understanding of an election, let us say, or a literary trend or a strike-vote.

However, I do see possibilities of profit for historians in what psychologists know about traits and values, and the data-base on which their study must depend. I pursue these questions for their bearing on motivation, my prime target: "why do we do what we do?"

Character or behavioral traits, as was recalled above, are ordinarily taken to exclude mental powers such as overall "intelligence" or perfect pitch or photographic memory, but they include a huge range of such things as honesty, aggressiveness, shyness, introversion, curiosity, optimism, sensitivity, generosity, or conscientious-

57 Quoted, R. Shweder in Kitayama et al. (2007) 137; re-phrased by Kim et al. (1994) 5, or Kitayama et al. (2007) 139, "a dynamic process of mutual constitution emerges between culture and self"; or Lehman et al. (2004) 689, "psychological processes influence culture. Culture influences psychological processes". On artifacts also, and tools, technology, and the like as elements of a culture, see, e.g., Triandis (2007) 62; "shared way of life", Berry et al. (2002) 225.

58 Opposing views about what is acquired vs. genetic open up a million references, e.g., Pervin (1994) 103ff. or Triandis (1989) 507 regarding the species, or Molitor and Hsu (2011) 94 regarding the individual.

59 On urges governing "the major part of man's activities," see, e.g., Malinowski (1947) 102, Caspi (1998) 312, 340, 342; Roberts (2009) 143, "children are born with a wide variety of temperamental starting values", and to the same effect, Molitor and Hsu (2011) 94; and Pervin (1994) 104 likewise sees "temperament" as innate.

60 On the complexity of our genetic selves and repudiation of the Standard Social Science Model (SSSM) of our make-up, see (persuasively) Cosmides (1992) 28, 93–99.

ness.[61] Control of traits like these, to restrain or stimulate them, falls under the social instinct. In everyday terms, all of us want the approval of those we live among – if not approval, then acceptance, or if approval, then better yet: applause and good repute. This was proposed on an earlier page as one of the goals to be expected in every population of the present or past, a "superfactor" – and not without good support. Darwin pointed out the "powerful stimulus to the development of the social virtues, namely the praise and the blame of our fellow men," and traced "the love of approbation and the dread of infamy" to its instinctual basis and the logic of survival.[62] Robert Hogan too looked to our hard-wired dispositions: "The problems of achieving status and maintaining peer popularity are biologically mandated"; and more inclusively, Peter Verbeek declared, "Sociality defines our species. The need to belong through interpersonal attachments is a fundamental motivation."[63]

Just how fundamental is evident not only in the remarkable body of observations produced for us by observing chimpanzees, bonobos, and rhesus monkeys and matching from among them all those acts and gestures which serve *Homo sapiens* in getting along with co-specifics – including ingratiation and deference and status-recognition. No, we can look beyond close relatives, beyond primatology, to see inborn social reflexes at work: we can look even among insects, just where Aristotle chose his illustrations, among ants, wasps, bees.

Add, cockroaches. Psychologists have noticed that people doing a job sometimes did it better if they had an audience, and sometimes did it worse. How come? Robert Zajonc wondered if the answer lay in their consciousness of competence. People quite sure that they could perform well rose to a higher level when they knew others were watching, but those not so sure just made more mistakes. To understand this paradox in simpler terms, Zajonc set 72 female cockroaches to run through an easy maze, and then through a tricky maze, being watched sometimes through a glass partition by other cockroaches, or sometimes accompanied by a co-specific; and the females

61 Defining "traits" such as neuroticism, see, e.g., the view not widely shared that they are "genetically based biological dispositions", so Löckenhoff and Costa (2007) 116 or Bergman and Magnusson (1990) 6; "disposition" equated with "tendency", A. Tellegen quoted in Roberts (2009) 140; or found in the "ordinary" sense of my own understanding, in Pervin (1994) 108, Asendorpf and Weinert (1990) 193ff., Schütz and Vater (2007) 994f., Costa and McCrae (2009) 299f. On "aggressiveness", see, e.g., Bergman and Magnusson (1990) 5, Asendorpf and Weinert (1990) 194f., or Brody (1994) 420; "shyness" and "timidity", e.g., Aken and Asendorpf (1996) 205f., Asendorpf (1999) 227, or Bergman et al. (2003) 137; on "intelligence" as a trait, see Mischel (1968) 35, 146 noted in Epstein (1979) 1098 and (1984) 222; also Caspi (1998) 322 and Oishi et al. (2008) 312; or generosity (altruism) in Trivers (1971) 45ff. (I distinguish between culture-bound traits as intended by Hofstede and his like, from genetic social characteristics of our species, of which I say more in chap. 3).

62 Darwin in *The Descent of Man*, quoted in Verbeek (2006) 424f.

63 Robert Hogan quoted in Smith et al. (2006) 131; Verbeek (2006) 423, 429, with extended observations of child-rearing years and experiences, and the "socioemotional and cognitive framework associated with the deep structure of communal sharing relations".

slowed down in the easy maze when they were conscious of having company, so to speak, and reacted to it, but handled the tricky maze more quickly with an audience, whether of one or many. The suggested explanation lay in arousal. The females knew they were acting out for others; what others thought of them distracted and excited them, with different consequences depending on their confidence in their performance.[64]

The co-specifics whose approval humans most and first desire are their parents, especially their mother, generally followed by another close member of the family, whether uncle or older sibling or grandparent; and then by more distant kin, neighbors, and generally acknowledged authority figures who embody the entire society as a school of trait-learning. "Early development, punishment and reward are delivered not only by the entities themselves," whether a kin-group or a nation, "but by parents and other elders and peers, who usually embody the social conventions and ethics of the culture to which the organism belongs" – so, Antonio Damasio, whose work will need mention later.[65] The social instinct is ever at work, in confined or public settings. From the instant of birth, we oblige, we observe and imitate, always to win approval. In the process our individual character is formed out of our innate potential; in the process and in the aggregate, the character of an entire people is formed.

So much for the role and importance of the social instinct, both in giving cohesion to a society and its ways, and in shaping the individual's behavioral tendencies. But further: measurement of these tendencies (as historians would like to know) can have predictive application. For example, mothers' forming of will-power in their little children, as Mischel noted, increased the children's likelihood of success in school. A number of other studies have been mentioned above, showing long-term costs or benefits nicely correlated with lifetime outcomes in marriage, social relations, career or health.[66] In brief, and quite obviously, how you are shaped as a child determines to a very significant degree how you will shape your course of life and the society around you – since these two are one.

These findings are clearly relevant to the historical discipline, but they can be specially illustrated from the work of ethnologists, who are interested in the whole picture. Jean Briggs and Esther Goody have closely observed (in Canada and Ghana) how mothers behave with small children.[67] Their object as always anywhere was to prepare the infant for success in life, which at the beginning means winning the mother's approval, and then in time most likely includes a male parent's as well,

64 Blascovich (1999) 68f., 75f.; Mendes (2007) 898; and studies among *Homo sapiens* to show better performance if watched, Leary and Allen (2011) 44.

65 Damasio (1994) 174.

66 Mischel and Gilligan (1964) 412f.; Ozer and Benet-Martínez (2006) 409, 412, a personality trait is a "strong predictor" of adult career success; and above at nn. 3f. and 22f.

67 Briggs (1970) and Goody in several publications, best in (1991) 106f., illustrating how dependence on group acceptance and good opinion is taught in childhood in a Ghanaian population, and in Japan.

and older siblings and grandparents and so outward from the core family to a wider and wider community, as maturation (which is socialization) continues – always, for approval, though least evidently in individualistic cultures like the American.

In a collectivistic one like the Japanese, the child is "carefully taught", Goody explains,

> to want to participate energetically in groups based in the neighborhood, school and work, and to seek the good opinion of group members. In order to be sure of acceptance s/he learns to be highly sensitive and responsive to the feelings and wants of the other members of these groups. However, as long as we work within definitions of particular cultures it is not possible to make very interesting observations about learning, since what is learned differs so widely. We tend to find ourselves considering the learning of norms *per se*. Is it possible to go beyond this relativity?

– and Goody engages herself in the attempt to discern larger truths, on the model of physics.[68]

Historians, however, are easily satisfied with less. What the ethnologists notice (especially Goody drawing a number of good comparisons) is quite interesting enough; the conclusions are as thought-provoking as they are acutely observed, for example: "many, probably all, societies consider that one of the major responsibilities of parents is the moral education of their children... based on precept, parable and proverb which specify how a 'good Gonja/Ashanti... man/woman' ought to behave... There are constraints of affect built up in the nurturance relationship, as well as constraints arising from the control the parent has over access to critical resources."[69]

Socialization of course continues beyond childhood. Something more will have to be said on proverbs in chapter 3, and, in chapter 2, on continuing moral lessons in adulthood that Briggs and Goody don't discuss. Their focus on childhood, however, is well chosen to bring out the emotional nature of socialization; "the primacy of emotion in morality," from parental hugs and tidbits to more adult demonstrations of approval for good behavior and the accompaniment of words to describe that behavior, so that the moral vocabulary is filled with feelings.[70] It is feelings, turning us toward or away from something, that are internalized and can motivate well-taught conduct. There is no reason to think motivation was governed or should be explained in any different way in times past, to which historians turn.[71]

68 Goody (1991) 106f.; centrality of teaching, 109ff., 114ff., 121ff.

69 Goody (1992) 13f.

70 Quoted, Verbeek (2006) 426, citing publications, and again, 439. See also Murray (1951) 454, "the seeds of attitudes (which are basically affective, rather than cognitive) are implanted in childhood"; and Hinde (1996) 371 instances many studies to show that Japanese maternal style invites closer affect and attention and uses more affect-salient speech to the child than American or European style, i.e., in a collectivistic society which in my view is the more likely character of societies everywhere, in the past (above at nn. 37f.).

71 Aversive/appetitive emotions accompanying immoral or "morally acceptable behaviors", in Bar-

To learn so much from psychology about traits and their relation to the core character of the surrounding society is very welcome, but a reminder, too, that there is no perfect fit between what historians need to do, and psychologists. The disjunction may be recalled, from an earlier page, between traits and values. We know that the former only describe conduct but "that values influence behavior"; "values guide action".[72] To get beyond observation into the mind of the person or people observed, and so to understand motivation, historians lack the living samples that psychologists can question. They must depend on written sources of which the most obviously promising are letters, diaries, memoirs, and in short, biography;but even a work of this genre, if it is to satisfy, must give some attention to the interaction between protagonist and supporting cast. Without the latter, the protagonist has no more significance than Hamlet at one of his soliloquies. For more serious historical interests, increasingly for a century and more it has been the life and actions of whole classes or populations that count; and, for their interpretation, the tricks of biography are of no use; of no use, much of psychology as a discipline, for all its achievements, in which it is the individual that is explained, not groups or masses. What is instead most helpful to historians is what psychology has to say about values. Its findings offer the best chance of reading the mass mind that lies behind mass behavior.

nett (2007) 586f.; Harris (1995) 474 or Hinde (1996) 371f. on Asian child-training suited to a collectivist culture.

72 The first quotation is from Bond (1994) 74, where the author is concerned also to show how "to integrate the cultural dimension into theories of behavior," and, as values like behavior differ according to culture, values are "the mediating variable of interest that connects to culture"; the second quotation is Schwartz (2007) 171, with good explanation of values as goals, as means of measuring proposed action, and as motivational, 170f.

2 Anthropology and Small Populations

In a journal that declares its mission to promote discussion between historians and social scientists, the most recent report is that, "though almost all historians profess to revere anthropological insights, the lessons of anthropology still seem to pass many by"; and a veteran of the social sciences, recently looking at all of them together, concluded his survey with the suggestion that they should perhaps listen more to each other. "It would be interesting to hear from historians," for example, "as to what anthropology could do for them."[1]

The invitation is welcome if for no other reason than its opening upon the past. For anthropology alone among social sciences has focused not only on living samples or populations but on those also that appear to be "frozen in time", as a newspaper account might put it. They offer for study ways of life that resemble those of long ago, while being at the same time susceptible to close observation and description in quantifiable, verifiable terms.

Yet anthropology and history are sister disciplines, exhibiting much overlap or at least close similarities and dealing with essentially the same subject matter: that is, mankind as individuals but still more in collectivities. Either discipline may, as naturally as the other, take in the empire of Shaka kaSenzangakhona in the Transvaal or, in North America, the long story of Plains warfare.[2] Other populations, although seen as primitive, nevertheless count their citizens in the tens of thousands, even in the hundreds of thousands: the modern Javanese of Clifford Geertz's studies, or many others of a size with the "nations" at least of ancient and medieval times.[3] Smaller tribes than these are reported as living for generations more or less constantly at war with everyone around them, and thus have had foreign relations in a conventional sense, if nevertheless hidden below the ordinary historical horizon. Examples include the Nuer, the "warfare societies" of New Guinea, and the much discussed Yanomami.[4]

---

1 Fernández-Armesto (2009) 217; Fish (2000) 552.

2 On Shaka, Ritter (1955) seems to me preferable to D. Wylie's *Myth of Iron* (2006); on the Plains Indians over some centuries, see Newcomb (1950), writing as an anthropologist; also Voget (1964) 487f. and Nisbett (1990) 259.

3 The Balinese were close to a million in the 1930s, cf. Barnouw (1985) 121; ibid. 37 on the Aymara Indians around Lake Titicaca, some 700,000 studied as one whole culture; and note the 350,000 Toraja in Indonesia, Hollan (1988) 55; 300,000 Bantu in western Kenya described by Wagner (1940) 202; and 170,000 Enga in Papua New Guinea, Feil (1988) 101.

4 The ever-raiding Nuer in Evans-Pritchard (1940) 48, 125; Boehm (1999) 95, New Guinean "warfare societies"; the ever anxious, gloomy Aymara of Bolivia, Barnouw (1985) 38; Nyakyusa in Wilson (1963) 80; Crow Indians in Voget (1964) 487; New Guinean Ok and neighbors, in Morren (1984) 173ff.; Yanomami in Chagnon (1997) 8f., 204 and Borofsky (2005) 121, 175; and Brazilian Mundurucu in Helbling (2006) 173f.

Normally anthropologists prefer their subject to hold still (history begs to differ). The greater part of their data is synchronic, caught in a snapshot not a video.[5] Quite aside from the convenience of this, however, it has some justification; for, where, by exception, preliterate cultures have been studied diachronically in the reports of earlier missionaries, travelers, and long-term residents (some, very careful), it is striking how almost unchanging many can be shown to be over very long periods.[6] They maintain the same integrity that may be seen in any small country such as, let us say, Switzerland. Kinship between history and the social sciences is thus reaffirmed. And if preliterate peoples are made the target of imperial intrusion, they will show a history just like Poland's, for example, or Macedonia's, in a great variety of responses.[7] They may resist to the very brink of extinction, or instead, they may accept an easy accommodation. There were, for illustration, Ghanaian LoDagaa or the Ivory Coast people, the Beng. The latter put up no opposition at all (though indeed they put up fervent prayers to their ancestors and the deified Earth) against French colonial forces, while their close neighbors fought back according to entirely different traditions.[8] Their story can be told in the same way as that of modern countries, applying the same rules of the historical discipline; and, vice versa, what anthropologists have to say in explaining these sub-significant narratives, historians can give heed to, and learn as they do so.

A good figure to learn from would be Franz Boas. A German emigré gaining a position in New York's Natural History Museum and then in the 1890s at Columbia University, he focused his investigations first on a people long in touch with the advanced nations and made familiar through their totem poles and potlatch. They were the

5 "Anthropologists's problems are generally synchronic", at least in past practice, Evans-Pritchard (1962) 52; Ortner (1984) 149f.; Kuper (1996) 7f. and 29 recording the criticism of Malinowski for caring nothing about the changes that might supervene in the lives of the people observed, since change always complicated his favored functionalist approach; but (p. 126) others like Evans-Pritchard and Gluckman have nevertheless found ways of using historical materials.

6 Generally, Schwartz (1980) 161 or Barnouw (1985) 67; the Bantu in Wagner (1940) 202; American Indians in Hallowell (1955) 127, 132ff., or Manson (1988) 92; Samoans in Freeman (1983) 158, 170; the Indonesian Kedang, in Barnes (1980) 87; the Kenyan Gusii in LeVine (1984) 71 (culture unchanged, 1940s-1970s); or the Pacific Islanders involved in the Kula, below, note 47.

7 Among countless illustrations, see e.g., Nader (1990) 8 on Zapotec village reactions to the intrusions of Mexican federal law; Wilson (1963) 17, 39, and 80 (on the credit loss of a traditional hero-type among the Nyakyusa of Tanzania); similarly among the Lugbara of Uganda, denied a life with war, Middleton (1965) 48; Hogbin (1970) 45 on the consciousness of a falling off from the glory days of previous generations of Solomon Islanders; Ross (1984) 90 on the Ecuadorian Achuara Jivaro; Fleisher (2000) 746ff. on cattle-raiding as almost a way of life in the earlier twentieth century along Tanzania's borders; Feil (1988) 107f. on the Tombema-Enga of New Guinea and (quoted) on Mauss. Mauss wrote about the *tee* in the 1920s, using data from Malinowski and others; and Hermann (1995) 155ff., 160, and passim, on the New Guinean cargo-cult.

8 Goody (2006) 23 on the LoDagaa; Gottlieb (2000) 55f. on the Beng; Rousseau (2006) 102 on the ever-peaceful Venezuelan Piaroa or the Brazilian Xinguanos.

Kwakiutl and their many neighbors of the same traditions. Because of the small size and independence of their communities they were specially suited to study. Of course the observer must be cautious:

> There are problems encountered in the investigation into the character of cultures. The more powerfully a master-idea (*Leitmotif*) dominates within a society, the more it finds expression not only in individuals in a given moment but also in many other members of the society, each with their own nature and in different ways. A somewhat clearer picture will only appear if the reigning form is so strong that it suppresses individual differences... I may perhaps offer an example, that of the Indians of America's northwest coast. The guiding principle here is the unlimited urge to gain and maintain celebrity status (*soziales Prestige*), and the intense feeling of inferiority if this is in the least little bit diminished. This shows as much through good as through bad actions. Though rank and wealth are prized above all, it nevertheless may happen that criminals (in the terms of the culture) compete with each other in sheer awfulness. Whatever looks like a loss of celebrity produces shame and can only be made good by treatment that correspondingly raises prestige; and, if that is beyond attainment, then – suicide.[9]

Boas' object was to grasp a people as one whole, and in this aim of course historians will happily join him, to understand collective behavior.

Among his students were two destined to make his views interesting to a very wide readership: Ruth Benedict and the slightly younger Margaret Mead, "towering figures" as they seemed a half-century later. Both took up and developed the idea that (in Benedict's words) "the study of primitive peoples" can help in the discovery of larger truths since "simpler cultures may make clearer social facts that are otherwise baffling and not open to demonstration".[10]

And with the phrase "social facts" Benedict reminds her readers of one of the great names of the time, the father of sociology as he was to be called, Emile Durkheim. He had used that key phrase to mean certain patterns of behavior which in realist fashion he saw as actual existing objects, out there on their own, first to be distinguished (or simply posited, I would say) and then used as tools of analysis. They were or are institutions, ways of acting that influence every individual alike, beyond the response of any particular person at any particular time. They might be a moral value, or the idea of fair exchange, conceptions of wealth, religious dogmas. "Treat social facts as things," he said; and he had many followers in the social-science world of New York as in London, too.[11]

---

9 Boas (1936) 262 and 267, in my translation, on the Kwakiutl, on whom he first published in 1925 and wrote to the same effect in 1928, as quoted in Barnouw (1985) 67. But his interest in the Pacific Northwest peoples went back to the 1880s.

10 Benedict (1934) 55; quoted on the two, Spain (1982) 166.

11 Durkheim (1982) 59, 69 – still the Great Teacher for many social scientists, e.g., Tooby and Cosmides (1992) 25, 27f., etc., accepting Durkheim's realist assumptions with consequent confusion.

Benedict paid her respects also to two philosophers even better known in her day: Herbert Spencer and Oswald Spengler. She acknowledged the popularity of their huge abstract ideas and generalizations, and offered her own, as for example, "Man, all down his history, has defended his uniqueness like a point of honor. Confucius..."; or again, "Greece... did not carry out... the distrust of individualism... which in Greece was scanted because of forces with which it came in conflict" (where her meaning is not immediately clear).[12]

She goes on about the usefulness of evidence from "primitive peoples", in the passage quoted above: "This is nowhere more true than in the matter of the fundamental and instinctive configurations that pattern existence and condition the thoughts and emotions of the individuals who participate in those cultures. The whole problem of the formation of the individual's habit-patterns under the influence of traditional custom can best be understood at the present time through the study of simpler peoples" – in contrast to understanding all the Greeks, all the West, all China across its millennia. "This does not mean that the facts and processes we can discover in this way are limited in their application to primitive civilizations." They can be applied to much larger entities. One might, for example, reason from the Zuni to the Greeks, or vice versa.[13] But the underlying objective in the study of Man remained the discovery of general laws in terms of which data could be assembled in some understandable form, just like the behavior of the celestial society of stars and planets, the latter made rational in their movements thanks to Isaac Newton. The model of the physical sciences was ever the ideal before such early students as Benedict and Mead. So it was and is also for their admired predecessors and their successors to this very day.[14]

If, however, the model of physics or mathematics should prove elusive, *nil desperandum*! Individual data could always be compared for points of similarity, suggesting larger ideas. As Alfred Radcliffe-Brown believed, in the early days of scientific anthropology, "the comparative method used as an instrument for inductive inference will enable us to discover the universal, essential, characters which belong to all human societies, past, present, and future. The progressive achievement of knowledge of this kind must be the aim of all who believe that a veritable science of human society is possible and desirable."[15]

---

12 Benedict (1934) 53ff., quoted; 78, on Spencer and Spengler; on Man, 4; on Greece, 80.

13 Ibid. 79f.

14 Boas' ideal was more empiricist and taxonomic than in the next generation of anthropology, cf. Bennett (1999) 952; but later and to this day, cf. Fish (2000) 553 on "the veneration of physics as the ideal of all science", with other illustrations in my Preface.

15 Radcliffe-Brown (1940) xi; and by successively wider comparisons we advance to "general similarities", "types", and so to "an abstraction only a little way removed from the concrete reality" (of a Durkheimian nature). In another illustration, two very influential anthropologists, Kroeber and Kluckhohn (1952) 181, warn that "as yet we have no full theory of culture. We have a fairly well delineated concept. But... concepts have a way of coming to a dead end unless they are bound together in

For this empiricist alternative to grand theory, an inspiration lay in the work of the Polish Bronislaw Malinowski, with whose study of the Trobriand Islands modern anthropology may be said to begin. His was a functionalist approach, as it has been called: he assumed that a society's norms and routines would develop in answer to basic needs within each people's particular setting. Thus, the setting and culture made sense and had to be understood together. Yet even Malinowski like others before him and after aspired to something beyond field notes. In italics (1916), he wrote, "*Only laws and generalizations are scientific facts*, and fieldwork consists only and exclusively in the interpretation of the chaotic social reality, in subordinating it to general rules".[16]

At mid-point in the last century, Max Gluckman, a leader among his fellow anthropologists by that date, could offer them a very satisfactory summing-up of their achievements to date. He recalled Ruth Benedict's familiar work, *Patterns of Culture*; like Benedict, he also reminded his readers of the Malinowskian attention to specifics and details that he himself especially favored. What they all amounted to was no mere jumble of tableaus of populations, every one more or less minutely portrayed but different from every other. That would be too much like history. What had been assembled was rather an information base from which could be inferred an order governing *homo sapiens* as a species. He saw his discipline in the same terms as his predecessors. Ultimately, the job was to be "scientific" in the conventional sense, aiming at laws, generalizations, taxonomy:

> "Faced by a truly enormous variety of tribes, living in diverse environmental situations... we had to provide a systematic morphology of the forms of tribal society and the patterns of its cultures. Our achievement has been considerable. Anthropological monographs in the last forty years have advanced knowledge of tribal politics, economics, domestic relations, ritual and religion and law, until the study of this field is a specialized, academic discipline in itself. Since these studies have raised general theoretical issues about the nature of social life and culture, the various branches of anthropology have been accepted as making a distinctive contribution within the social and human sciences, and have been deployed on peasant and modern industrial societies. In addition, the studies of tribal life by anthropologists helped to eliminate among the most educated people the idea of tribal society as mere savagery."[17]

a testable theory."

16 Gluckman (1965) 28ff.; Kuper (1996) 22ff., 33, 149; Malinowski (1979) 1 and 9 (quoted); Stocking (1986) 38ff., Malinowski's empiricist approach even to Freudianism, in the 1920s; and Bennett (1999) 951, choosing Malinowski's long article of 1916, later a book on the Trobriand Islands, as "the first modern, theoretically informed ethnological monograph"; and Shack (1985) 18 choosing "Malinowski's *Argonauts*[1922] as probably the single most influential publication in the shaping of modern anthropology".

17 Gluckman (1965) 176.

And if anyone should ask why this spokesman and his colleagues "*had to* provide a systematic morphology", the answer would no doubt be, that anthropology, psychology, or any of the "-ologies" devoted to the study of Man must aspire to membership among "real" sciences. It couldn't be doubted that the goal was attainable and suited to become the discipline's best contribution to knowledge.

But in this same interwar period, before the job could be finished, the forces of change advanced upon the more remote regions of the world with ever-increasing insistence, giving rise, now, to two answers for every question the visitor might ask: "Yes, that's how it is nowadays with the traders" (or "with the district commissioners", or "state courts", or "prospectors", or "missionaries" or "developers"...) "but our old ways were different". The face of the people turned toward the outside was being transformed, necessarily, with effects eventually registering on internal structures. The whole was no longer itself. Rather, it was made up increasingly of various compromises on the way to becoming modern history. Benedict's "simpler cultures" were destined in all but the most obscure corners of the earth to undergo a complicated deformation; anthropology must include in its observation not only the familiar aspects of life, kinship and so forth, but also "such forces as mechanization, industrialization, suburbanization, and internationalization through tourism and the mass media."[18]

An unlucky, almost comical illustration can be seen in the account of Jean Briggs. Early in the 1960s, being interested in studying shamanism, she sought out the most isolated Eskimo group she could identify; with enormous effort and at some personal risk she reached it and settled among them; only to discover they had been somehow evangelized over several decades previously. They had all become devout Anglicans, embarrassed by and estranged from their own past.[19] Marcel Mauss, Durkheim's nephew and follower, saw the consequences of such processes in a certain social custom of New Guinea: "When the gift exchange system of the *tee* is no more, as Mauss lamented, a new sort of man will be born".[20] And for a third witnesses, I may quote my friend Weyer in the 1950s: "The last of the truly uncivilized natives are nearly gone. Just when the techniques of anthropology and psychology have reached a useful stage, we find ourselves almost without any primitive people to try them out on".[21]

---

18 Kottak (1983) viii, in a volume intended to introduce college students to the discipline.

19 Briggs (1970) 2f.; and 4, the Utku are taught to turn their back on their history. It is "bad". For a well analyzed description of the cultural impact of similar colonializing pressures, to be seen among the Sinhalese, cf. Kapferer (2002) 6–17.

20 Kuper (1996) 148 on problems posed to study by colonial influences, and above, n. 6.

21 On the discipline's "ludicrous, not to say tragic, position", see Malinowski (1922) xv; Weyer (1955) 73, 120 (quoted); Southall (1970) 29, on "the melancholy paradox of anthropology"; Marcus and Fischer (1986) 24, on "salvaging cultural diversity, threatened with global Westernization... All peoples are now at least known and chartered"; 36, "the kind of field sites anthropologists have traditionally

In more recent decades anyone interested in the varieties of human society untouched or little changed by Western exploitation, by missionizing, and *cocacolonisation,* could only reach out to that "purity" (call it) through the written record of earlier observers, not through living among them like a good ethnographer. As an example, the Hawaiian natives' sacrifice, if it was that, of Captain Cook in 1779; or by using a description of Iranian nomadic pastoralists of the 1950s and earlier, one might attempt, a half-century later, to reinterpret that record according to the latest theories and *comparanda*; but the hard evidence all lay in the past. Or one might instead describe the "untouched" as they responsively transformed not only their institutions but their very history to make a better fit with the Western world.[22] The study of the primitive thus gradually drew to a close, or almost, and with it, the catalogue of specimen societies through which to understand our more complicated ones.

Here had been – here once lay – what historians must surely find useful. Hence my emphasis on the anthropological scene of a generation ago and more, before the world went global. In more modern times what has been increasingly seen around the world has been the reflection of our Western selves, a fact acknowledged in the anthropological discipline itself by adaptations in its goals and methods. But, as "purity" in the target populations has been lost, so lost also are social phenomena similar to whatever is not modern in the peoples and periods that historians study; that is, tribal practices on a small scale, very closely observed. So one might compare chieftains' feasts with a medieval baron's table, or ideas about honor and kin among the peoples of the Pacific Northwest coast, with duels and feuds still in Andrew Jackson's day.[23] Even more valuable than *analogies* for the purposes of historians are anthropological *approaches*, methods, or theories, both those that seem to work and those that don't; and best of all, the idea of *collective personality*. This last holds out the most promise, in my view, as it is sought and defined by anthropologists.

---

sought can no longer be found, or even imagined without dissonance", and in the "shrinkage" of the world, all are interdependent, none can be treated as "totally alien"; Bennett (1999) 951, for whom the 1950s and 1960s "marked the end of tribal society and culture"; still more obviously in 1992, when N. A. Chagnon saw how "the world is shrinking and 'unknown' tribes or villages are now very rare" (quoted in Borofsky 2005, 25). See further in www.uncontactedtribes.org for exceptional survivors (mostly in Brazil, also Peru and Colombia).

22 On Captain Cook's death in 1779, Sahlins (1995) 5f., Obeyesekere (1997) 194 and passim, and Bolyanatz (2004) 109ff.; Salzman ((2000) 49–53 on the Bassari in southern Iran known through a book of 1961; Gordon (2004) 64 and passim on the Zambian Lunda and their new "traditions"; Kapferer (2002) 16ff. on the Sinhalese; or other illustrations of ethnography rescued from much earlier publications, Boehm (1999) 95f., Ames (1995) 163–69 or Fleisher (2000) 746f. on the Tanzanian Kuria. By my privileging of early (generally pre-1960) reports of non-European cultures to serve in my discussion of collective personality, it will be clear where I stand on the vexed question of any indigenous collective essence and its possible recovery from a pre-colonial past (on which, see, e.g., Dirlik 1996, 9ff., 23f.).

23 On feasts, see for example Hayden (1995) 22f., quoted further at n. 48.

I discuss approaches, first, before turning, last, to the matter of a collective character or (in Franz Boas' term, above) Leitmotif.

Interpretive schools in anthropology of the traditional sort have continued to appear in support of rationalism, functionalism, neo-Freudianism, structuralism, empiricism, post-colonialism, or other. The danger of agendas driving interpretation has been duly noted: for example, "actively unscientific" misrepresentations in furtherance of "ideology", in order to support cultural against biological determinism. Boas and the Columbia school had been a too close-bound, in-turned research community.[24] Prospects of Newtonian certainties we have seen gradually fading. A wit took note of the process: "all the *isms* had become *wasms*".[25] That was in the 1990s in the midst of a contest between the proponents of cultural relativism as against universalism, a contest invoking Marxism and Capitalism and sustained by the best academic presses into the present century. It will need mention again, later.[26]

But beneath theory there remained the techniques of science. These had naturally been applied from the earliest days, even back in the nineteenth century by Franz Boas. A more modern instance was Jessie Bernard's testing (1945) of Margaret Mead's work, which was by that date hugely admired and solidly established in the public mind. Mead had drawn conclusions about sex-differentiation from the comparison of three "preliterate cultures" where, in one, the people "as a whole are maternal and feminine in temperament". In a second, she found them "ruthless, aggressive, and positively sexed;" and in a third, men were like women and women were "dominant, impersonal, managing partners". Without Bernard's challenging Mead's assumption that an entire population may have a personality that can be sensed and described, nevertheless the vocabulary of her analysis was open to misunderstandings: "feminine", "masculine", and so forth. He wondered,

> How could one set up a scientific study to test her generalizations? First of all, there must be some clear-cut definition of terms. What do we mean by 'temperament'? Do we mean acquired

24 Freeman (1983) 282, 302, and Crook (2007) 125–54 on the relations of Boas, Benedict, Mead, and Mead's second husband Reo and romantic partner Gregory Bateson, very much a Bloomsbury group; Roscoe (2003) 583, 585, on Mead's bringing a "theoretical gestalt" to Papua New Guinea and in fact finding just what she wanted within a few days of arrival; response by Leonardo (2003) 593ff. with reference to various agenda-tilted treatments of the Arapesh in New Guinea; Tooby and Cosmides (1992) 44 on what might be called scandals even in anthropology, beyond Mead's faults; Bennet (1998) 954 on difficulties confronting attempts at restudies; but corrections to field notes sometimes successful, as e.g., in Knauft (1987) 458, reviewing several "peaceful" characterizations.

25 Quoted, Kuper (1996) 188. It is striking, how introspectively unhappy the discipline appears in its publications, witness, e.g., Spain (1982), Kuper (1996) 52f. and passim, Bennett (1999) passim, or Fish (2000) 553, 559, and passim.

26 See in Chap. 3 nn. 35f., 51, and 54, regarding the nature of rationality in preliterate societies, argued in books from the 1980s onward, by M. D. Sahlins (e.g., 1995) and Obeyesekere (1997) with a continuation in, e.g., Bolyanatz (2004), who presents it as "*the* anthropological debate of all time" (109).

> traits like 'bravery, hatred of any weakness, of flinching before pain or danger'...? Obviously, if we define temperament in such terms, there can be no question of cultural conditioning. Not even the most confirmed believer in innate characteristics would, I believe, argue that these traits were inherited... these are not matters of temperament so much as of mores."

And Bernard goes on to imagine a biaxial measurement in which the line "choleric-phlegmatic" crosses that of "melancholic-sanguine", and Mead's three preliterate peoples can each be situated in the picture. Yet "no one," he argues, "ever claimed a sex bias in these temperamental types in our own culture. Women as well as men have about as good a chance to be one as another... At any rate, once temperament is defined, the next step is to measure it", by such things as basal metabolism tests or tests of glandular function. These could be applied then to Mead's three populations. Where, however, no such measures were in fact made available, they are badly missed, and when, rarely, they were attempted by Mead herself, the numbers translated into nonsense. "In brief, what we really hunger for is not only the fascinating cases that Miss Mead presents so well but also frequency distributions, measures of deviation, and dispersion, etc." With still further discussion, her findings about sex roles and temperament dissolve into nothing.[27] Bernard had (as Freeman was to do, many years later) in effect applied replication as a test.

In aiming at rigorous argument it was natural to extend it with that other standard instrument of the scientific inquiry, quantification, even of quite unlikely subjects. An example is the *tee* mentioned above, or continuity of marriage customs among the people of Kédang in Indonesia – though of course too much quantification could be ridiculous.[28] It served very well in controversies. Derek Freeman in 1983 – after his own years of residence in Samoa, talking with Samoans old enough to remember the times and customs that Mead had described in 1928 – took issue with Mead's lines of reasoning, as Bernard had done; but, in addition, he questioned the reliability of her observations, which Bernard had accepted as the starting point of his criticism. Just how well had Mead been able to do her job among the Samoans? Her field notes could be taken as the database; but they revealed a very brief and incomplete immersion in Samoan life; also an ignorance or disregard of many (and discrepant) descriptions of that life by previous observers over a full century preceding her residence. Measured against statistics from twenty years later, Mead's statements about suicide, adoption, and so on didn't hold up.[29]

---

27 Bernard (1945) 176f., on Mead's New Guinean Arapesh, Mundugumor, and Tchambuli, and 179f. on their study (quoted); further criticism of her Procrustean treatment of evidence to make it fit generalizations, or careless mis-reporting, in Brown (1965) 164–71; and Sullivan (2004) 184.

28 The *tee* at note 7, above; Feil (1988) 104; on Kédang near Timor, Barnes (1980) 87. In Gouldner and Peterson (1962) 375 and passim or Gluckman (1965) 35f., examples of "mensuration gone mad"; Novick (1988) 383ff., on the vogue of quantification setting in among historians post-WWII.

29 Freeman (1983) 123–71 passim, 203ff., 185 and 202 (virginity-tests), 221 (suicides), 259–67 (teenage delinquency and crime). Since nineteenth-century observations and those that Freeman could quan-

A second prominent instance of quantification in controversial matters concerned "the Fierce People", the Yanomamö (Yanomami) of the Amazon basin around the Brazilian-Venezuelan border. It was Napoleon Chagnon who most fully reported on them in 1968 and subsequently. He lived among them for decades, particularly among those found in one certain large area (Kaobawä). Here, "warfare, violence and abduction of women have been extremely important factors in their history as far back as I can trace it with informants who are very old – perhaps in their 70s or 80s – in 1964 when I began my work. They have long since died". In about a dozen villages with a population of nearly 1,400 in 1988, he made a careful count of those who killed more than once, or themselves had suffered a violent death, or had lost kin in such a way.[30] It was an unusual sort of census, unusually precise, in answer to critics who had challenged the characterizing of this people as "the fierce".

Questionnaires could yield quantifiable assessments of tribal values, asking about human nature (is it good? or bad? and how do we relate to nature, or to the past or the present?).[31] For practical purposes, polling was used by David Smock in a district of Nigeria, where the government in 1966 proposed to establish and fund communal palm plantations. Where would such projects be most likely to receive good support and attention from the residents, given that no harvest from the investment could be expected for five or six years? Which villages had a collective character best suited to succeed, qualifying, for instance, as "more self-reliant", "more likely to believe that by working harder they can improve their position", or "more fully imbued with the puritan ethic and the entrepreneurial spirit"? "The puritan ethic came out in a questionnaire asking whether respondents thought it advisable to forego immediate pleasure in order to achieve more lasting satisfaction in the future". The point of the exercise was to identify in percentiles the traits that would be "predictive".[32]

Rorschach testing, too, was used to detect personality traits in a given culture from the 1940s on. In illustration: gross differences could be measured between two groups of European descent in Western America, and two groups that were Indian, but also differences between the two members of the latter pair. It was possible also to distinguish in numerical terms some of the dominant aspects of character among

---

tify fitted well together, there was no reason to think that Mead's Samoa had really been different.

30 Chagnon (1997) in the fifth edition, with changes from the first of 1968, at page 204. The controversy over "fierceness" became embroiled in serious charges principally against a certain Neel but also Chagnon, brought by a journalist Tierney (2000), and supported in a sourcebook and syllabus with stimulating questions for students by Borofsky (2005), the whole collection being tilted against Chagnon. However, a supporter R. Hames (121ff.) is quoted on the Chagnon side, and Gregor and Gross (2004) add still more to correct the balance.

31 Henrich (2005) 799f. on testing for reciprocity-values in very remote villages of several continents; similarly in Newson et al. (2007) 462f. on market-values; and further, questionnaires put to a range of wealth-levels, Haidt (1993) 614, 617f.

32 Smock (1971) 60–72 passim.

Eastern American and Canadian Indians and how deeply rooted these aspects were in the psyche of persons tested. A. Irving Hallowell made the case, with due caution:

> *If* it be assumed that personality structure is, in large part, a product of training, experience, and psychological integration that is directly related to the cultural variables that constitute the individual's group-membership situation; and *if* it be assumed that reliable information on personality structure can be inferred from the manner in which the subject responds to the stimuli presented by the Rorschach figures, *then* it must be granted that the data obtained in this way are psychologically significant...

and Hallowell continues, that without such anchorage in shared perceptions, "the individual... could not function effectively". As others put it, in the absence of value-coherence (which *is* the culture), the "social system would cease to work".[33] Thus by scientific testing the most essential collective traits could be shown not only to exist but could show how they came to exist, through being internalized.

The existence of collective character remained a given, and its resemblance to national character was noticed, too. Anthropologists not unreasonably arrive at and share their overall impression of their subjects, drawn in broad strokes though needing improvement over the course of longer residence and deeper inquiry. It is assumed that in every people there really is a collective character to be discovered. The notion pervades anthropological publications and analytical discussions.[34] "It

---

33 Early Rorschach use by A. Kardiner and others, cf. Manson (1988) 70f.; Hallowell (1955) chap. 3, esp. 39 (quoted), 42f., 143, 149; Kaplan (1954) 329; Spiro (1999) 12 adding nuance to Kaplan's studies, where also by a different method (a questionnaire) Kluckhohn and Strodtbeck (1961) 80–90, 138, and passim, had found similar significant differences. On the absolute necessity of value-coherence, see statements in Fortes and Evans-Pritchard (1940) 20 (quoted, "cease to work") or Strauss (1992) 8; or Kaplan (1954) 320, Kuper (1996) 52, or Rousseau (2006) 76, saying shared values insure conformity and communal harmony.

34 Above, nn. 4, 29; the Zuni "a ceremonious people", Benedict (1934) 59, 78; "war alone is the dominant concern" of the Prairie Indians, Boas (1936) 266; "the will to superiority" is central in Kwakiutl character as Benedict saw it, Codere (1956) 334; "proud, excitable, dramatizing," the New Guinea Iatmul, Bateson (1936) xxii; the "callousness" of Balinese, in Mead, quoted, Wikan (1989) 297, who are "progressive and unconservative," Manners (1956) 165, and "measured, controlled, graceful", Hollan (1988) 52 or Just (1991) 290; among the Nuer, "simplicity, single-mindedness, and conservatism," etc., Evans-Pritchard (1940) 30, 130, 151; the Ilongot loud, eager talkers, gesturing, exclaiming, expressive, Rosaldo (1980) 14; the Camayuras "a happy people full of good humor", Weyer (1955) 121; the "coarse and dull" Mailu of the Trobriand Islands, Malinowski (1979) 5; the Kede "adventurous, courageous," etc., Nadel (1940) 195; the Borneo Ibans "the wickedest headhunters in the whole world", Vayda (1976) 48; the Northeastern American Indians "stoical", Hallowell (1955) 133, 144; the "passivity and docility" of the Swazi, Nader (1990) 296; "self-control and restraint" of the Javanese, Just (1991) 290 or Geertz (1960) 367; "harmony, reciprocity, and moral behaviour" of the Venezuelan Piaroa, in Rousseau (2006) 102; or on Manus island, "a puritanical, materialistic, driving people", Crook (2007) 132. In a survey of perceptions of "cultures" across the last century and a quarter, Triandis (2007) 64f. and passim assumes the separate, distinguishable existence of cultures in scores of thousands

is a common impression of those who visit foreign countries," wrote Gregory Bateson apropos Ruth Benedict's work, "that the natives are either faster or slower, brighter or duller in their reactions than the members of the observer's community. This impression is no doubt due to some form of cultural standardization of the personalities concerned."[35] Or again, the conclusion is drawn from a variety of cultural anthropologists, that "most cultures have a few basic principles that classify and evaluate broad ranges of behavior and/or emotion. Such key orientations establish ideals and values, and can be crucial to an understanding of motivation."[36] And, looking a little more deeply, we have Victor Barnouw in his description of the Navaho and other Indians: "modal personality [may be] defined as the sum total of learned cultural behavior" and "the theory that modal personality patterns play a significant role in historical events seems important and one wishes that historians would take note of it". Marshall Sahlins agrees: "The claim is not that culture determines history, only that it organizes it."[37]

To take the next step and apply a further lesson from anthropology, a key term here needs clarification. Should "cultural" be treated in rationalist fashion, and as the active, shaping force of its member-population? Instead, is culture itself shaped by a modal personality? Or (in nominalist fashion) perhaps culture *is* the modal personality aggregated? Boas, Benedict, Mead and many others had made such questions familiar. In criticism, on the level of logic, the circularity of their reasoning could be pointed out; and it could be added, as a matter of observed fact, that "any culture is a system of expectancies: what kind of behavior the individual anticipates being rewarded or punished for... For this and other reasons (e.g., the strongly affective nature of most cultural learning), the individual is seldom emotionally neutral to those sectors of his culture which touch him directly". By this latter formula the whole matter of collective personality is firmly seated in the living minds of the society's members, not in the imaginary world that lies beyond the philosopher's cave.[38]

world-wide.

35 Bateson (1936) 177 (quoted).

36 Knauft (1985) 61, and (2) as illustration, his finding among the Gebusi "the dominant ethos is one of self-effacement, easy humor, and friendly deference;" again (1987) 459.

37 Kaplan (1954) 334; 319, instancing a student of Clyde Kluckhohn's, V. Barnouw (1950) on the Chippewa; and Sahlins (2004) 11, quoted.

38 The "modal" personality, in Kroeber and Kluckhohn (1952) 166, Kaplan (1954) 319, 334, Kuper (1996) 149 on Malinowski's "people's model", Spiro (1999) 7f., or A. F. C. Wallace cited by Sullivan (2006) 643; 641, on Mead's perceived equating of individual personality with culture; Mead's characterizations in Bernard (1945) 176 or Freeman (1983) 90, and Benedict's in Benedict (1934) 131 of the Dobuans. On the circularity of supposing that culture shapes individual behavior, where culture in fact is shaped by individuals, see, e.g., Freeman (1983) 74 on Benedict's and Mead's "theory of culture as 'personality writ large'"; Codere (1956) 334, quoting Benedict (1934, 222) on "the ideal man" of the Kwakiutl. See also Kuper (1996) 184 on Boas' students; better, Kroeber and Kluckhohn (1952) 157 (quoted, on "expectancies"); and Bennett (1999) 952. Impatient of all "stereotyping" as he sees

But whether it is to be found in the living mind or is rather modal, the personality prevailing in a given culture must have as its foundation whatever can be found in every culture, demonstrably universal. Quite aside from urges or drives, Darwin pointed out how contractions of certain facial muscles in Man (as also in other primates) convey identical emotions cross-culturally and, on this foundation laid in 1867 and 1872, the most recent discoveries by psychologists have built, to confirm his findings beyond dispute and to greatly extend them, too.[39] A half-dozen emotions are favorites (anger/rage, fear/anxiety, disgust, sadness, joy/happiness, interest/surprise) but others must be added. Laboratory means can show them to be mostly under the control of the autonomic nervous system and distinguishable from each other, in whatever age of subject or cultural context. Of the six most often listed, anger can be shown to last longest; most obviously, to spur action; and to do so most strongly. Heart-beat, breathing, and skin temperature are affected. It seems likely, however, that facial expressions, or the raised voice or tears or "any component of emotion can assume this initiating role".[40]

Hard-wired behavior, so far as it shows in facial expression, might sometimes appear to deviate from the accepted universals according to the people studied, as, for example, in displays of anger.[41] Appearances, however, are deceiving: the feelings really are there but it may not be the choice of a people to let them show. What will be reported by observers trusting only to their own eyes must be corrected by laboratory tests and comparative findings; and these will better reveal the universals. It is only tradition and custom that make them look different.

The extent to which universal elements control patterns of behavior and account for the shape of whole cultures, anthropologists have debated as much as psychologists. I reported some of their discussion in the preceding chapter; I return to it in the next chapter, too.[42] In both disciplines, discussion has lingered on the significance of behavior deviating from perceived norms and on the degree of plasticity in human

---

it, Hofstede (1994) xi declares flatly, "a culture does not consist of modal personalities; culture is no king-size personality".

39 Darwin's article in *Notes and Queries on China and Japan*, 1867, precedes his *Expression of Emotion in Man and Animals*, 1872, where Tassinary and Cacioppo (1992) 28 date the beginnings; cf. MacMullen (2003) 59; and on proposed basic emotions, 53f., 59f., as also in Levenson (1992) 23f., Zajonc and McIntosh (1992) 72, or Fish (2000) 556; and on universals, above, chap. 1 nn. 1 and 29–34, and below, n. 43.

40 On forceful anger, Levenson (1992) 24 or MacMullen (2003) 77; and quoted, Levenson (1992) 26.

41 Fish (2000) 556; on the role of display rules and consequent differences which can be shown up as cultural by lab tests, see, e.g., Tassinary and Cacioppo (1992) 28f., and Ekman (1992) 35 or MacMullen (2003) 71, anger displayed by Americans compared with Japanese.

42 Perhaps first in Benedict, see Freeman (1983) 74, culture is "personality writ large"; later, Kuper (1996) 184; or the two can't be kept separate, Hallowell (1955) 33, and Eggan (1954) 55 agreeing; or socializing forms personality (so, Mead and Benedict), in Voget (1964) 484, 486, Nadel (1940) 195, Sullivan (2004) 188, or Murty and Vyas (2006) 627. Further, see below, nn. 54ff.

beings in the process of their socialization. Were they susceptible of absolutely any formation by their parents and other members of their community? Nature was proposed as at least very important in the outcome; then nurture commanded the field; more recently, champions of nature seem to be again ascendant.[43]

To illustrate plasticity, consider two cultures in the southern Pacific. One of the pair is found in Tahiti; the other, well to the west of Tahiti but with the same climate, in Truk. This latter is a lagoon embracing a number of tiny islands. While both members of the pair present "an image of the tropical paradise", the Truk population must venture beyond the walls of the lagoon for each day's subsistence, out in the open water, with effort and risk. The men are a fierce, macho folk. In Tahiti by contrast, males show none of the Truk competitive and possessive behavior. Relations between the sexes in the two populations reflect these differences also.[44] It would be easy to point to other pairs like the Tahitians and Trukites, showing how one and the same human material can be made into two quite different ways of life in response to their surroundings.[45] Response will reveal an existential or functionalist logic.

But not entirely and not always. A second pair show quite different adaptations to essentially the same environment. Among the Kede people along the banks of the Niger, those upstream do some fishing but mostly farming while those adjacent to them downstream have extended their fishing to trade and transport. These latter over time have become the carriers of everything that moves on the river, thanks to their willingness to take risks, embark on trips of many weeks, and venture among quite other populations. They "are adventurous, courageous, possessed of a spirit of enterprise."[46] The differences within the two Kede peoples developed from within the community without regard to subsistence or what might appear to be the logic of the situation, at least in any subsistence-driven fashion.

Still further along the spectrum of nurture-shaped ways of life, the Kiriwinan islanders and the surrounding Melanesians offer a good example in their *kula*, described as "a pursuit of immense importance to the natives, and playing on almost all

---

43 On deviance as observed and how it should be explained, see Wagner (1940) 202f.; Bernard (1945) 179f.; Brown (1965) 165; Manson (1988) 114; Kuper (1996) 149–52; Brubaker (2004) 49ff.; and Sullivan (2006) 603. On a tilt toward hard-wired universals, see, e.g., on Mead or Benedict, Voget (1964) 484, or Sullivan (2006) 644; the differing emphases noted by Helbling (2006) 156, 168f.; on universals being favored, see, e.g., D'Andrade (1992) 24, Cosmides and Tooby (1992) 207f., Spiro (1999) 9ff., and especially Barkow et al. (1992) passim. Zajonc and McIntosh (1992) 71f. review the good neurological evidence for distinct mental states identifiable as appetitive or aversive, cross-culturally; further, on these and universals, Levenson (1992) 23f., Ekman (1992) 34, Fish (2000) 556, or Rousseau (2006) 76, on "values that form part of our species' make-up: food, sex, sleep, security, company".

44 Nisbett (1990) 259f.

45 E.g., Newcomb (1950) 318ff. on Dakota, Cree, and other Indians, or Ross (1984) 90f. on different branches of the Peruvian Jivaro.

46 Nadel (1940) 195 (quoted) and passim.

of their social passions and ambitions." Its origins lie some hundreds of years in the past.[47] Bronislaw Malinowski is quoted in a book that first brought attention to the *kula*. The custom or institution recalls one common in American high society a century ago, in which people left calling cards with their friends and acquaintances, sometimes adding a few words of greeting; and it was a thing to be proud of if one's silver plate on the hall table had lots of cards left there to show the next visitor how sought-out the recipients were. Similarly the *kula* enlisted the whole population of scores of little maritime communities on scores of islands of which the Trobriands are the best known. Emissaries from them sailed around to each other in outrigger canoes, in the less perilous seasons, leaving off and receiving in exchange decorative shells, often inscribed. The shells were of two species, and the carriers of the one coasted about in a counterclockwise direction, taking weeks or months on the circuit, while those of the other species went clockwise. Shells were valued for their previous owners, whose lineage could be traced and would be well remembered. Carriers who returned home with specially storied shells to be worn or displayed in their home drew praise and prestige upon their communities and themselves. Leadership status in their homes depended significantly on one or another aspect of the *kula*.

Yet it had nothing to do with subsistence. Deeply penetrating the lives of everyone directly or indirectly involved, holding its place in that remote Pacific world over the course of countless generations, the *kula* exemplified in remarkable fashion just how much a way of life could be constructed without material logic. As Malinowski insisted, it "contradicted in almost every point" our modern economic literature and notions of exchange.

> All its main transactions are public and ceremonial, and carried out according to definite rules. It is not done on the spur of the moment, but happens periodically, at dates settled in advance, and it is carried on along definite trade routes, which must lead to trysting places... the Kula is not done under stress of any need, since its main aim is to exchange articles which are of no practical use.

The point Malinowski wanted to emphasize here he made again through his description of how the same people took care of their basic subsistence. They depended principally on a staple, yams, that men grew in the family garden. What struck the observer most was the pride that was taken in making one's garden not simply productive, but pretty and neat and embellished. At the end of the season, too, it should produce a yield sufficient to feed all dependents, all guests, absolutely anyone who asked; and in fact a great deal was left to rot, since there were no takers. The owner could expect general applause for all this; that was his reward. In contrast,

47 Malinowski (1922) 73; on a *kula* article datable to between 500 and 2000 years ago, see Malnic (1998) 16.

> A notion which must be exploded, once and forever, is that of the Primitive Economic Man of some current economic text books. This fanciful, dummy creature, who has been very tenacious of existence in popular and semi-popular economic literature, and whose shadow haunts even the minds of competent anthropologists, blighting their outlook with a preconceived idea, is an imaginary, primitive man, or savage, prompted in all his actions by a rationalistic conception of self-interest, and achieving his aims directly and with the minimum of effort. Even *one* well established instance should show how preposterous is this assumption that man, and especially man on a low level of culture, should be actuated by pure economic motives of enlightened self-interest.[48]

What brought Malinowski to a boil was the dismissal of the primitive as hardly human, on a level beneath that wonderful invention of his own academic world, *homo economicus*. The Kiriwinans whom he knew and some of whom he valued as friends were in their fundamental nature no different from himself. What, after all, was meant by "rational", the term of praise? It looked only to "practical use" and "utilitarian purposes". In his own observation, social institutions, structures, or the modal personality (not that he used the term) could not be explained solely through subsistence needs, material benefits, security against hostile neighbors, or similar factors. They developed in more complicated ways out of a different logic. They were much more the invention of a community, over time, and require a wider definition of rationality – a matter reserved for the next chapter.

To this point, my discussion has been concerned with the external features of generally small, preliterate populations, as they appeared to visitors from a more complicated world – my object being to note whatever these latter noticed that might also illuminate the large populations of more formal history. The most striking observation made by visitors, it seems to me, is the governing personality they are able to identify, or think they can identify, in whatever group they may be studying. From this, observation will turn to the constituents of that personality, of which some will be universal and of our species, and will dictate behavior directly: as, for example, the reproductive urge. Others, for example governing speech or nurturance, find expression in traits particular to a culture.[49]

They are the product of that most delicately interactive relation whereby each individual helps to define the collective way of life while being at the same time

---

48 Malinowski (1922) 59; and in other writings always insistent that "while the 'savage' may be no more rational than ourselves, he is at least as reasonable" (summed up thus by Kuper 1996, 23). Compare the similar *tee*, "'irrational' in the logic of modern economics thinking", in Feil (1988) 108, or "the essentially nonutilitarian, or surplus, nature of feasting" in various tribal settings, Hayden (1995) 22, often noted, cf. e.g., Malinowski (1922) 172; care taken by Harris (1984) 113f., not to call Yanomamo belligerence irrational simply because it was not materially profitable; similarly, Newcomb (1950) 319, on warfare as seen and waged by several of the Plains peoples, not really "an economic war"; and more generally on "nonmaterial dimensions of behavior," Blanton (1995) 106.

49 A debate of little concern to me, but see Newson et al. (2007) 454, 457, indicating its outlines and the proportion of causality, split between the hard-wired and the culturally acquired.

shaped by it – a never-ending process which anthropologists go on to explain in more detail, focusing above all on the coherence of the result. On this, as they say, existence itself depends (above, at n. 33); according to its rules everyone must do things the same way. It is expected. Conformity is taken to be, at least in part, response to the existential demands of the immediate environment; yet function by no means explains everything, neither *tee* nor *kula* nor rituals of many sorts which have somehow become, and so simply are, the custom. They determine proper conduct in whatever role or position one acts: as parent, child, warrior, medicine man, forager, wood-carver, but above all, as a good group member.

In the forming of a collective character, no moment could be more unguarded or revealing than childhood. Here, observers have been on the watch for the first signs of personality typifying a people and destined to develop into adults who will reify that people's most distinctive values.[50] At one extreme have been the investigators who thought they could see a group personality emerging from the very earliest months of upbringing. In consequence, much analysis of weaning was needed, and of sphincter control and of what a non-believer mockingly called "diaperology".[51] In time, interest in anal and oral experience and other Freudian elements in the forming of the members of a culture, and so of the culture itself, seems to have faded, but without diminishing interest in the guidance provided to children by parents and close kin. Emotional ties and rewards and how they worked and their huge importance in the forming of little children have been noted;[52] observation and imitation of others as well, quite unguided at every young age;[53] the forming of teenagers also, as for example among the New Guinea Iatmul, where a public celebration will be staged

---

50 Begin with childhood: so, Margaret Mead in Sullivan (2004) 189, Kaplan (1954) 334, Lutz (1988) 107f., Strauss (1992) 8, or Murty and Vyas (2006); ferocity taught to Nuer children "from their earliest years," Evans-Pritchard (1940) 151; to Iatmul children, Bateson (1936) 4; to Maori, Vayda (1976) 81; to Yanomamö children, Chagnon (1997) 127; to children of New Guinean "warfare societies", Boehm (1999) 95; generosity and sharing, to Bemba children, Gluckman (1965) 52, to Solomon Islanders, Hogbin (1970) 35, and to Murngin children, Peterson (1993) 863, 866; club-forming to Nyakyusa boys, Wilson (1963) 67; suspicion of strangers, to Kayan children, Rousseau (2006) 77; non-competitive behavior to Samoans, Freeman (1983) 88; no fighting, to Zuni children, Whiting et al. (1956) 95, or Briggs (1970) 137 and passim on the Utku; civil, peaceable manners to the Balinese and Toraja, Hollan (1988) 52–55, and to Dou Donggo, Just (1991) 298ff.; and the group personality stubbornly perpetuated in children, Hallowell (1955) 39. But notice the report of Goody (1991) 120, "Most of the patterns of learning prosocial behaviour... have not been the result of formal teaching. It is seldom possible to know what the adults had in mind when they shaped... behaviour because the ethnography seldom addresses the question".

51 M. Mead even pronounced personality types to be characteristic of a group by inheritance, genetically, see Sullivan (2004) 187f. Especially Abram Kardiner championed Freudian theory in culture-formation, see Manson (1988) 52f., 96f., Kaplan (1954) 319f.; also Quinlan and Quinlan (2007) 168; and "diaperology", Manson (1988) 106.

52 For example, in Briggs (1970) passim or Goody (1991) 106–19 and (1992) 13f.

53 Haidt (2001) 828.

by a proud mother for the daughter who returns from her first successful fishing attempts, or among the Malawi Nyakyusa:

> ...often a man would say to his son 'Don't you hoe for me, I'll do the hoeing myself, you go and swagger about.' Sometimes a man would sell a cow and buy a huge-bladed spear and give it to his son. Then, if he heard that his son was a fierce man in war, and always quarreling with and spearing his fellows, he would say with pride: 'He is my son!' And if he heard people saying: 'The son of so and so is a fierce man', he would rejoice.[54]

In these latter pictures the whole community is seen functioning as a school, teaching lessons in the behavior most approved by adults, to adults. Their value system can be sensed in their myths and stories. Public symbols, rites and speeches are equally useful and open even to an outsider.[55]

What is taught at the knee, respect for one's elders, is a value spelt out in larger terms by the prominence, or often the special privilege of speaking to one and all, that belongs to older members of the community.[56] The privileges of age shade off into ancestor worship. This in turn shades off into an awe that is the proper tribute paid to all inherited tradition.[57] Awe invests the spirits, the gods, and those living mortals, elders, priests, medicine men, or chiefs that know their lore. Such persons act to affirm and protect things as they are.[58]

Often instruction is in a positive form, that is, through noisy advertisement of something or someone perceived as good: the "furious competition" of potlatch, the parade of successes in *kula* or *tee* exchange, or the display of trophies from a raid on a neighbor.[59] The community serves as the audience to learn an individual's "claim to a place in society". Status is didactic: there are the more honored ones, speaking while

---

54 Bateson (1936) 17; Wilson (1963) 79f.

55 For myths and stories with a moral, see Nader (1990) 55 or Mathews (1992) 127ff., 159; the community as teacher, especially in Bateson (1936) 4, 141, and passim, also Hogbin (1970) 37f.; Boehm (1999) 73f.; Munn (1986) 211, 234–66 on "didactic speech", or Just (1991) 299f., 303.

56 In Melanesia, Malinowski (1922) 37; among the Ibo, Meek (1937) 112f. or Jones (1971) 67f., 71; among the Zuni, disrespect for elders is punished, Whiting et al. (1956) 102; an Arab "theme", Barclay (1971) 292; age privileged among Zambesian Lozi in judges' panels, see Gluckman (1965) 39; also among Arusha in Tanganyika, Gulliver (1963) 38, and the Brazilian Camayuras, Weyer (55) 108, and the Gawans, Munn (1986) 42; and elders are better fed at feasts, Wilson (1963) 71.

57 On "the weight of ancestral custom" among the Bantu, see Wagner (1940) 202; "ancestral authority" among the Ibo, Jones (1971) 65; fear of angering ancestors, e.g., among Solomon Islanders and Admiralty Islanders, Hogbin (1970) 45 and Crook (2007) 132.

58 Arab veneration for holiness, Barclay (1971) 303; among the Ibo, the foundation of law, or at least sanctions, rests in religion, Meek (1937) 20; power based on monopoly of religious lore among the Hopi, in Rousseau (2006) 182, cf. Plog (1995) 193, more generally on the pueblo; similarly among the Tsimshian and Kwakiutl, Ames (1995) 175, and the Hopi, Plog (1995) 193.

59 The potlatch-quotation, Gluckman (1965) 77; public defense of the *tee* system, Feil (1988) 107; "claim to a place," quoted, Voget (1964) 487 and 492f.

everyone else is silent. As a child observes and learns from observing and *mimesis*, one must bow to them, uncover one's head, kiss their hands. "When the chief sits down, no one would dare to stand."[60] Teaching may also be through negatives. What is seen as wrong invites the shaming of the deviant. Most of this goes on more or less informally but it is nonetheless effective.[61]

We hardly need to be told why. Talcott Parsons and Edward Shils pointed out how "the need to be approved and esteemed is a fundamental motivational basis for the acceptance of socially necessary disciplines... the core of the reward systems of societies is to be found in the relevance of this element of the motivation of individuals." It is a truth as old as Aristotle, and a very foundation-stone in the social theory of France's well known Pierre Bourdieu, who quotes the Greek philosopher: Man is, of all species, the most prone to copy his cospecifics, *mimetikotaton*. He learns by doing what others do. And just as a whale is a marine animal, so Man is also a community animal, *politikos*, and within that community, depends on its support. Bourdieu offered many vivid illustrations of this and other ideas out of his anthropological work in North Africa, where "doing one's duty as a man means conforming to the social order" and where the culture's general "dispositions" govern not only what a person intends but how he anticipates others will respond; for everyone responds to the same expectancies.[62] More recently Claudia Strauss drew such observations together: "Given that human action is certainly underdetermined, if not undetermined, by innate drives, we do indeed have to examine the cultural sources of motivation, including the social behavior people observe, the instructions they are given, and the constructed realities they bump up against."[63]

Socialization is of interest to other disciplines than anthropology, of course (see chap. 3, below); but as to the objection that one of them, psychology, might be better

60 Kiss the hand, etc., the Aymara in Bolivia defer to the Mestizos, Barnouw (1985) 40; quoted, Malinowski (1922) 52.

61 Shaming and mockery noticed among the American Indians, cf. Hallowell (1955) 133; among Tonga of Rhodesia, Gluckman (1965) 98, and Samoans, in Freeman (1983) 89; Kabylians, also, in Bourdieu (1977) 162; the cost to the shamed, above at n. 9.

62 Quoted on "the need to be approved", in Parsons and Shils (1962) 150. In Aristotle, *Politics* 1.2.9, 1253a, *politikos* is often translated "social"; further, his *Poetics* 1448b, in Bourdieu (1977) 96, with the statement in Malle (2008) 275, that "humans are the only species in which members instruct each other by demonstrating a novel behavior and inviting the other to perform it in turn. Complementarily, humans are exceptional observational learners". Further, Bourdieu (1977) 161, drawing on Kabyle observations to make concrete the "various ways of reasserting solidarity" with one's society, through conformity, where anything else is suspect; 72 and 214 on "the system of dispositions" which he calls *habitus* and its function in determining individual strategies of behavior; Hunt (1989) 13f., defining Bourdieu's *habitus*; and Goodman (2003) 783–86 on Bourdieu's understanding of proverbial wisdom as fossilized values; and on the individual's action emerging from a cultural structure, cf. Ortner (1989) 13.

63 Strauss (1992) 8; and on motivation, further, above, nn. 31f.

heard from, there is a good answer. Psychologists indeed command laboratory science in all its enviable depth and exactitude; but they generally focus on the young men and women they find handy in their own classrooms, and such a test group can constitute only "an extremely narrow cultural base on which most broad behavioral generalizations are constructed".[64] Better, then, an approach through the comparative study among very different, simpler populations, looking for consistencies without necessarily looking for natural laws.

Consistencies are barely detectible among hunter-gatherers, the least cohesive of peoples; but elsewhere they are essential (above at n. 38). Agreement, prescribing the loyalty owed to one's kinfolk, begins with one's immediate family and then reaches out through marriages. On this, the most general Leitmotif, our species has devised endless variations. They are of particular interest to anthropologists; for, whatever culture is studied, its members so often manifest a quite extraordinary knowledge of who their agnate and cognate relatives are or were, in distant generations, and, therefore, who in the community is owed this or that particular service – who has a right to it. As an extreme instance, witness the Gahuku-Gama of New Guinea, among whom there is no general ethical system at all, no single set of rules about right and wrong, but only according to familial relation; so it is bad to kill your mother's kin in a fight with the neighboring tribe, but good to kill anyone else.[65]

Of networks thus fashioned out of a definition of duty, a clan can make a workforce or a war-force. It may then accumulate wealth and prestige. Its success validates the ties of obligation that may be extended beyond the clan through a system of exchange or the like, to *tee* brothers, eating clubs, or age groups.[66] In this manner a "structure", a "simpler culture", can emerge. Within it, everyone knows where he or she fits and what is due to whom.

The term "structure" opens up a very large technical literature and all its discussions over a full century. How various its forms could be appears among the North Coast Indians that Boas studied, and others after him. The unit of control was determined not only by descent but by residence as well, each with its chief; and

> chiefs had considerable power to organize production, public ceremonial, and ritual. They had the power – and obligation – to accumulate and display the wealth employed for potlatching. This power is balanced by their lack of power over free individuals and the limits imposed on their power by councils, and by the ability of household members to vote with their feet by leaving the household, or even to establish a new House.[67]

---

64 The fact bears repeating from chap. 1 at n. 35; Fish (2000) 553 is quoted), adding "e.g. 80% of the articles in social psychology journals are experimental studies of undergraduate psychology students".

65 Shweder and Bourne (1984) 167f. (observations of the 1950s).

66 Feil (1988) 104; Nyakyusa, Wilson (1963) 68; and on Arusha, Gulliver (1963) 28.

67 Ames (1995) 178.

Power thus has an objective existence, at least as it is seen here. Like muscle, you may simply have it, much or little. But the underlying assumption here is realist, not nominalist. While it serves most descriptive purposes well enough, for analytical purposes the fact must be confronted that nobody *has* power. In all respects, "sociocultural systems can be said to exist *concretely* only in individuals".[68] Power is a relationship without existence outside the minds of any two or more of its members, the one directing, by what the other acknowledges as a right, while that other complies; and compliance is seen as a duty. Leaders, if they are accorded obedience, do indeed control muscle that may be sufficient to compel others who belong neither to the clan at all nor to the club. Against compulsion, appeal can only be directed to some other part of the network, as for instance to a council, or to an entirely different structure of obligations, as for instance that larger community that embraces the whole House – thus, for example, in the potlatch people just referred to. Members of this larger community will approve or disapprove of their chiefs' decision. Their decision will or will not have power – or muscle. We would say it amounts to law, which in its own turn has power to the extent its commands are approved – that is, are seen as right. The only recourse from the law, as the passage quoted indicates, is to quit the society entirely; and such an act for a *zoon politikon* is very difficult.

We thus arrive at the Social Contract – hardly a novel finding, older indeed than Aristotle (Plato, *Crito* 51f.). But anthropology has something new to add on the nature of obligations that constitute the contract and control behavior. Adam Kuper calls these "*sentiments* of social solidarity [which] must be maintained in order to make people play their appointed parts."[69] They explain leader and follower; they explain council members and appellants who fail in their suit but accept that failure. In all these can be sensed "an identification with the moral order, a respect for legitimate authority, and a *feeling* of disinterested obligation to live up to expectations". It can be illustrated, for example, by "motivational patterns" among the Zuni.[70] They allow an insight into those *feelings* and *sentiments* and the role of the *irrational* in motivation in which not only anthropologists but historians as well are interested, and which will need mention often in the pages that follow.

The words italicized by myself, above, bear on a discussion among anthropologists about their most familiar term of art: "culture". What exactly does it mean?

---

68 Kaplan (1954) 320, quoted ("concretely", my italics), gathering the views of a number of anthropologists; cf. the psychologist Hinde (1996) 368, "'Culture' is thus best viewed as existing in the minds (separately and collectively) of the individuals in a group".

69 Kuper (1996) 53, a formulation "plausible enough" but needing to be carried further; on solidarity, above, n. 62.

70 Parsons' thought which Kaplan (1954) 323 applies (quoted) to the Zuni, as an example; compare Evans-Pritchard (1940) 171, on clan support for fractious behavior among the Nuer because "it is recognized that a man ought to obtain redress for certain wrongs... if he is right." On "expectancies", see above, n. 38.

From some hundreds of proposed definitions, a consensus emerged a half-century ago: "the essential core of culture consists of traditional (i.e., historically derived and selected) ideas and especially their attached values".[71] *Values*, proposed as culture itself and crucial to a society's function and survival, in turn would be those sentiments and feelings that Kuper speaks of (above), and which Robert Aunger further explains as "cultural knowledge [which] is not just transmitted information but the internalized derivatives of others' social inputs. [It] depends on the entire personalities of each individual: cognitive, evaluative, and affective. Through this process, some cultural information acquires emotional and directive force, and thus determines an individual's behavior".[72] True, the debate continues, whether knowledge of this sort is really internalized; but it certainly forms an integral part of the individual's make-up; and the individual is himself also a part of that texture of reflexes, thoughts, and feelings that surrounds every member of the culture.[73]

As to "emotional force", it is especially marked where the sense of entitlement is violated. For this, the Ifaluk even have a particular term, *song*, meaning not plain anger but "justifiable anger", where a right has been denied.[74] *Song* and other emotional states that accompany moral claims or reactions to others' behavior of any sort can be generally read in quite visible signs. They are known thanks to the universality of facial expression. The yield of anthropological observation may thus fairly be called scientific in the sense of being verifiable (as, for example, from photographic records).

Now, to sum up: beginning, some pages past, with the *kula* and Bronislaw Malinowski, three common anthropological observations were recalled in a series to describe or, better, to explain "simpler societies". First, in such societies a collective personality can always be perceived and is most often the starting point for a full account of their lives; and on this, Boas' *Leitmotif*, my chapter focused at the outset. Further, this personality is formed across time, in each rising generation, through nurture, group approval, and various rites and symbols. Lastly, coherence or consistency in that collective personality is a consequence of a general agreement about right and wrong, which directs behavior and is motivational in its affective wrap-

---

71 Kroeber and Kluckhohn (1952) passim and 181, quoted; the number duly noted in White (1968) 15; and of course endless revisiting of the definition-problem, e.g., in Kitayama et al. (2007) 138f.

72 On the crucial place of values recognized among anthropologists, see above, at nn. 31, 33, 36, 49, 53, and 67; values as the constituents of a morality, e.g. in Boehm (1999) 245; further, Aunger (2000) 448, views illustrated passim from observations in the Ituri Forest.

73 Though Kaplan (1954) 323f., 328 has doubts, he acknowledges that internalization of values is usually assumed, cf. Aunger (2000) in n. 72; and "deeply ingrained" is similar, in Vayda (1976) 81 on the Maori; above at n. 49; and after all, monkeys betray feelings of guilt, which can only be internalized, cf. MacMullen (2003) 72.

74 Lutz (1988) 165, quoted; MacMullen (2003) 67; illustrative of the range of sanctions in Wagner (1940) 203; and on anger's force, note 40 above.

pings.[75] So individuals choose their ends or goals, making their decision on how best to achieve these – while, for everyday purposes without social implications, cognitive operations come into play. It is right and wrong – that is, collective values – that are the most basic causal factor in the course of life of collectivities, to the extent that Man, not the environment, is in control.

In these three elements of our humanity thus summarized no doubt there is nothing novel; nothing new is intended. They fit with much that is commonly agreed in psychology, sociology, and economics, as I hope to show in later chapters. But in anthropology it is possible to look at them more closely *and in societies different from ourselves*. Let these be just such as historians must deal with, in all their strangeness: Salihid Arabs or Bogomil congregations. Here it is that anthropological insights afford good guidelines. Those most useful are not to be found on high among theories and abstractions, but rather on the plane of the concrete and objective, "writ small", and especially in the area of values.

75 Many references to thumb-nail sketches or summings-up of a people, in n. 34, above; socialization at nn. 43, 46–56, above; social coherence the great object, nn. 21 and 54, above; agreement internalized, n. 73, above; and motivational wrapping, nn. 33ff., 63f., above.

3 Reason and Decision-making

3.1 Economic reason

The preceding chapters about the social sciences were meant to bring out various turns of research and interesting questions – interesting for historians. One of those questions with especially wide implications was addressed by Malinowski: Does *Homo sapiens* generally act out of his well calculated material interests? Is he *sapiens* because, and only when, he is *Homo economicus*? Is that how to explain who we are and why we do what we do? Depending on the answer, explanation will draw on evidence of a rational, instrumental, cognitive sort or, instead, on the exploration of the surrounding world of values and loyalties. For the historian, these are very important matters. The choice of interpretive strategies is crucial. These are what I would like to examine, briefly, in this introductory section.

Malinowski rejected the assumption by our enlightened selves, that material benefit determines our own actions and that it does so even among unenlightened primitive man, or savages. The idea was preposterous! *Homo economicus* was a mere "figment". That was the position he took in a debate already active a century ago. In time, more participants stepped forward from the social sciences and especially from a field much favored in recent years, behavioral economics.[1]

The point at issue, being about motivation, was and is necessarily central to historiography. Over the course of time, what Malinowski objected to so strenuously instead gained in favor among historians and their readers, and became thoroughly familiar, in part of course thanks to Karl Marx. If Marx was not wholly right, still, he was not wrong, either. If historians would not accept the argument that all change is driven by economic factors – by the essentials of work and wages and profits and the struggle for a share in the rewards – yet such things certainly do have some role to play in all social relations and every existential decision, across all time. When exactly it was that economic interpretations recognizing this fact became prominent in Western historiography is an idle question; but we now accept the consideration of material benefit even in situations where we don't quite expect it: in the Crusades, for a large instance; for a smaller one, in the eventual success of Vincent whom we would never have heard of had there been no Theo Van Gogh to buy his paints for him.

The historiographic story in itself, however, is not what interests me so much as the mode of thinking that has determined its outcome. That mode is "scientific". At its

---

1 Malinowski above, chap. 2 at n. 48; compare the similar impatience of Marc Bloch in the early 1940s, quoted in MacMullen (2003) 152; and for a glimpse into the surrounding questions controverted in the later twentieth century, see, e.g., Gray (1987).

best, at its most authoritative, it finds expression in numbers. In numbers there can be no ambiguity. Six is always less than seven and a thousand bigger than a hundred, beyond dispute. Therefore the person whose argument can be expressed in such terms, and who can demonstrate its superiority to any alternative, numerically, has won; the sum of agreed-upon knowledge has been increased.[2] Such clarity of results historians value as much as anyone, and it might be expected that they would favor it in their style of analysis, as in fact they have done, increasingly, for a good half-century.[3] An associated consequence is the emphasis on those aspects of motivation that can be presented in numerical terms, meaning calculations of risk and returns as opposed to urges, wants, passions, drives, and impulses.

To illustrate what our choices of analytical approach may involve, there is a convenient illustration, well known a generation ago. Eugene Genovese wrote that slave owners in the American South still in the 1820s through the 1850s held on to their way of life despite its unprofitability because that way gained them and their family ease, honor, attainments and place in their world. His view, accepting of "noneconomic objectives" and "irrationality", was denied by Robert Fogel and Stanley Engerman in 1974.[4] To oppose these two, Herbert Gutman published a critique the following year; and this latter volume in turn was answered, or some would say disposed of, by many subsequent studies, foremost among them, a massive work of 1989 by Fogel himself.[5] He and Engerman saw the slave owners as "shrewd capitalistic businessmen", calculating in a hardheaded way exactly how much profit could be wrung from their labor force.[6] All this back-and-forth among scholars is of course radically simplified here so as to bring out the two contrasting views, that the motive supporting the institution of slavery to the point of secession and war was, as one might say today, "soft" and cultural, or to the contrary, that it was profit-driven and rational.

---

2 See MacMullen (1990) 21f. for some expansion of the thought.

3 Fogel (2003) 21 suggests the middle of the past century as a time of change.

4 Genovese's views are described and quoted in Fogel and Engerman (1974) 64f., but without references (despite the claim to the contrary, Fogel and Engerman [1974a] v, 54); but see, e.g., Genovese (1989) 3, 8, 295; 16, "irrationality"; this, the prime weakness in the consensus picture corrected by Fogel and Engerman (1974) 4; actual profitability of the slave economy, Fogel and Engerman (1974) passim, and Fogel (2003) 44, 47, 62ff.; the Genovese picture apparent in, e.g., Wyatt-Brown (1982) 14, 68,72. A second contention of Genovese, that slaves could be and were imbued with a work ethic accounting for very high productivity, was accepted by Fogel and Engerman, only to be later opposed by Fogel (1989) 162, as Levine (2003) xvif. points out. My lack of specialist knowledge leaves me on the edge of this controversy, where it is only apparent that the understanding of human motivation is not a natural target for cliometrics.

5 Gutman (1975) passim and Fogel (1989), the latter work crowned by the Nobel prize in economics.

6 Fogel and Engerman (1974) 232; cf. 73f., "hardly likely that twenty-six-year-olds were priced [as records show] twice as high as ten-year-olds because twice as much honor and prestige were attached to the owners of the older than the younger slaves".

Fogel and the other new voices that joined him called their method cliometrics, "the systematic application of the behavioral models of the social sciences and their related mathematical and statistical methods to the study of history", aiming at "'scientific' reinterpretation".[7] To date, their successes have been many. Fogel himself was recognized by a Nobel prize in 1993.

It was awarded in economics, not history. In history, the object is to explain things that count, not simply things that can be counted – no matter how welcome and sometimes essential it is to get the relevant figures right. The question raised by Genovese in explanation of the "why" of slave-state history was in fact very important; yet it was never addressed by Fogel and Engerman. They simply assumed that, if plantation owners could be shown to have been "good businessmen", they could not have concerned themselves at the same time, or perhaps even more, with "soft" issues. To do so would have been "irrational", which could not be imagined of any significant population of *Homo sapiens*.

But yet, history shows entire civilizations built on the very considerations that Genovese posits, those that are irrational. Money merely subserves them. It can be a means not an end, an instrument enabling *noblesse* to *oblige*. A subordinate role of this sort is certainly conceivable in the setting that Genovese terms "precapitalist".[8] Still it may be asked, did he have it right? For my purposes it is irrelevant whether he or Fogel better saw the truth, measured against the much greater interest of the question, whether *sapiens* must always and entirely mean "rational". This was what Malinowski opposed, quoted above and perhaps never quoted or really noticed by anyone else but myself; for my reading has not turned up a single mention of his views. Certainly they have left no mark on the flourishing business of cliometrics and economics. Yet they certainly seem useful in explaining why people did what they are known to have done.

The anthropologist spoke as he did looking out from a wide, wide window on the world, in which our species was not seen as all college students and capitalists. They might instead be hunters, gatherers, nomads, among whom "mobility and property are in contradiction," as another anthropologist, Marshall Sahlins, pointed out long ago; for among such peoples, ever on the move, no storage facilities could exist, the impulse to accumulate is therefore never institutionalized, and there can be no wealth. As Sahlins said, "Economic Man is a bourgeois construction."[9] Or as Malinowski said, a "figment".

---

7 Fogel (2003) 19f.; 21, "'hard' scientific methods".
8 "Precapitalist" quoted in Fogel and Engerman (1974) 64; for an example of a civilization of the sort, "irrational" in valuing money in order to give it away in exchange for non-monetary rewards, see the *magnum opus* of Paul Veyne (1976).
9 An example in Australia, Gammage (2011) 132; Sahlins (1972) 6ff., 12ff., 20f., 85, and passim (14, quoted, on Economic Man); Lutz (1988) 163 on the impact of a sudden cash inflow on the moral code and institutions of people living in a more primitive economy.

The figment is nevertheless welcomed in economics, particularly in the sub-specialty *microeconomics*, as immensely useful; for, so great has been the press of questions and answers generated in the discipline over time, so many the arguments and doctrines accumulating around habits of buying and selling, they absolutely require some artificial simplification at their center if they are ever to be understood in any scientific way.

To begin with, the figment serving as a sort of template, in which to contain and arrange the discussion, must be *sapiens*. He must be conceived of as pure intelligence focused purely on the satisfaction of his wants and interests, using pure truth (that is, only sound facts) to determine his choices of action, and unconstrained by extraneous forces or rules in estimating the likelihood of the best choice to gain what he desires. Add, that what he desires is a matter of general interest: money. Objection might be raised against the choice imputed to him, meaning what would seem most desirable to him (its "utility" in the technical language of microeconomics); for what is imputed must in fact be a subjective judgment on the part of whoever is the analyst manipulating him; and in addition, there may be some doubt about the realism of his mental operations.[10] Never mind (to repeat), the imagined *sapiens* is useful.

Just how useful appears not only in the obvious dependence of microeconomic literature on the working assumption of rationality, but also in what the specialists have had to say about it. In 1989, "Academics who write about financial markets today are usually very careful to dissociate themselves from... psychology", meaning anything beyond strict facts and logic; they abjure the concept of "social norms" and sociology; into the current millennium, still, "Traditionally, microeconomic decisions have been modeled on broad notions of rational choice whereby entities attempt to maximize their utility or expected satisfaction". And the gospel survives barely challenged in the business school community.[11] Theorists evidently have had much dif-

10 For an introduction to *Homo economicus*, see, e.g., Eatwell et al. (1987) 1.585–88 (J. M. Buchanan, s.v. "constitutional economics"); 4.68–76 (A. Sen, s.v. "rational behavior"), and 776–78 (R. D. Collison Black, s.v. "utility"); ibid., also Shafer (1988) 193f., on the subjectivity of what is desirable.

11 Shiller (1989) 8, quoted ("Academics"), adding that it is "hard to find in the large literature on the efficient markets hypothesis any social psychology"; on "social norms", and sociology being quite ignored by economists, see Coleman (1987) 133; and quoted next, Kenrick et al. (2009) 765, citing scholarly studies from the 1990s and going on to say (766), "the purpose of microeconomic models has been to mathematically represent basic elements that underlie aggregate preferences and choices". Notice, "the modern theory of decision making under risk emerged from a logical analysis of games of chance rather than from a psychological analysis... not as a description of the behavior of real people," in Tversky and Kahneman (1988) 167 – who add (186), "The assumption of rationality has a favored position in economics. It is accorded all the methodological privileges of a self-evident truth...". The statement no longer holds good, cf. Loewenstein et al., below, n. 67. On the business community as seen by an insider, see Stickney (2009) 4: "the prevailing view is that emotionality is the antithesis of rationality" and decision-making entities are seen as "fundamentally rational places" (Stickney herself subscribing to the newer views of A. Damasio, J. P. Forgas, and others).

ficulty in thinking of *Homo economicus* as a fallible being, for to do so could only introduce unwelcome complications into their theories.

This risk, however, was exactly what Daniel Kahneman decided to confront, beginning in the 1970s in many short essays often co-authored with Amos Tversky or with other younger colleagues, putting the case for the imperfection of Economic Man's rationality.

To show, now, in four illustrations, how their case could be made: first, some hundreds of graduate students in psychology at leading U.S. universities were asked to guess the relative size of enrollments in nine different academic programs. Further, they were to guess which of these nine was most likely to attract a certain described student. In the outcome, their choice did not reflect in a mathematical way the chance dictated by their own program-size estimates. Instead they tried to fit the description of the individual into their idea of a typical member of one of those nine disciplines (lawyer, computer scientist, etc.), with results that "drastically violate the normative rules of prediction". A search tool, a "heuristic", was applied to sort through our memories more quickly, indeed too quickly, with a stereotype as the unfortunate result. "People," the study continues, "are prone to experience much confidence in highly fallible judgments, a phenomenon that may be called *the illusion of validity"*.[12]

Or second: someone is shown two parallel lines drawn each with a pair of short lines sticking out at each end; but the pair on the top line stick out to make a "Y", while the pair terminating the lower line are folded back to make a "V" like an arrowhead. Which of the two lines is longer? As shown, in fact the lower one is longer; but in a quick glance it looks shorter. Or they may be equal, but not seen as equal. It is a well known visual trick, an optical illusion, showing how we can make up our minds through instantaneous comparison of an image with similar ones in memory, and feel sure that similar is identical; which turns out to be false.[13] We trust a first impression, an "intuitive" judgment instead of slowing down to examine the matter more carefully.[14]

And a third illustration with yet another form of fallibility:[15]

> The hypothesis that people generally make risk-averse choices has been widely accepted by economists who normally assume that a consumer or an entrepreneur will choose a risky venture

12 Kahneman and Tversky (1973) 237–41 (quoted, 239, "rules", and 249, "fallible"); the illusion-argument illustrated, Kahneman (2011) 209–12.

13 The Müller-Lyer illusion in Tversky and Kahneman (1988) 179f. on "certainty and pseudocertainty"; also Kahneman (2011) 27.

14 "Intuitive" and "bounded rationality" in Kahneman (2002) 449.

15 Kahneman and Tversky (1982) 160f.; Kahneman (2011) 252, 327ff. The study of loss-aversion occupied Kahneman in many publications representative of his method, e.g., in Kahneman and Tversky (1979) 268f., 278f., down to Tversky and Kahneman (2000) 150f.

> over a sure thing only when the monetary expectation of the venture is sufficiently high to compensate the decision maker for taking the risk. Psychological studies, however, indicate that risk-seeking preferences are common when people must choose between a sure loss and a substantial probability of a larger loss... We propose that people commonly adopt a limited view of the outcomes of decisions: they identify consequences as gains or losses relative to a neutral point. This form of mental accounting can lead to inconsistent choices, because the same objective consequences can be evaluated in more than one way.

As a fourth and final illustration, expanding on the third: in a comparison between suffering a certain loss only by a hair, and suffering the exact same loss by a large margin, students who were polled showed the bare miss to be the more painful of the two "although their objective conditions are identical". What made the difference was the pleasure-measure or, as Kahneman terms it, "the psychophysics of hedonic experience" reckoned in "hedonimeter totals".[16] It was no quantifiable difference but mere feelings that weighed down one side of what should have been a perfectly balanced question. One may anticipate such feelings in advance of some choice through imagining what it will be like, and thus be influenced in making up one's mind. The operation has been the object of neuroscientific studies, placing it in the seat of emotions where we review and react to the recall of past financial experiences, good or bad. I return to such studies in the section below on scientific reason.[17]

Imagination and intuition were not what Economic Man brought to bear on economic decisions, at least not according to traditional microeconomics; but Kahneman like Tversky was a psychologist. Despite his Nobel prize in economics and despite generally publishing in the periodicals of that discipline, it was natural for him to take account of more mental activity in decision-making than was strictly mathematical, even though his pages and those of his school overflow with equations, charts, and games that assume sophisticated numeracy, sometimes in explicit opposition to the average person whose "irrationality" must be explained.[18] A consequence of their research and publication was the blurring of the outline of Economic Man, or, one may say, the bridging of the gap between that strictly rational figure and the real world of real people.

On the one hand, it was the assumption of classical economics that *Homo economicus* was not subject to distractions, remaining a purely analytical construct; and

16 "Psychophysics" in Tversky and Kahneman (2000) 157; "hedonimeter" in Kahneman (2011) 380 (*hedone* is Greek for pleasure, as it is assumed everyone knows already).

17 Kahneman and Tversky (1982) 170, "imagine" or "imagination" occurring nine times in six little paragraphs, to bring out the non-cognitive action in the mind; further, on regret and other feelings attending and influencing an assessment, Kahneman and Tversky (1982a) 201, 204, 206; Tversky and Kahneman (2000) 155ff.; Kahneman (2000) 758f., 766. Psychological conjecture has been affirmed and amplified by neuroscience: see Bechara and Damasio (2005) 339, 341, 358f., 368, and passim.

18 From a hundred examples, see Kahneman (2011) 314ff., 434ff.; Jennings et al. (1982) 212, paying tribute to Kahneman, and 224 on bivariate data; and Benartzi and Thaler (2000) 302f., 307.

besides, collective economic behavior as opposed to individual was never meant to be within the purview of this paragon. On the other hand, the layman hardly needed to be told that decisions about money are sometimes made on the basis of imperfect information or imperfect mathematics or that, on occasion, all-too-human urges or emotions will intrude, causing, for example, a panic. Panics are a matter of common knowledge, and Bubbles, too, that often set them off. Anyone who had high-school history has heard of them. They are big events. Hence of course a historian's interest in Kahneman.

Collective actions such as market movements have always been of general concern. Taking account of these phenomena and of much more besides, Keynes' work in 1936 is as well known as any. He was percipient, too, in anticipating as he did the place of sheer simple "urges" in our financial decisions. "Animal spirits," he called them also, and "fears of loss" and "hopes of profit" as opposed to mathematical expectation.[19] His plain-sense view of humankind in time lost favor to that more convenient caricature *Homo economicus*; but it could be very profitably revisited, as analysts have more recently come to see – among them, Robert Shiller.

Shiller's examination of some of the more erratic market moments and their causes, recent or further back to the 1920s, has attracted a wide readership. To explain certain factors he has drawn support from Kahneman and Tversky and similar studies.[20] Some were social-psychological as best applied to collective conduct; others involved studies of small groups questioned individually. Professional or large-scale single traders were reached by telephone or questionnaire to invite their recall of just what was going through their minds in the day, or two or three days, immediately preceding some major decline in stock prices, so as to account for their joining it. The rather predictable findings served to show how little susceptible such group behavior must always be to ordinary psychological testing. Too many people will be involved, and too many influences on their decisions; too much will have been hardly thought through if not simply irrational.[21]

Such challenges to analysis made it hard to arrive at scholarly consensus. The gap, as it was termed above, separating optimal calculation from actual market beha-

---

19 Keynes (1973) 161ff., feeling he must temper his description of the important causal role played by emotions, by adding, "we should not conclude from this that everything depends on waves of irrational pyschology", since in the end we depend on "our rational selves choosing between the alternatives as best we are able".

20 Shiller (2000) 137, 144, citing Kahneman and Tversky (1974).

21 Social-psychological, Shiller (1989) 41, 57; network telephoning, herd behavior, scare parallels, 380–90; all these again in Shiller (2000) 46, 60f., 67, 77, 89f.; on social-psychological factors, Akerlof and Shiller (2009) 53ff., 61f., 65f.; and Shiller's phone polling, Shiller (2000) 77, 89 (N = 889), cf. (1989) 380. As to the predictability of contagious alarm at moments on the market, and the size of the investor-population involved, a standing reminder is "the Chicago Board Options Exchange Market Volatility Index", "often referred to as the *fear index* or the *fear gauge*", cf. Wikipedia s.v. "VIX".

vior, marked off opposing views of how investment choices are made; for it couldn't be supposed that the norm is literally thoughtless. Of course not. While not a sort of adding machine on two legs, no investor would admit to decisions that had no reason at all behind them. Shiller took note of one side of the gap, to be found in "many of the major financial textbooks today, which promote a view of financial markets as working rationally and efficiently... These books convey a sense of orderly progression in financial markets, or markets that work with mathematical precision".[22] Like the cliometricians (above) aiming at "'scientific' reinterpretation", the most admired economists thus hoped to arrive at Newtonian truth through the most exact science of all: mathematics.

Not too far from this ideal, Shiller found an intermediate population of informants. Some were experts or semi-experts among major professional and private investors who really know the markets. Others were those sources on whom academic pollsters chiefly depend, namely, their own students; and these latter are, as often as not, postgraduates not undergraduates and not in the easiest of colleges and universities, either.[23] In contrast were the ordinary people that Keynes took account of. Shiller acknowledged these, too, en passant, reminding his readers that "the general public has not by and large taken Economics 101";[24] and social psychologists have added that, "The rational Homo economicus often does not 'get' the seemingly strange behavior of normal people. Despite or, perhaps, even because of his unbounded computing capacities in terms of, for instance, Bayesian updating of probabilities and backward induction, Homo economicus is out of tune with us, mere mortals."[25] In sum, analysis of market behavior discovers, and cannot ignore, different degrees of rationality in decision making.

3.2 Common reason

Though the layman is hardly aware of Economics 101 while academics on the other hand pay little mind to the general population in all its confusions and susceptibilities, it does not follow that these very different actors in moments of economic choice are, any of them, irrational; for "reasonable" may mean one thing for the specialists and academics, another thing for the layman of Keynes' description or of Shiller's, just quoted. "Decision theory neglects all the reasons for action that can only be

---

22 Quoted, Shiller (2000) 67.

23 Above, chap. 1 at n. 35 and elsewhere; and Stanovich (2002) 126, showing incidentally (146) how the author equates "smart" people with academics.

24 Shiller (2000) 38, quoted.

25 Hertwig and Herzog (2009) 662; to the same effect, Kenrick et al. (2009) 781.

understood through seeing how agents are embedded in their social and cultural contexts."[26]

Who it is that makes a decision, and in what situation, certainly needs to be considered in comparing the two types. It has often struck me that my own response would be both rational and irrational, if it were provoked by the riddles that Kahneman and his discipline so often use to open up a subject's mind. For, where a choice may be "rational" that is consistent with some reasoning behind it (and this is a common part of a definition of the word), what if the reasoning is misinformed through no uncommon fault? Or perhaps it is verifiably correct although generally seen as wrong? The problem in fact is familiar. It introduces into the equation, in place of a figment, a human being whose decisions respond to all sorts of implications and personal experiences that no amount of modeling can take account of.

As an illustration, Kahneman gives an account of a project he once undertook with associates to design a syllabus for a new subject at the high-school level. After a year's joint labor, they asked a veteran in education how long their work might take them to complete, and he gave an estimate of six more years, more or less, without even a very good chance of success at the end. They disregarded the estimate, went ahead, and eventually did finish. Nevertheless, Kahneman in retrospect calls the decision to persevere "not reasonable... embarrassing... irrational... Facing a choice, we gave up rationality rather than give up the enterprise".[27] He presumes to judge not only his own decision but his team-mates' as well; but surely they might have been swayed by other considerations than his own – by the obligation, for example, not to let down those who needed to persist for career reasons, or by the shame ("embarrassment") predictable in their research circle, for quitting after wasting a year. And so forth.

Such layman's thoughts seem to me the sort that anyone on the team might have offered, being questioned, and might have defended as entirely sensible and decent; therefore, in terms of common values, reasonable; but they obviously expand the definition of "reasonable" beyond material rewards, to include the intangible; beyond cognition, to affect. For the expert, this is wrong. Reason is simply reason. If you don't know that, then, "Get a grip on yourself. You're too emotional to think straight." This is how people talk, as Seymour Epstein imagines.[28]

---

26 Nozick (1993) 64, quoting Bertrand Russell, that "'Reason...' signifies the choice of the right means to an end that you wish to achieve". Here it is evidently one's preference of ends that governs, hence, the choice must be subjective. To the same effect, see Bermúdez (2009) 2 quoting C. Korsgaard on "expected utility", where the chooser decides whether something is desirable (= has "utility"); and 2f., quoted, on "decision theory". Kruglanski and Orehek (2009) 646f. give due weight to cultural differences in what is "rational", concluding, "the concept of rationality does not have an *absolute* sense, but rather is relative to someone's subjective vantage point".

27 Kahneman (2011) 247; and for a broader consideration of how such factors are involved, see Blossfeld (1996) 183f.

28 On the reason/emotion, cool/hot contrast, so long familiar, see, e.g., Williams (2000) 58f. or Pe-

However, a well-known jurist, Richard Posner, saw it differently. He was recently asked about his decades on the bench, and answered,

> If a case is difficult in the sense that there is no precedent or other text that is authoritative, the judge has to fall back on whatever resources he has to come up with a decision that is reasonable, that other judges would also find reasonable, and ideally that he could explain to a layperson so that the latter would also think it a reasonable policy choice. To do this, the judge may fall back on some strong moral or even religious feeling. Of course, some judges fool themselves into thinking there is a correct answer, generated by a precedent or other authoritative text, to every legal question.[29]

The wisdom of the reply lies first in its accord with prevailing thought over many centuries, at least in Anglophone legal systems. Their practitioners (it is quite extraordinary) will not say or even ask themselves how "reasonable" ought to be defined.[30] Though Posner goes on to acknowledge that sometimes personal biases may be invoked, nevertheless his thought is clear: the Western institution of trial by judge and jury ultimately rests on the assumption that rationality pervades our human society. Everybody shares in it – all, laymen. True, some who are specifically trained will be elevated to a deciding role on the bench; but if their judgments are challenged, it is the reference-points accepted by society as a whole that must serve them in their defense.

Philosophy can be called on for help if the general assumptions of rationality seem overly sanguine and summary. John Rawls accepted them as the basis for his *Theory of Justice* (1971).[31] His work gained wide attention from the start. Into the new millennium he continued to engage his critics and inspire new defenders, serving as advocate for a second figment: the vision of society as a whole, rational. This, like

---

ters et al. (206) 79ff. Quoted is Epstein (1994) 710, in comparing the rational and unthinking process; Damasio (1994) 166 (the full statement quoted below, n. 79); and a partial definition of "intellect" as relevant knowledge, memory, and language, minus affect, in Bechara and Damasio (2005) 338.

29 Posner quoted in Segall (2011) 47; cf. MacMullen (2003) 151 for similar statements by jurists and law-professors, that the base rock of legal wisdom (what/who is "reasonable") cannot be defined (!).

30 MacMullen (2003) 53 with note 2; Devine (2012) 88f.; and compare Gazzaniga (2011) 201, reflecting doubts about any requirement of perfect accuracy and the assumption that "the standards for law and science are the same, which they are not".

31 Rawls (1971) 41, morality is rational, "our judgment supported by reasons" (which are unexplained); "first principles" simply exist universally (30), that everyone would accept (53), "recognized" as "legitimate" (74) and "intuitively clear" (98), etc.; and "the most reasonable principles of justice," according to Rawls, "are those everyone would accept or agree to from a fair position," Stewart (1999) 774. On Rawls' defense of the objectivity of his constructions, see Kitcher (1995) 221f.; further, on Rawls' "enormous influence," Rogers (2011) 183. Compare the assertion by M. Nussbaum, "human beings are above all reasoning beings" (1999), quoted in support of moral theory by Turiel (2006) 9; or Kitcher (1995) 211, "an ethical statement is true if it would be accepted by a rational being".

Homo economicus, originated in the realist perception of a certain quality in human behavior – uncomplicated reason – which can be then treated as if it had a separate, actual existence. It makes a good fit with that other perception so generally accepted, too, that the act of reasoning or logical thought will show us the right answers whenever it is undisturbed by our passions or "hot" thoughts.

The hot nevertheless can't be ignored, as Keynes saw and, more recently, Epstein, Kahneman, and Shiller among others. The fact, thus recognized, is nevertheless resisted by many psychologists. They insist still on the dominance of cognition in the common understanding of that word, as a distinct process that defines our species: we are singly and collectively *sapiens*.[32] The better science that refutes this position must be acknowledged in later sections of this chapter.

In the contrast between pure reason and the merely human, one anomaly needs to be mentioned. It is a kind of irrationality that reflects or implies its opposite. It appears in Western thought as the belief in the ghosts, myths, rituals, and gods that others acknowledge but which we, enlightened observers, dismiss in total as "superstition".[33] Yet they constitute a very great part of past civilizations. A compendium of illustrations compiled by James Frazer toward the end of the nineteenth century, in two hefty volumes later expanded into twelve (1906–1915), opened up to its readers the wide world of religious ideas and practices. *The Golden Bough*, once so famous, offered a convenient entry-point to this whole area of thought. Frazer collected just about everything known and relevant, ancient and modern, Western and Eastern, all discoverable in the library of the British Museum. In the jumble he so richly provided, he took delight in showing what the Victorians could only perceive as The Other – really weird! – in intimate juxtaposition with Ourselves. There was indeed much to think about here, and much that was very unsettling. Surely there were lessons to be learned from the many bizarre practices more or less identical in the most widely different settings, seeming to join heathen to Christian, and Antiquity to our present times. Was there not, in consequence, some "general conclusion to be drawn from the melancholy record of human error and folly which has engaged our attention in these volumes", as Frazer said in summary?[34]

---

32 For a selection of recent authorities insisting that there is no affective presence in thinking, and that cognition and affect are immiscible, see MacMullen (2003) 54ff.

33 Epstein (1994) argues for two quite distinct modes of "processing information," one the familiar cognitive, the other "intuitive-experiential". Of this, the best example is "superstition" like belief in ghosts, which is "nonrational thinking" (710, 712). See also Camerer et al. (2005) 22 reporting on brain experiments where stimulation of the temporal lobe "produces intense religious feelings – e.g., the sense of God or Christ, even in otherwise unreligious people" – with Dawkins (2005) 48. Haidt (2012) 45, 48, and passim seems to me to confuse the discussion of rationality by proposing two kinds of "cognition", as both "intuition" and "reasoning", where the former is "automatic".

34 Frazer (1959) 648; and, in a good discussion of the work, Vickery (1973) 71, 134, 137f., the view that, as contrasted with the author's rationalism (18), "The Golden Bough yields to no book of the

For a generation and more, his work provided a talking point among the educated. He was knighted; Malinowski asked him to write an introduction to his own first publication in ethnography; and indeed anthropology in the years after the expanded *Golden Bough* afforded a gathering flow of illustrations and amplifications of Frazer's work – as, for example, among the good Christians of Ethiopia for whom the leopards in their region also counted as good Christians who kept the usual Christian fast-days.[35] Or that the Tahitians when Captain Cook turned up took him for the avatar of the god Lono. Fantastic! An entire population out of its collective mind![36] The so-called cargo-cult in the same huge area of the Pacific, in the decades after WWII, taught belief in a common, benevolent ancestor-world, from which was to be received a shipload of wonderful things; but it had been hijacked by the wicked Europeans. One priest or prophet of the cult, Yali by name, was particularly active in spreading this message. Europeans who sensed the growing anger and consequent danger around them took counter-measures, bringing to bear their police and missionary powers in combination. Recurrent unrest was serious but, at the same time, it was contemptuously dismissed in the media as mere "madness", "frenzy", "fanaticism", and "irrational".[37]

The distance between our Western position and all such wild, childish delusions can be even better sensed if we try to see ourselves and our own reasonableness as others do. Consider the so-called Pauli exclusion principle, propounded by the Greeks and, at the atomic level, in our own times, too, that two objects cannot occupy the same space at the same time. The contradiction is unimaginable; the principle stated is rationality in the purest form. Yet we have no trouble imagining a second self inhabiting each one of us, even occasionally making itself known to us while remaining intangible and invisible; and, when its host, ourselves, expires, it continues its existence through infinite time in the infinite company of other like entities: all, souls.[38] Still more irrational, the idea of a Being that is simultaneously three, "the inherently prelogical core of Christian theology itself," as an anthropologist puts it

last two centuries in its sustained and graphic indictment of human folly and barbarism" (22). But the same dismissal of primitive culture can be found in Frazer's contemporary, Emile Durkheim, speaking in 1912 of Australian rites and beliefs, ridiculous, frenzied, "fantastic and even bizarre", quoted in Moscovici (1998) 217.

35 Sperber (1975 [1974]) 93ff. on the Dorzé.

36 Sahlins (1995) 5f., with bibliography and comparison to the American Indians, earlier, seeing the Spanish invaders as gods; Obeyesekere (1997) 194, 220, 230ff., in violent disagreement with Sahlins' "relativism"; and Bolyanatz (2004) 109ff.

37 Hermann (1995) 118f., 123, 143 (Yali) and 157–166 (perception in the missionary press); and 190–98 (counter-measures).

38 Shweder and Sullivan (1993) 510, pointing out the various conceptions of the soul, Christian but also Hindu; Uhlmann et al. (2008) 75, showing that 96% of Americans, 37% of Germans believe in souls.

(C. Scott Littleton): "the notion that God is at once singular and plural".[39] A Tlingit, Herman Kitka, not so many years ago but as a very old man, and a fierce champion of his people of the Pacific Northwest throughout his whole life, recalled how even as a child that heritage had been opposed by government and its agents.[40]

> Even when I was going to school [in the years around 1910], if I spoke Tlingit, you know the teacher plastered my mouth and made me stand in front of the class with the plaster over my mouth. They were that strict. They wanted all the Tlingit culture wiped out. What they kept saying was that they didn't want the Indian pagan worship existing. But we never worshipped any idols. The Tlingit, they prayed to the Holy Sprit only – just one. Western man came among us, the missionaries told us there were three that you pray to. My grandfather, when we caught fish in Deep Bay, stood on the sandbar and prayed to the Holy Spirit.

And in another glimpse of the same region, a young Inuk reported to his friends what the missionary had tried to explain to him about immaculate conception, and "by the time he had finished, all the Inuit were laughing so hard that tears were running down their cheeks."[41]

The priest's doctrine pressed on them was ridiculous measured against what they had always known for sure. What was known was manifest in what everyone around them always said, including many persons who were generally accepted as good judges and were thus to be believed. Disagreement, even doubt, would have been unreasonable. Paul Veyne carried the argument further and to a distant point, in a remarkable little book, asking "Did the Greeks believe in their myths?"[42] Greek thinkers, in the Western view, were certainly capable of rational thought; yet what are we to do with their Olympus and its goings-on? Our most commonly accepted ideas about religion don't seem to fit around the Greek reality.[43] Veyne found the answer in the readiness even of the most thoughtful to believe what was said according to who says it. Their Ancients, those venerated authorities of an ageless past from whom mythic traditions were passed down, deserved a special credit according to a standard all their own.

Littleton was quoted, above, in comment on Lucien Lévy-Bruhl, renowned for confronting the collisions of rationality such as those here indicated and others that Lévy-Bruhl discerned, both in the *Golden Bough* and in works of anthropology of that

---

39 Littleton (1985) xliv.

40 Thornton (2008) 195, the interview in the 1990s (the Tlingit in Alaska).

41 Ehrlich (2000) 219f.

42 Veyne (1988) xi, instancing the Ethiopian Christians and their leopards; 5ff., 15–18; 48, 96f., and passim; and Lloyd (1990) 20, 44f.

43 See Versnel (2011) 546–59, an exceptionally deep, wide-ranging exposition of the Western struggles with ancient Greek religion and the entanglement of descriptive language in Christian assumptions (but, 553, for the Greeks, the gods were "part and parcel of their social knowledge").

early period.[44] They had what could be called a rationality, but one different from ours. The idea of such a thing provoked a great deal of academic discussion which is not pertinent to my interests, once definitions are agreed on – that is, in our modern terms, most obviously, our agreement to respect what can be observed and verified in nature, thus answering to our "science".[45]

By such a definition, however, we exclude religion. Here indeed is a problem. Frazer's worlds may certainly be different. Let their inhabitants be as strange as they wish, then; but to distance ourselves from our own prevailing faith or call in question its doctrines is another matter. They are not such superannuated beliefs as the king's touch, last witnessed two full centuries ago,[46] but living beliefs like Virgin Birth, the Holy Trinity, our very souls! All these are of today.

The problem touches on historiography, my own concern, where there exist certain "No-Go" zones. I instance one of a respectable size: the rationality of the ancient world, as it can be known from the Bronze Age down to the fifth century, down to Aristotle and into the millennium and more that followed – so, our own Western world. The opening period of this development is sometimes called the Greek "Enlightenment", marked by certain assumptions that remained a part of mental life among the most highly educated for many centuries. The term Enlightenment is of course borrowed from the development originating much later in the rediscovery of ancient texts and their eventual incorporation into accepted, eighteenth-century thought.

What remains obscure in every sense is the "Darkening" that intervened between the two Enlightenments. How and when did it first appear and become established? In answer: beginning with the third century of the present era – thus, well before our Dark Ages and inclusive of Rome's eastern empire as well as the western. It remains un-named (the name in quotation marks is my own invention) and attempts to define it in simple, concrete terms, and to suggest how it set in, haven't stimulated any interest. Occasionally the alarm is raised, instead, that any Darkening that began back in the third century, just when Christianity was taking on its defining shape and mass,

---

44 See a dense section on "childlike" ideas of cosmology, disease, etc., among primitives, Lévy-Bruhl (1985) 38–43; on this theorist, defending the consistency of a different mode of thought, see Guimelli (1999) 33f.

45 Various positions taken, to call "rational" the mode of thought that differs from the Western, e.g., Guimelli (1999) 33, or to find the non-Western (i.e., irrational) at home in ourselves, see, e.g., "We have learned from ethnography not to impose our Western distinctions of science versus religion and natural versus supernatural on the beliefs and concepts of non-Western peoples," LeVine (1984) 79; and Shweder (1977) 637f., drawing in Claude Lévy-Strauss – who distinguished between the content of a belief (which might be different from any Western one) and mode of thinking which would be the same, cf. Kruglanski and Orehek (2009) 649.

46 Burke (1986) 443f.; and compare the belief among the Romans of the second and third centuries, that their emperors' touch could heal, MacMullen (1997) 50.

suggests too close a link between that emerging faith and "superstition". Voltaire, Hume, and Gibbon can be sensed lurking in the wings again, intolerably. It is best to leave the whole subject alone.[47]

The nature of rationality as it emerges from all that has been said thus far seems at first sight to be too confused and disputed to be of use to historians in explaining motivation. The definition of the key term itself is disputed. If it were agreed on, there would still be doubt about where in the world to find it, whether among "laymen" and "everyone" (as Rawls says) or instead, among academics and philosophers; and historians would draw up their accounts differently according to the one choice or the other. There is the charge that people *en masse* are simply incapable of logical thought, as a recent polemic declares, aiming at our modern societies.[48] In contrast, as was described in the previous section, the truly rational being is to be found among students in Econ. 101 (as Shiller says) – so often responding to their professors' tests and games – or can be found among the professors themselves, still more select and aloof: "Econs" as Kahneman calls economists for short. He goes on to characterize such mandarins of the mind through their way of thinking. They are "internally consistent. A rational person can believe in ghosts so long as her other beliefs are consistent with the existence of ghosts... Rationality is logical coherence – reasonable or not. Econs are rational by this definition, but there is overwhelming evidence that Humans cannot be".[49]

We humans nevertheless are prone to give ourselves good marks for making good choices, as Kahneman himself points out. Defining "rational" only as the way economists think, he concedes that ordinary people all too often invent plausible factors leading to a decision, post-facto, to make it look "presentable".[50] Other times and communities are no different – witness what anthropologists have sometimes repor-

---

47 See MacMullen (1990) Chap. 11, the English original which Roberto Lopez volunteered to translate for the *Rivista italiana di storia* (1972), with my notes 55f. on Arnaldo Momigliano's essay of the same year, and a final version in MacMullen (2006) Chap. 4, esp. n. 29 and p. 50. The Momigliano essay, focusing only on historiography, was entirely compatible with my own essay, as I explain. I also explain and emphasize that the "darkening" affected all of the empire's people, not Christians or any other group in particular. My conclusions are not much at odds with Grant (1952) who writes with very different aims and texts, or with Festugière (1970) 1.xviif., likewise, or with Theissen in 1974 (in English, 1983, 31, 276).

48 See, in 500 pages, "The Age of the Crowd" so described by Moscovici (1985) passim; Krueger (2009) 635, on divisions among psychologists "on the rationality of ordinary people", which many deny entirely.

49 Kahneman (2011) 411f., borrowing the term "Econ" from R. Thaler and C. Sunstein.

50 Quoted, Fortes and Evans-Pritchard (1940) 20, going on to say, that natives "generally state it [a political relation] in terms of its utilitarian and pragmatic functions"; Rousseau (2006) 138, quoted on "rationalization"; Kahneman (2011) 415, quoted on "presentable"; and Haidt (2001) 815, 817, 822, and Haidt (2012) 46, building an argument on our tendency to think up rational causes for our acts *ex post facto*.

ted even of the simplest cultures, that "natives stress the material components" when they discuss moral questions. Facing a choice of explanations, "they themselves offer the latter rationalization". To see through such misrepresentations is not easy. Apropos witchcraft among the Azande, Adam Kuper notices "the problem of rationality" that appears in anthropological discussions. They sound no different from our own.[51]

We don't want to forfeit anyone's respect. That's why we explain ourselves in terms that others around us won't disagree with. We even credit our species with sound sense so pervasive that our lives and property can be safely entrusted to a randomly selected panel of twelve of our fellow beings. In the common view, reason isn't the preserve of specialists or particular authorities: it is literally *common* sense. A famous judge, a famous philosopher, have been heard agreeing to that as a foundation for civil society. "Rational" thus can be defined quite conventionally to mean backed by good reasons and consistent with a person's general beliefs. Personal beliefs must themselves comport with the consensus to make one a reasonable person in the first place.[52] At the end, then, reason is a *social* thing. As a necessary consequence, it reflects a given way of life.[53] Each culture is its own self, pervaded and governed by its own reasonable beliefs: "different cultures, different rationalities", as Marshall Sahlins reminds us. Another ethnographer, Alex Bolyanatz, adds: "One cannot do good history, nor even contemporary history, without regard for ideas, actions, and ontologies that are not and never were our own."[54]

That is the point of my chapter, to see what ideas about human motivation seem most likely to produce "good history". My cultural-historical approach thus takes me past cliometrics and microeconomics, past *Homo economicus* and almost past *Homo sapiens*; for it does appear that the assumption in that latter title, *sapiens*, allows for a great jumble of beliefs that pass for sound within our society, whatever their real quality as it might be judged by some outsider. Are they really to be trusted?

As a resource in decision-making at the level of the individual, each of us has a miscellaneous fund of knowledge, of experiences and solid opinions, some of them

---

51 Kuper (1996) 74 (quoted) to 77, "trying to persuade that these beliefs were in some way reasonable", and Novick (1988) 550, noting how in the 1970s "the spectre of thoroughgoing cognitive relativism hovered over the continuing debate among English and American scholars concerning the rationality of Azande witchcraft". Compare Haidt (2001) 814, "moral reasoning is usually an ex post facto process... one becomes a lawyer to build a case... it becomes plausible to say, 'I don't know. I can't explain it, I just know it's wrong'"; cf. 822, and Cushman et al. (2010) 48.

52 See, e.g., Nozick (1993) 64, "rationality is a matter of reasons. A belief's rationality depends upon the reasons for holding that belief".

53 An interesting comment, that "Subjects in their daily life make use of ways of reasoning which do not induce false conclusions but only *different* ones, characterized by a validity fitting to their place in society," Guimelli (1999) 25.

54 Sahlins (1995) 14, quoted in Bolyanatz (2004) 110, with Bolyanatz' next step (111).

simple and caught in popular dicta and proverbs, American or Russian or Algerian: "Spare the rod and spoil the child," "Punctuality is own brother to good business", or (to teach group solidarity), "Don't we all eat the same barley?"[55] At a moment of choice we refer to this knowledge, wondering, "What do I know that's relevant? What do most people think? I need some good sane advice" – and it can generally be found somewhere in that common fund afloat in the common mind of which we are a part.

At the level of whole societies, and characterizing them, are much more complicated and consequential elements shared in by the members: prejudices, ideologies, stereotypes, culture-heroes, belief-systems, interpretive theories, and the like.[56] As an object of study, singly, they may be called mentalities (*mentalités*, favored by the so-called Annales school),[57] "themes", "attitudes",[58] "social representations", "axioms", and still other terms among which there is no need to make a choice.[59] Being generally supported, they form character, individual and general, since individuals and their surrounding world interact in ways that anthropologists especially describe. All together, the totality of shared knowledge may be compared to "the cloud" in cyberspace. In the collective brain, it is a grander equivalent of that nano-cloud found in the individual. Much has been written about this inchoate mass of experiential memory and opinion, how it is acquired and how brought to bear on collective decisions that in turn lead to action. It plays some part in history, undeniably; yet no one reflecting on it has paid much attention to its rationality. That term seems somehow irrelevant.

The historian's focus on "why?" – meaning ultimate motivation whether of individuals or collectivities – directs my interest to those elements or aspects of all this social knowledge that are most closely associated with behavior; that is, associated with what people all together *do*. Doing is evidence, plain to the senses; by its means, social science can show how human beings as a species seek each other out to form clusters, and from the clusters, communities, just as Aristotle said, and how, once in clusters and communities, they are prone to conform to what they see around them,

---

55 The second of these proverbs along with many others in Tolstoy's *War and Peace* (trans. C. Garnett), Part 12 chap. 13; Part 13 chap. 11; the third along with others in Bourdieu (1977) 161; and many others of many peoples, regarding wine, "better for you than water", etc., in Lo Monaco (2009) 93–97, 269–72.

56 Whole populations are like individuals, see, e.g., Oelze (1991) 74; and on "modal personalities" and the associated discussions, see above, chap. 2 at nn. 37f.

57 For an introduction to *mentalités*, see Bintliff (1991) 10ff.

58 Rokeach (1968) 116 and passim (grouping attitudes with beliefs and values).

59 On "social representations", see Moscovici (1984) 17; (1987) 518f.; (1998) 216ff., 220ff., and passim; Farr (1987) 345, 355 protesting at the vague definition of key terms; Burke (1986) 439ff.; and Reiser (1987) 411ff.; as an example, the idea of saintliness in a community's heroes, Giordano (2005) 60f., or of madness, studied in a French village, Jodelet (1991) passim, or of *machismo* in Mexican populations, Diaz-Guerrero and Diaz-Loving (1994) 134; and Cranach (1998) 34, 37. On axioms and values, see Leung and Bond (2009) 1.

being innately imitative, as he also said. In consequence, in that mass of common knowledge called common sense, it is no surprise to find that the greater portion is *social*, having to do with human interactions. It follows that the *social* sciences will devote their research most particularly to these points, and to the most widely shared ideas of what is sane or foolish, right and wrong according to a given culture. Here, now, historians have the most to learn.

A convenient point at which to begin is one touched on above by Shiller, that is, the finding that market alarms develop out of people's urgently checking their thoughts with each other, and worrying over them in moments by themselves, and checking again, all in a hurry, in the not indefensible belief that ideas shared among many are likely to be more sound than whatever occurs only to some single individual; in short, as Shiller says, "herd behavior".[60] Panics are social phenomena. Across intervals of time, however, the same dependence on what others are thinking also operates on us less urgently as "custom", "tradition" or "convention".[61] To an observer, daily routine seems to proceed almost unconsciously, whether in our response to what others expect of us, or our lending of a helping hand or recall of proverbial wisdom in comment on whatever is at hand. Action verges on reflex.

Thus Kahneman describes what he calls our mental System #1: it "generates impressions, feelings, and inclinations", "operates automatically and quickly, with little or no effort, and no sense of voluntary control", "sometimes substitutes an easier question for a difficult one (heuristics)", "responds more strongly to losses than to gains (loss aversion)".[62] Even in this sampling from his more extended definition, the process can be identified that was always the principal focus of research for himself and his associates: that is, on the blind spots and little tricks that our minds play on us, especially statistical aberrations, and the consequent blurring of the lines that define perfect rationality and *Homo economicus*. In retrospect, he sees advances in the better defining and qualifying of System #1 as a real breakthrough.[63]

---

60 Shiller (2000) 86, "cascade effects"; 90ff., "psychological feedback loops"; 150, "herd behavior" since all those other people could not be wrong; Kahneman et al. (2000) 320f., 324, gouging is acceptable if "everybody is doing it"; also Hertwig and Herzog (2009) 684; or Loewenstein (2001) 278f., the vicious circle of panicky behavior. Coates (2012) 129–234 passim, written from the point of view of a seasoned stock trader, invents scenarios to illustrate how excitement can be described and explained by neuoroscience, but since he assumes his model traders will behave "rationally", i.e., so as to maximize profit, their reactions don't explain motivation, only excitement.

61 On these guides to conduct, see Malinowski (1922) 62, regarding "a very complex set of traditional forces, duties and obligations, beliefs", etc.; "convention," in Moscovici (1984) 8; *habitus* in P. Bourdieu, cf. Henry (1994) 90ff., 99; and the conclusion offered by Westermarck and quoted below at n. 124, that "the Headmaster" in "society as a school... is Custom".

62 Kahneman (2011) 105 – this, defining his System #1 along with a score of other criteria.

63 Kahneman (2002) 467f. and 470f.: "The failure to identify the affect heuristic much earlier [than the 1990s], as well as its enthusiastic acceptance in recent years, reflect significant changes in the general climate of psychological opinion. It is worth noting that in the early 1970s the idea of purely

He distinguishes a second mental process, his System #2, which he describes as slow, conscious, deliberate, effortful thought, including the computational. Opposed to affect, it invites the term "cognitive". The two Systems are, as he explains, figments, like two persons inside our heads invented for convenient conceptualization.[64] Such constructs or metaphors have long been familiar in describing our own mental life and can be observed in descriptions of animal behavior, too, of which illustrations are scattered through these pages, past and to come.

For my own purposes, however, it is important to notice only this: that both Systems may be fairly termed "instrumental". They have to do, not with motivation that sets us on to some purpose, but rather with our quickly sorting out the choices offered toward that end. The ultimate causes of action that lie at a deeper level in our minds are not Kahneman's concern. They are the concern rather of biologists and neuroscientists.

3.3 Scientific reason

Ants, cockroaches, rats, and higher species act in ways suggesting the wide range of hard-wired responses within our own species as well. To these observations, the study of the brain as a physical object has contributed. It too has taken for granted the distinction between instincts that dictate a great deal of behavior, on the one hand, and on the other hand, the urges we feel whether to act on them or not, and how. These we would say are within our control. The existence of such feelings cannot be doubted: they produce physical symptoms like palpitations, sweaty palms, dilation of the pupils, changes of facial expression. Action then supervenes, or not; it can be observed and quantified, or its absence noted. The experience from start to finish may be over and done with in a fraction of a second, recalling some of the phrases used by Kahneman to define "fast thinking" in his System #1; or it may be more leisurely, lasting minutes, even hours or days, like his System #2.[65]

---

cognitive biases appeared novel and distinctive, because the prevalence of motivated and emotional biases of judgment was taken for granted by the social psychologists of the time." Again, (2011) 12, in analyzing how an investment decision is made, "a broader conception of heuristics now exists, which offers a good account. An important advance is that emotion now looms much larger in our understanding of intuitive judgments and choices than it did in the past". The two Systems are close to the pair proposed by Slovic et al. (2002) 397f. and others before this team, though without proposing a large role for affects.

64 Kahneman (2011) 13 (the Systems "as if... two characters in your mind", cf. again, 21), 19ff. (deliberate), 26 (impulses), 28 (feelings) and 103 (emotions); generally avoiding the term "cognition" but cf. 35f. and the quotation at n. 63, above.

65 For a short history of the development of this field, see MacMullen (2003) chap. 2, with some indications of early bibliography in Davidson (1984) 327f.

In the 1980s, Robert Zajonc and Peter Lang, independently, illustrated the sequence at its simplest and most urgent through a person's seeing a snake, and then assessing it in the light of similar remembered images as a good thing or a danger; next, instantaneously, feeling fear and taking flight.[66] A different sequence, regulating for example a choice of one's career, would involve a great deal of imagining of possible outcomes and how each might fulfill or disappoint – that is, how each would feel. Feelings or emotions would be the guide; they may be said to enjoy primacy among other mental powers, even in control of cognition.[67]

Not that there need be no thought at all; but Zajonc was conscious of being a pioneer in elevating the role of affect in decision-making:

> What I want to argue is that the form of experience that we came to call feeling accompanies *all* cognitions, that it arises early in the process of registration and retrieval, albeit weakly and vaguely, and that it derives from a parallel, separate, and partly independent system in the organism.
>
> ...It is generally believed that *all* decisions require some conscious or unconscious processing of pros and cons. Somehow we have come to believe... that if a decision has been made, then a cognitive process must have preceded it. Yet there is no evidence that this is indeed so. Quite often 'I decided in favor of X' is no more than 'I liked X'... We sometimes delude ourselves that we proceed in a rational manner and weigh all the pros and cons of the various alternatives. But this is probably seldom the actual case.[68]

This much was the yield of the usual self-reporting; but much more could be learned through the study of the brain as a physical object. A first lesson, long ago, was in the essentially digital or binary economy of any decision or choice. It can be made once and done, or it may result from a sequential proliferation of choices: Yes/No, On/Off, Good/Bad, Appetitive/Aversive, Like/Dislike, each with its associated feelings. The fact could be confirmed in cases of brain damage, where one hemisphere (as also in other species) produces more aversive responses if it is the undamaged portion while in other patients the other half that survives intact produces appetitive responses.[69]

---

66 Zajonc (1980) 156; Lang (1984) 197.

67 Zajonc (1980) 153ff., "perhaps all perceptions contain some affect"; Izard (1984) 17; Zajonc (1984) 117f.; (1998) 591, "emotions are of prime importance" among all mental processes; Forgas (2001) 16, as to Zajonc's findings, "evidence for the primacy of affect in social reactions is stronger than ever"; a similar endorsement in Haidt (2012) 55; Turner (2000) 139, "thinking and decision making cannot occur without emotions," as Damasio says; also Smith and Kirby (2001) 76, that since the 1980s, the "critical importance" of emotion is recognized as we "evaluate, reason, and make decisions", and Loewenstein (2001) 267ff. to the same effect, in the realm of economic decisions, and again as quoted in Kopcke et al. (2004) 17.

68 Zajonc (1980) 154f.

69 Davidson (1984) 327; hemispheric differences summarized, 344ff., including for the first time the affect-connection; 357, physical symptoms differentiated according to some emotions – though per-

Modern lab techniques show emotion to play a part, apportioned between the two halves of the upper forward brain: in the right, negative thoughts, sadness, depression and the associated expression on the face; in the left, positive thoughts, laughter and happiness. It could be concluded by the 1980s from even earlier work that emotions, as they might be experienced and described in response to electrical stimulation of the brain, are or contain information in clusters of remembered sensory data such as images, along with the impulse to act in some certain way.[70] All of this has of course very wide implications.

In time, it became clear also that what might be called the more basic emotions were concentrated in an inner lower part of the brain (the limbic or limbic-related). In the upper forward parts lies the governance of emotions that are more adaptable, including the social. These make history, producing new behavioral patterns in response to changes in environment. What counts for my purposes is the fact that the motivationally decisive factors are indeed feelings, often of a quite perfect simplicity, not reasoned positions or rationality in the usual sense.

This truth seems now to stand. Even though the way in which the brain works is often described as complicated beyond any comprehension, the present consensus accepts some major points of understanding that bear on motivation and decision-making, thanks especially to Antonio Damasio. His more technical work in the 1980s continued into an article offering important insights on somatic markers (explained below) and so to *Descartes' Error* of 1994, a book that has won a remarkably enthusiastic reception, translation into dozens of languages, and a claim equal to anyone's, to have put neuroscience on the map.[71] From this rich survey of research, from the conclusions at which it arrives, and its suggested interpretations that add to its intel-

---

haps not the social like pride or sympathy, Weiner and Graham (1984) 171; also Davidson (2003) 318f. Davidson's work (1992) is credited among the earliest to show the correlation of negative in the right hemisphere, positive in the left, in Zajonc and McIntosh (1992) 71; 140, 174, asserting the Yes-No simplicity of the flow of thought; more recently, Bechara and Damasio (2005) 356f.

70 Lang (1984) 197, 221 ("there is no clear demarcation between affective and nonaffective behavior"); Izard et al. (1984) 5, "under most circumstances cognitive factors contribute heavily to every aspect of the emotion process"; and more recent studies cited in MacMullen (2003) 153f.

71 On somatic markers, see Damasio et al. (1990) 84–90. Conjecturing "emotion as information processing" had led Lang (1984) 220 to a view of what Damasio later developed; and Kahneman (2002) 470 accepts it, ignoring Damasio and attributing its discovery to P. Slovic. Discrimination among the somatic marks of different emotions had been asserted by William James in 1884 but later established in tests, e.g., by P. Ekman, cf. Davidson (1984) 357; but there are exceptions to this finding, Oakley (1992) 19. Accepting the somatic marker proposal, see, e.g., Peters and Slovic (2000) 1466, Loewenstein (2001) 273f., Haidt (2001) 824f., Davidson (2003) 318, Camerer et al. (2005) 26, Arsenio (2006) 583, Zak (2008) xiii, Haidt and Kesebir (2010) 801, Wong et al. (2011) 86, or Coates (2012) 97f. J. Haidt and his associates at Princeton acknowledged the important influence of Damasio (1994) on their work: see Haidt (2001) 824, Greene and Haidt (2002) 517f., and Greene et al. (2004) 389.

ligibility, my own interests draw out only what relates to decision making, reasonable or not. My focus, however, is not far from that of the book itself.

To begin with, Damasio applies the term "emotion" to our experiencing of bodily sensations in our reaction to an external stimulus. Very much as in the illustration above (Zajonc or Lang, describing our sighting of a snake), the experience first produces a quick appraisal ("What is that thing?"), a quick "primary" emotion (aversive or appetitive, No or Yes), and physical changes some of which we are aware of, like our pulse-beat, while some are beneath the level of our conscious sensing. Connection is made with the inner brain for memory and instructions. That may be all there is to it. It is reflexive, what any animal will depend on for survival. The aversive or appetitive emotions arise from that inner system, the most ancient in terms of evolution, and especially the amygdala. Of this, more, later. But we humans may also, and often do, feel consequent physical changes. Awareness of these is not so instantaneous.[72] It may allow a more attentive assessment in which comparison can be made with some representation from the past (a visual image, a tactile feel, a smell, sound, or taste). Then follow, next, our ("secondary") emotional responses to the recall of the representation, as we bring before our attention the image (especially visual) of doing something we have done before, testing if it felt good or bad; and we may repeat the process through a succession of representations. They originate in the upper front parts of the brain but connect with the older, central parts. Each representation has a feel to it, and the feeling is judged good or bad in the light of our goals.[73]

Among our constantly increasing store of representations, we choose analogies or models to guide us. The store is gigantic, as is suggested by the sheer size of our prefrontal cortex. Let us say it amounts to a third of the brain's 100 billion neurons (and more).[74] Here, principally, must be lodged the yield constantly fed in to us from our five senses. For survival purposes, however, our storage capacity would be useless without an efficient retrieval system. The need is not only obvious but confirmed by the size of the reviewing area, our short term memory, in which there is room only for quite small gobbets of data at a time. The limits appear most familiarly in the length of our thought-units in speaking, even of academics at their lecterns. We simply can't handle much more than twenty words in a row without a break in attention to take it

---

72 "Emotion" defined in terms of a dedicated brain system, its somatic effects, and their registration as what we perceive as a feeling, cf. Bechara and Damasio (2005) 339; on the inner, limbic system, Damasio (1994) 118; "emotion" and "feeling" kept separate, 146 n. (but this is "not orthodox").

73 For useful pages on these processes, see Damasio (1994) 130f., 133 ("feeling your emotions"), and 133–48 passim. Loewenstein (2001) 268 proposes a similar distinction between different sorts of emotions ("anticipatory" first, then "anticipated") in an appraisal process.

74 Brain and prefrontal cortex size, Miller and Cohen (2001) 168, 185; a smaller number, a mere 20 billion, in Marcus (2004) 2; and 85 billion with approximately 1000 connections each, in Helmstaedter (2013) 501.

all in.[75] For efficient retrieval, the key is emotions as color-coded tabs (so they may be called). They are Damasio's hypothetical "somatic markers" – the physical sensations associated with representations that allow us quickly to sort through our experiences by "algorithmicity".[76]

Even in this very crudely compressed description of complicated, half-understood mental processes, with a great deal of Damasio's account clipped away in Procrustean fashion, one novelty stands out: namely, the role of emotions. Herein lay Descartes' error. The philosopher had supposed that animal spirits, the passions, every form of undisciplined mental activity must be of the body, while higher powers that distinguish thinking Man exist quite separately. In fact, however, it is through our feeling the internal physical responses to alternatives that we can then make choices and so progress toward a decision. Of course another name for that progress is "thought" or "cognition". It issues from, it assigns a cooperative role to, the physical self that Descartes scorned. Body and mind must work together as a team. While some behavior obeys innate reflexes, "most somatic markers we use for rational decision-making were probably created in our brains during the process of education and socialization... based on the process of secondary emotions" – for instance (I add) created at a grandmother's or mother's knee.[77]

And much that Damasio offers only as hypothetical would find a ready agreement among the Balinese. "Who can think but with their feelings?" – this was a common saying long ago among this people. Among the Papuans the one word *inatimang* still means both "feel" and "think". Now we have Zajonc and others to the same effect. It supports an essential part of my argument, that why we do what we do can be understood only with the cooperation of the observer's feelings, so as to identify and match, at least in some degree, the affective element in human decision-making. This much is for historians. Further ambitions to map the brain, I think I may leave to the neuroscientists.[78]

Where Damasio went beyond his predecessors was in the interpretation he gave to a famous instance of frontal-brain injury, that of poor Phineas Gage in 1848, with other similar cases in the modern literature. They present a remarkable puzzle. How was it that such victims of accident or disease retain a normal command of facts,

---

75 Damasio (1994) 174 ("immense number of scenarios" stored) and 196f. ("a vast store of factual knowledge"); but limited staging area, 198f. On the science explaining thought-units, see MacMullen (2001) 8–11.

76 The quoted term in Damasio (1994) 168.

77 On somatic markers, Damasio (1994) 173ff. and elsewhere, esp. 177 (quoted).

78 Wikan (1989) 297, the Bali quote, and Hermann (1995) 200, the Papuan New Guinean. On neuroscientific ambitions, see, e.g., Seung (2013) hoping to explain "how the brain's wiring makes us who we are", and (58) mentioning decision-making, or Helmstaedter (2013) and the volume in which Helmstaedter's study is published, along with contributions there by more than a hundred other neuroscientists; but I don't see how to apply any of this work to my own discussion.

including knowledge of social norms and conventions, but are unable to cope with the ordinary needs of life among their fellow beings? Somehow they lack the ability to apply knowledge to action. They are tactless, improvident, impulsive, insulting, irresponsible, ungovernable in their employment; they cheat and lie. But before the damage, if they had not been born with it, they had been altogether different! Furthermore, when tested for their response to interviews, questions, or descriptions of scenes that should have elicited an emotional response, none such will be detectible. The patients' affect is always utterly flat. From which Damasio concluded, as the only possible hypothesis, that the damaged area of the brain was the principal site of emotion, or at least a very important one, and that emotion was necessary for what might be called social thinking or coping such as we all command in the course of our interaction with others. He was conscious of opening a new window on "reasoning and deciding", with the implication of action that would follow.[79]

Appraisal, he saw, is deliberative and consequential, cool and slow. It discerns the best path toward a goal, as will be apparent to us in some representation; but it does not *impel* us to *do* anything. Explaining *action* requires what Damasio next brings into the picture, namely, the involvement of the elements in our nature that are essential for our survival.[80] They are instincts: for the preservation of life and aggression in the process; for reproduction and nurturing; to satisfy hunger and other physical needs; or to win acceptance and approval from our conspecifics (especially those close, as kin) on whose support we depend. As a part of our social instinct, we are even hardwired to control aggression – beyond certain limits.[81] At moments of choice through representations of possible action, together with their associated affect, we can test if these and the like goals will be attained by choosing "A" not "B", imagining what each would feel like, good or bad. Instinct and situation thus are matched. We *think* through *feeling*, exactly as the Balinese and Papuans could have told us. The process is what we know as *cognition*.

We apparently handle even essentially numerical calculations with somatic markers. Damasio offers in evidence a gambling game with cards color-coded to yield

---

79 Damasio (1994) 166, as to the quoted two terms, "not a whisper [in anyone's previous analysis] is ever heard about emotion or feeling"; 175, "partnership between cognitive processes and emotional"; and "even more telling" (57), study of brain damage in infancy, affirmed, e.g., by Anderson et al. (1999) 1032, 1035ff., or by Dolan (1999), though without mention of Damasio's work.

80 Damasio (1994) 179: "The neural basis for the internal preference system consists of mostly innate regulatory dispositions, posed to ensure survival of the organism. Achieving survival coincides with the ultimate reduction of unpleasant body states and the attaining of homeostatic ones, i.e., functionally balanced biological states. The internal preference system is inherently biased to avoid pain, seek potential pleasure, and is probably pretuned for achieving these goals in social situations."

81 Hare and Tomasello (2005) 441ff., conjecturing socialization by natural selection, as observed in foxes that can be bred for acceptance of humans – thereby a model for wolves turned into domesticated dogs. Further, Tomasello (2011) 15 and 20f.

good or bad results, but in so puzzling a way, literally it can't be figured out. Nevertheless, normal subjects engaging in it bit by bit learnt what color paid off, though modestly, without risk of penalties but without any chance of a big win. This color they preferred, prudently, and stayed with it. Gage-syndrome subjects in contrast impatiently went for big gains, suffering big losses and, before long, bankruptcy. Realistic calculation of long-term success in the game, as Damasio emphasized, was impossible for anyone; but he supposed normal subjects somehow developed a "hunch" about the dangers in big gambles as opposed to a sound, sensible course. Kahneman might agree to call this risk-aversion, and intuitive, but the neuroscience in support was cited above.[82]

About choice, a great deal of research has been published to explain its latter, instrumental stages, but without getting very far into the early stages. For illustration: in an excellent discussion by two neuroscientists, the rules of the road in Britain are recalled, at odds with the American; but for tourists in London the two words LOOK RIGHT will be spelt out in big letters on the street-edge next to a pedestrian-crossing, and Americans seeing the warning will override the knowledge they would otherwise trust, registering the British rules in their prefrontal cortex to guide them. This area of the brain serves as "active memory in the service of control", as can be known from patients who have suffered damage in this area. They cannot maintain the override for any length of time, in the face of all the contrary representations that must be sorted through.[83] Research and analysis, however, generally pick up only after the point where a choice of conduct has become a goal – that is, the next thing that the pedestrian wants to do. The goal is not only to cross the street but to do so safely. Nothing less than survival is at stake; for everyone knows that the street is a dangerous place. Representations of that fact are held in memory along with the associated emotion. It is fear that controls the override and insures in the unimpaired mind the needed attention to the novelties of traffic flow. Absent fear, there is the risk of a wrong step. The fear is existential, instinctual, which I note as the marker of those deeper levels of motivation distinguished in the Preface, above.

To override can be the chosen strategy, not out of fear but in response to some other feeling, as can be illustrated in other species.

> In a common experimental paradigm, hungry laboratory rats may be offered a choice of two rewards, perhaps a pellet or two of chow available immediately, against a larger reward (say

82 Damasio (1994) 212ff., cf. 42; Bechara and Damasio (2005) 345–51; some confirmation in Camerer et al. (2005) 44; accepted in Wegner (2002) 327; and the neuroscientific discussion cited above, n. 17. Even here, envisioning outcomes and reacting with a primary emotion may be the explanation – witness the ability of birds and other animals to count, i.e., to understand a numerical sequence where four is bigger than two, etc., in return for reward, or that choosing a small number of repeated acts is better than a large number, cf. Freidin and Kacelnick (2011) 1001f. (starlings' behavior in foraging).
83 Miller and Cohen (2001) 170ff. (quoted, 173).

> eight pellets) delayed by ten, twenty-five or thirty seconds. The rat can express its preference by pressing either of two levers in a testing chamber or by scurrying to one or another goal box across the arms of a simple T-maze; the experimenter records how often an animal selects the later, larger reward and thus obtains a measure of the rat's relative tolerance for delay.[84]

What is required of the rats for the better reward is the ability to develop and hold in the field of control a representation of the desired reward while learning the path to it through trial and error. They thought it out in their animal way. It appears little different from the human.

3.4 Moral reason

Our powers of thought now appear much better understood than they were only a generation ago. For historians, the most useful advance has been achieved by psychologists like Zajonc and neuroscientists like Damasio. The former have ultimately relied on the self-reporting of subject groups or individuals, though they apply many devices of laboratory investigation. The neuroscientists add data directly accessible to the investigator's five senses checked against the subject's actions, thus bypassing whatever the subjects might say was going on, mentally. Despite their differences in method, the two schools agree on the singular influence of emotion over our actions, with or without our thinking them through.

The finding is resisted on one front. It is our common conviction in many moments of everyday life – and among these, the most important – that our choices are not determined by any agency within us that is not in our control. In that sense our will is free. We are in charge, giving deliberate thought to what we are about to do. The belief seems universal and virtually ineradicable; we simply know that in the process of decision we are functioning as rational, morally responsible beings.[85] Yet Daniel Wegner insists that these mental sensations are themselves not a reality but a delusion. "Conscious will is an *emotion of authorship*", a feeling which in turn may stimulate still others like guilt or pride. The sense or feeling of authorship counter-intuitively *follows* rather than precedes the decision.[86]

To demonstrate the fact, choice may be examined not solely through self-reporting, meta-cognition, auto-inspection, or whatever the preferred term. Instead,

---

84 Manuck et al. (2003) 159; on the control element, not to lose the goal in mind, see Baumeister and Vohs (2003) 202f., 210. The marshmallow tests by Mischel (above, chap. 1) are exactly similar.

85 Wegner (2002) 2, "The conscious will explanation... has a much deeper grip on our intuition. We each have a profound sense that we consciously will much of what we do, and we experience ourselves willing our actions many times a day"; cf. 325, and the same view accepted, e.g., in Gazzaniga (2011) 2, 6f., 75, or 105; and on delusions, above, nn. 50f.

86 Wegner (2002) 318 (Wegner's italics), seeing his proposition as "a useful new perspective"; 341 (guilt, pride); and x, 26, 60, 341f., and passim, "delusive".

it can be by-passed through the examination of what we *think* or sense we are doing. Laboratory experiments on this have been going on since the 1960s. For example: a person is rigged up to show brainwaves and then is to push a button; and in a certain part of the brain, (1) electrical activity changes, indicating readiness potential, RP; (2) the subject is aware of wanting to push the button and (3) then, of actually doing so; thereafter (4) the finger moves. Notice, something has certainly gone on in the brain in the interval, which varies from a fraction of a second to as much as ten seconds, before (2) we would say we have willed anything at all.[87]

While we are not aware of it, this period of time may accommodate any of innumerable mental phenomena that are unconscious, such as hypnotic responses, split-personality actions, mis-remembering or mis-speaking, hallucinations, every sort of involuntary movement and autosuggestion. What is, however, most interesting to a historian in this interval is the point of origin it offers to impulses that are innate and instinctual. They are predetermined; some of them are touched on in the pages above and below; and many more are illustrated by Wegner. He says cautiously of brain-activity in pre-conscious seconds, "we don't know just what that is".[88] I would rather say, with the evidence, that the interval serves the findings of Zajonc, Damasio, and biologists at large, for whom reflexive feelings are very much a part of motivation.

The sequence (1)-(4) is deterministic if "determined" means not subject to our will. At issue are free will, the teachings of St. Augustine, penal policy, malice prepense, sin, and all such serious matters of law and religious belief; also the degree to which morals are conceived to be thought through – to what is universally right or wrong and so formed into rules – or whether instead they are right or wrong only for this or that people. On these matters a seasoned scholar should be heard; and such a one is the philosopher, Elliot Turiel.

Elliot Turiel, without defining the term, champions "reasoning" of a high order. Predictably, too, he rejects Damasio's ideas that seem to confuse thinking with feeling: Damasio, before he got into his neuroscience, should first have examined and explained the everyday social coping practices that brain-damaged persons can't manage; he should have talked more about "theoretical formulations", "complex judgments and understandings", "valid conceptions".[89] In short, he didn't treat his subject like

87 Experiments well surveyed by Wegner (2002) 49–59; further, with updates, Gazzaniga (2011) 127ff., 199f. He posits two different things, brain and mind (4f., 218ff.), without ever defining let alone explaining the latter; and through this latter he escapes from the implications of "determined" (i.e., physically caused) mental activity.

88 Innate value choices, above, nn. 80f. and below, 103; Wegner (2002) 29–61, thereafter, passim; and 53, quoted.

89 Turiel (2006) 15f. on "Damasio's errors" and insistence on the importance of "moral reasoning" in individual decision-making; 10, "morality is not primarily driven by emotions... [nor] is it mainly emotions that guide the formation of judgments about right and wrong"; and 11, upholding the Piaget-Kohlberg view that moral rationality [not specific values] is innate though not apparent in humans

a philosopher. Offering these criticisms, Turiel can forego further discussion and turn to his target of favor over a full half century: the rationality of morality.

He finds what he seeks at two levels: in evolution and in individual maturing. The latter process, of more interest, is discoverable through the close study of how children as they grow up conceive of right and wrong at different ages, becoming more and more analytical. The subject was explored by two well known psychologists, Piaget followed by Kohlberg. Turiel, a colleague of the latter in his own earlier years, expanded on the work of these pioneers by drawing a clearer distinction between the two social constructs he discovered in morality: convention and principle.[90] Convention is what even children can understand, based as it is simply on what is received and expected in surrounding society. Principles on the other hand rest upon or are expressed as universal concepts of honesty, rights, fairness, welfare, harm, and the like. They are, in Turiel's view, the product of abstract moral reasoning; they are the "higher" as opposed to what are the "lower", the "primitive" and "underdeveloped" ethical systems of mere convention.[91] He pronounces the capacity to understand moral rules as such, superior; and for this superiority he finds confirmation in testing children and young people through interviews. The older ones show an understanding of the universal above what is merely accepted.

Jonathan Haidt also addressed the distinction between convention and principle, and the question of universality. His intent, resisting the rationalist interpretation, was "to test the idea that affective reactions may play a role in moral judgment", and to do this among "issues and actions on the basis of their ability to offend, or 'feel wrong,' even when victimless" – for example, using one's nation's flag to clean one's toilet.[92] A far larger sampling than Turiel's was interviewed, and one that was more heterogeneous, too, representing both rich and poor people in three very different cities. These were Philadelphia, and as a second the struggling city Recife in Brazil, and Porto Alegre also in Brazil as the third, with its relatively prosperous population largely descended from European immigrants. In interviews, answers to various questions in percentile terms ranged all the way from 3 up to 87, or from 7 to 97. The higher the socioeconomic status of the person interviewed, and especially in the U.S., the less likely that moral disgust registered, and the less likely, any perception of any moral violation. The effect of class was even more marked than citizenship. Contrasting his results with Turiel's, Haidt concluded that the latter's "studies of college students may be misleading" and will produce "an exaggerated impression of cultural

until the end of childhood; the same views championed and examined, Turiel (1977) 78.

90 Turiel (2006) 11 on the question of a higher, Western morality.

91 For the terms quoted, see Turiel (2006) 30 and (1977) 78–82; further, Haidt et al. (1993) 614, also Nado et al. (2009) 622f. on Turiel's belief in the "objective prescriptive force" of "moral rules", as seen in work of 1979 and 1983, and 625f., that Haidt's subjects acknowledged moral differences across time.

92 Haidt et al. (1993) 615, quoted; 613, emphasizing "the comparatively neglected role of affect in moral judgment".

uniformity."[93] Both warnings were more than warranted.[94] In fact, the chief determinant in Haidt's study was local preference, here varying from one country to another. True, all of them were of today; but across time an equal range of preference could be safely assumed. And, just as historians must do, the people Haidt interviewed did see and could accept differences in moral standards between their own world and that of three centuries ago.

Elliot Turiel's rationalist view on moral judgment was thus deprived of a foothold in the empirical evidence. Indeed, he conceded that "people do have strong feelings about their moral convictions and do go to great lengths to implement their moral views", that is, in acting out their feelings.[95] On earlier pages, above, microeconomists also have been shown to acknowledge, though somewhat gingerly, the participation of emotions in decision-making.[96] As to psychologists who are surely the best judges in the matter, they all seem to subscribe now to the primacy that Robert Zajonc assigned to our feelings, a full generation ago, so long as he left room for the distinction between deciding, on the one hand, what exactly is the nature of a given stimulus or experience, and on the other hand, what action to take, appetitive or aversive.[97]

From all three disciplines, then – philosophic and social scientific – something like a consensus can be inferred, which gives weight to affect in behavioral analysis and incidentally serves my own particular objective; for historians may find guidance here in their handling of their materials. They must decide how much of the past should be explained in terms of theological or political doctrines, calculations of utility, published tracts and sermons, authoritative proofs, and all such frigid materials of reason, or whether instead they should search about in the clouds of love, ceremonies, common sayings, shame, and other nebulous influences discoverable in any given culture. The two bodies of information must be apprehended by quite different powers of the analyst's mind.

Consensus among the disciplines, just outlined, suggests how best to look at the matter. Particularly in regard to moral reason, it helps to narrow the focus to feelings. The longest lasting of these is anger. For the study of motivation, I note that it is anger that impels us to action the most forcefully, too, and is the most intimately involved in moral judgments. It flares up as indignation when someone is perceived as attacking not only our personal rights but the general moral code itself; for rights asserted by

---

93 Haidt et al. (1993) 613ff.; tables to analyze results, 619–22; quoted, 625; and Haidt (2012) 15f., 21f. Turiel and Killen (2010) 48 dismiss Haidt's work as "reductionism" but concede (35f.) that "emotions involve evaluative appraisals" – which does approach the emerging consensus.

94 See above, chap. 1 at nn. 34f. and elsewhere.

95 Turiel (2006) 30.

96 Above, Kahneman, Shiller, and others in nn. 17, 19, 21.

97 See, e.g., a relatively early statement in Dienstbier (1984) 486; more recently, Camerer et al. (2005) 18, wording the contrast as ""go/no-go" and "true/false".

the individual without validation by society at large can only be meaningless.[98] In addition to anger, however, there are also fear and disgust and (sometimes) surprise often proposed as the strongest of our feelings. The four of course are not all moral nor are they the whole story; for there is curiosity, too, and longing, happiness, sadness, gratitude, shame, guilt, sympathy. It is a long list to consider in the abstract, separating out if possible, and setting to one side, the further sensations of mood, drive, and attitude.

Moreover, looking around in our contemporary world, certain emotions can be found in one society but not in another. It is simply by chance, through the interest shown in comparative psychology by Japanese researchers, that *amae* is most often mentioned, unique among the Japanese: a "sweet dependence", "playing baby", as it has been described.[99] *Amae* is relatively well known compared to the thin random scattering of other feelings identified as peculiar to other societies. An example would be the special term for moral indignation, justified wrath, *song* as it's called among the people of a tiny island in the seas far north of Australia; similarly, *popokl*, "outrage over the failure of others to recognize one's claims" among the New Guinean Hageners.[100] Such unique words and what they designate prompt the belief that some particular variation in affect-capacity must characterize many or even all societies, and are in fact their own creation. Certainly the acceptability of expressing one or another feeling is a social construct, and a legitimate object of study in cultural history.[101]

Underlying cross-cultural variation in emotions are innate and invariant universals, according to one school, while another can see only proofs of the mutability or plasticity of our tendencies. Debate extends to the realm of moral reasoning. Discussion at the level of theory may be left to philosophers,[102] but at the empirical level both psychologists and biologists see the need to consider the innate. Among psycho-

---

98 On the forcefulness of anger, see MacMullen (2003) 77; and Kroeber and Kluckhohn (1952) 157 speak of "the strongly affective nature of most cultural learning [so] the individual is seldom emotionally neutral in those sectors of his culture which touch him directly"; on rights and anger, see, e.g., Trivers (1971) 49ff., Brown (1986) 575, de Waal (1991) 336, Epstein (1994) 710, Fry (2006) 403, or Akerlof and Shiller (2009) 23 (sociological literature); and on the real nature of an acknowledged right as against a mere claim, Coleman (1991) 500f. Further, below, n. 100.

99 On *amae*, Harré (1986) 10, quoted; Fiske (1992) 698; Kitayama et al. (2000) 110; Markus and Hamedani (2007) 9; Triandis (2007) 69; on *kanashii*, Tov and Diener (2007) 695; on Japanese *oime*, uncomfortable indebtedness, Ellsworth (1994) 38; a Balinese term, Rosaldo (1984) 142f.; a number of Eskimo terms for feelings not matched in other languages, in Briggs (1970) 311–76, as, e.g., *unga*, affection felt for someone in a particular degree of kinship; *verguenza ajena* in Spanish, Crespo (1986) 214, embarrassment felt at a wretched performance.

100 Lutz (1988) 44 and 163 on Ifaluk *song*; (1985) 38, quoted, on *popokl*.

101 MacMullen (2003) 71ff.; and notice "emotions as historical factor", a session in 2010 at the International Congress of Historical Sciences.

102 On plasticity or its denial, see, e.g., 500 pages of polemic in Pinker (2002); or, grounded in social and biological science and also wide ranging, Marcus (2004) 33–45, 147–58.

logists, Jonathan Haidt and his associates have proposed that (as also for numeracy or language-acquisition) we are pre-programmed or "prewired" to respond selectively to experience and thus to learn forms of behavior that our own particular society will call moral; and in fact we can sense this instantaneity in some of our judgments. These, Haidt would call intuitive, that is, emotional or at least not cognitive in the usual sense, though often preliminary to more deliberate assessment.[103] Rather than supposing moral assessments to be purely rational, he sees them as partially affective. Thus a role for surrounding cultures opens up, which teach right and wrong and everyday behavior.

Haidt instances how we see incest, which every people will reject with disgust and without need of reflection. He could perhaps have recalled a passage in Plato's *Laws* (838af., trans. Jowett) where the matter comes up in conversation between an Athenian and a Spartan Megillus. The Spartan is predictably cast as the one in need of enlightenment.

> *Ath.* We are all well aware that most men, in spite of their lawless natures, are very strictly and precisely restrained from intercourse with the fair.
> *Meg.* When do you mean?
> *Ath.* When anyone has a brother or sister who is fair; and about a son or daughter, the same unwritten law holds, and is a most perfect safeguard, so that no open or secret connection ever takes place between them. Nor does the thought of such a thing ever enter at all into the minds of most of them... And is not the reason of this that no one has ever said the opposite, but everyone from his earliest childhood has heard men speaking in the same manner about them always and everywhere, whether in comedy or in the graver language of tragedy? When the poet introduces on the stage a Thyestes or an Oedipus, or a Macareus having secret intercourse with his sister, he represents him, when found out, ready to kill himself as the penalty of sin.
> *Meg.* You are right in saying that tradition, if no breath of opposition ever assails it, has a marvelous power.

The role of surrounding society in affirming an instinct at every stage of a person's life could hardly be more acceptably explained; but it is easily replicated in anthropological literature which, if one goes back far enough, shows us an ample cross-section of human behavior not yet homogenized by the industrialized West. It can almost serve historians as a surrogate for time travel.

So much for the need to acknowledge some element of the innate in moral reasoning, as it has been seen by psychologists ancient and modern. Among biologists who take up the question, it is common to point out how animal behavior resembles the human, as, for example, in what a certain kind of ant does to succor its conspecifics.

---

103 Haidt (2001) 814, answering rationalist interpretations; allowing a role for the genetic, 824, 826, 827, "even if moral intuitions are partially innate, children somehow end up with a morality that is unique to their culture or group"; see also an associate with Haidt, Greene and Haidt (2002) 517; Greene et al. (2004) 389, 397f.; Haidt and Kesebir (2010) 798ff., 802–07; and Verbeek (2006) 439.

If humans were observed in such conduct, they would be called compassionate; so ants exhibit compassion, a moral emotion, just as the behavior of cockroaches was seen earlier to resemble what among humans would be called social anxiety; likewise rats, as has been shown in a dramatic little experiment that brought out their susceptibility to fellow-suffering and their anxious efforts to relieve it.[104] In insects and little rodents, to say nothing of infinitely closer similarities in higher forms of life, the playing out of impulses matches how we humans act, and it is a common inference therefore that in our species also such impulses are instinctual. They include some that are social, very prominently. There is even neuroscientific evidence, too, for the existence of prosocial control in those regions (the limbic system, especially the hypothalmus and amygdala) which lie deepest in our brain, constitute the command areas oldest in our evolution, and are shared with innumerable other species.[105]

We can sift through the large body of data of this sort, where observation shows non-human behavior in relation to conspecifics that can reasonably be called social. There is, for example, mating for life; that would be monogamy in human terms. There is some bar to copulation with an animal's own offspring, that is (in human terms), a bar to incest; there is special treatment reserved for pregnant females, that might be called respect for life; and there is some bar against an animal's eating its offspring (cannibalism in human terms) – though not among pigs, cats, and (to the horror of pet owners) among hamsters. All these and other forms of regulation of animal behavior are evidently inborn. A selection among them can be made to define the most basic.

A primatologist, Frans de Waal, nominated four, emphasizing, however, that in our own species they were not determinative of behavior in detail. Rather, as he says,

> In discussing what constitutes morality, the actual behavior is less important than the underlying capacities. For example, instead of arguing that food-sharing is a building block of morality, it is rather the capacities thought to underlie food-sharing (e.g., high levels of tolerance, sensitivity to others' needs, reciprocal exchange) that are relevant. Ants, too, share food, but likely based on quite different urges than those that make chimpanzees or people share food. This distinction was understood by Darwin, who looked beyond the actual behavior at the underlying motivations, intentions, and capacities. In other words, whether animals are nice to each other is not the issue; nor does it matter much whether their behavior fits our moral preferences or not.

104 Sanderson (1941) 146, describing leaf-cutter behavioral patterns, well known; on cockroaches, above, chap. 1 at n. 64; Bartal et al. (2011) 1428ff., on rats seeking relief of stress at seeing a conspecific trapped, and sharing of food, cf. de Waal (2005) 17 or among owls, altruism in food exchange shown by dominant owl nestlings toward younger siblings, in Roulin et al. (2012) 1229f. For succouring behavior in pigeons, wolves, etc., see, e.g., de Waal (2005) 12, invoking Darwin, or Verbeek (2006) 443 (still more often witnessed and reported among cetaceans and especially elephants).

105 Wilson (1995) 153, 161f.; Davidson (2003) 319f., but 328, mother love in the orbitofrontal cortex; de Waal (2005) 32; Verbeek (2006) 425f.; Vuilleumier (2009) 225ff., 235f.; especially Buchanan et al. (2009) 289, 291ff., 304ff., and 309; and on the social functions, Bickart et al. (2010) 163.

> The relevant question is whether they possess the capacities for reciprocity and revenge, for the enforcement of social rules, for the settlement of disputes, and for sympathy and empathy.[106]

De Waal's mentions of reciprocity and sympathy follow easily from the observations that have been made of ants, rats, and other animals, too, as will appear. Nevertheless, his appeal to Darwin might seem awkward. At least to the layman, Darwin means natural selection. What is there in being "nice" that serves this end? The answer is, that what counts is not the survival of the individual but of the gene; hence, allowance, and more than allowance, a privileged status for prosocial affect among species whose members may depend on it for their very lives.[107] Consideration for conspecifics is well known and widely illustrated, not least among primates, while anthropologists report the same findings and underline their huge importance among the peoples they observe.[108] Darwin even expressed the belief, better called the hope, that "the social instinct – the prime principle of man's moral constitution – with the aid of active powers and the effect of habit, naturally leads to the golden rule", though among primates as well as our own species it is common to see the rule applied selectively according to rank or relationship.[109] Reciprocity presents no problem, then, to an evolutionary explanation.

The same may be claimed for altruism. In Darwinian terms, helping others quite selflessly and giving to others without thought of repayment may seem decidedly counterintuitive. But in fact the case is easily made for this latter claim, too, "in hundreds of experiments from around the world",[110] and the sense of fairness in distribu-

---

106 De Waal (2005) 13 (I have omitted two references from the passage); (1991) 336, using the term "precursor" to describe certain primate behavior similar to the human; 348, doubts about a chimpanzee's awareness of its species' "rules"; and his choice of the "four building blocks" of morality observable in non-human species, in Brosnan (2006) 168: "sympathy-related capacity (e.g., attachment, cognitive empathy), a norm-related capacity (e.g., internalization of prescriptive social rules, social expectations), reciprocity (including moralistic aggression), and getting along with others (e.g., peacemaking, intentionality in relationship maintenance, negotiation)".

107 Difficulties reconciling individual survival-fitness with other-oriented behavior, Verbeek (2006) 425 and Pizarro (2007) 588; gene-survival, cf. Wilson (1995) 153 and Verbeek (2006) 425.

108 See, e.g., Fiske (1992) 689, 697f., or Fry (2006) 399, 401, 417, quoting *The Descent of Man* (1871); 400 and passim, on the wealth of anthropological data.

109 Haidt (2001) 826, on reciprocal, i.e., delayed, altruism; selective unselfishness, e.g., favoring kinsmen, in chap. 2 n. 66 above, Shweder (1984) 29, Hastings et al. (2006) 484, or Haidt and Kesebir (2010) 809, with nonhuman examples in de Waal (1991) 315 and Brosnan (2006) 161f. For a non-human (primate) deference to the rights (access to females for copulation) enjoyed by a dominant male, indicated by anxious apologetic behavior toward a dominant male by one lower in the hierarchy even for a breach of the rule that had not been observed, see Elster (1999) 49, "pangs of conscience" (or, better, expectations of punishment which is what we call guilt).

110 Henrich (2005) 795, quoted; 799 (using, e.g., test games in small societies in Mazambique, Zimbabwe, Borneo, Paraguay, etc.) and passim; an early such study, Trivers (1971) 45f.; Damasio (1994) 176, pointing out possible selfish rewards from altruistic acts; and de Waal (2008) 64ff., finding both

tion, and distress or anger at unequal sharing, shows up even in early childhood. Why should it not declare its innate character in humans, when primates and other social animals further down the evolutionary scale display their outrage at treatment different from their expectations, that is, different from their sense of right? De Waal's collaborator Sarah Brosnan has presented the evidence with much interesting detail.[111]

Reciprocity and altruism may both be in accord with adult, thought-out rules of ethical behavior; but the trigger for such conduct must be sought in our inborn capacity to empathize with others. Generous impulses, outgoing affection and trust, can be shown to be, not obedient to conscious moral reasoning but initiated rather by our circuitry and chemistry. Those warm fuzzy feelings can be greatly increased by injection of a certain neural stimulant, oxytocin.[112] The more deeply that science peers into the human mind as a physical object, and the more recent the scientific publications, the more remote the older rationalist views of morality thus appear.

At the same time, the particular importance of our *social* evaluations is evident in our everyday mental operations. By far the greater part is devoted to our interpersonal relations and to problems that especially require affective input, sizing each other up, divining others' thoughts about ourselves, choosing what to do within the bounds of what is acceptable. What is acceptable is, by another name, "right and wrong", our "code of ethics", and morality; "emotions provide the main support of social norms," as a sociologist says.[113] Emotions may thus be said to lie at the very center of moral systems, as Edward Westermarck pointed out more than a century ago. A prescient man, Westermarck! – omnivorous reader in biology, history, psychology, and (with field experience) especially in anthropology; so his ideas drew on abundant data. He is now forgotten. In opposition to current rationalist theory, and more than a century ago, he wrote,

---

selfish behavior/thoughts and reflexive altruism almost simultaneously in humans, and comparable behavior in primates.

111 Lapsley (2006) 52f. or Killen et al. (2006) 160, 166, on children and fairness; Trivers (1971) 45f. on reciprocity observable in "all known cultures" and 49, "injustice, unfairness, and lack of reciprocity often motivate human and indignation," with anthropological literature; Tomasello (2009) 33ff., supposing the sense and display of fairness to be innate in *homo sapiens* alone among primates, though in fact non-human species including birds also display this sense, cf. Brosnan (2006) 168f.; further, Brosnan (2006) 155, 158f., 161f., 168f., on emotional outbursts at violation of "social rules", for example, chimpanzees' "tantrums"; 162f., observation of hierarchies, e.g., dominants and subordinates among baboons or wolves; and (165) special treatment for pregnant females.

112 For the individual-specific focus of loving/giving emotions as a subset of altruism, stimulated by oxytocin, see Damasio (1994) 121f., Kosfeld et al. (2005) 673, Zak et al. (2007) passim, Barraza and Zak (2009) 182, and Mehta and Josephs (2011) 177f.; on the "warm glow" rewarding altruism, Harbaugh et al. (2007) 1622f.; on altruism and wish to protect as innate in our species, Tomasello (2009 6ff.

113 The primacy of interpersonal thought in running our lives is implicit in Damasio (1994) 8–12 and passim, but found also in Kemper (1978) 4, 43, and passim, or Zajonc (1998) 604; quoted on emotions, Elster (1999) 98, with further discussion, 99ff.

> That the moral concepts are ultimately based on emotions either of indignation or approval, is a fact which a certain school of thinkers [meaning utilitarians] have in vain attempted to deny… Men pronounced certain acts to be good or bad on account of the emotions those acts aroused in their minds… [In conclusion] The theory was laid down that moral emotions belong to a wider class of emotions, which may be described as retributive; that moral disapproval is a kind of resentment, akin to anger and revenge, and that moral approval is a kind of retributive kindly emotion, akin to gratitude… acquired by means of natural selection in the struggle for existence.[114]

Westermarck's choice of emphasis fits not badly with what de Waal had to say, quoted earlier, that is, picturing morality in high colors and strong contrasts; and de Waal, himself prescient as well, went on to predict "a much larger shift in theorizing that will end up positioning morality firmly within the emotional core of human nature".[115] In fact that shift has been remarked on since the 1990s not in biology but in psychology, and an active champion of it has been Jonathan Haidt. Like de Waal he has attempted to distinguish the more basic social proclivities, those called "capacities" by the primatologist and "foundations" by Haidt; but Haidt argues for five, not four, that define "morality". They are innate at least in their outlines, however varied cross-culturally in their details.[116]

3.5 Moral culture

So far as regards the individual, basic morality is inculcated in the home by mother, father, and other close kin. Depth of ethical understanding increases as children mature, as Piaget and his successors have shown. In America, childrens' peer pressure, especially among teenagers, is a formative factor, though in other countries not

---

114 Westermarck (1906) 1.4; repeated and expanded, 2.738; again, anti-utilitarian, (1932) 23, arguing for hard-wired moral "intuitions".

115 De Waal (2005) 34, quoted; also 14, "if anything, morality involves strong convictions. Those convictions don't – or rather, can't – come about through a cool rationality: they require caring about others and powerful 'gut feelings' about right and wrong"; similarly, Haidt (2012) 25, "we *just feel* it's wrong". On the prediction, compare Greene and Haidt (2002) 517, "the affective revolution" in recent years; and Haidt (2012) 25 and 67, dating to post-1998 the change in the discipline of psychology, to "become a lot more emotional".

116 On de Waal's choice, see above, n. 106. Haidt (2012) 128–54, chap. 7, posits five "foundations" (131) four of which overlap with much of de Waal's (*care* shown in nurturing, *loyalty* shown to kin, *fairness*, and *authority* in a hierarchy); and Haidt likewise supposes all to be "innate", but in a form sufficiently flexible to require the term "prewired". His fifth item, however, *sanctity*, he illustrates in terms that gather up what I instance among animals (under "cannibalism", "incest", etc.) and therefore do not seem to be uniquely human, though they may be expressed or institutionalized in what we call religion. We cannot enter the brain of a fox, or of a Neanderthal man, for that matter, in response to the perception of fire, great winds, or lightning.

so much.[117] Anthropologists have been quoted, in the preceding chapter, to show how it worked in pre-industrial peoples; a historian may reach further back to Regency England and the extraordinary career of George "Beau" Brummell, to whose magical influence at the time we owe our own modern male power dressing: the dark well-cut jacket and trousers and necktie of today's banker, diplomat, or corporate counsel *comme il faut.*[118]

We can look even further back, to ancient Athens. Plutarch tells us of the education of Alcibiades, that city's most glittering teenager:[119]

> When he came of school-age he generally paid attention to his teachers but he refused to play the double pipes, thinking it ignoble and fit only for slaves... When a man blew the pipes with his mouth even his best friends couldn't recognize his face... The pipes blocked off the mouth and robbed him of his voice and speech alike. "Let those Theban youth play the pipes," he said, "since they are no good at speaking"... Thus jokingly but at the same time in earnest Alcibiades freed himself of these lessons along with the other young fellows as well, for word soon got out to them that Alcibiades was disgusted with pipe practice, rightly, and ridiculed those who were learning it. So it happened that the double pipes were totally excluded from the program of gentlemanly studies and fell into disfavor with everyone.

The "ceeee-leb", the idol, the mold of fashion, the personification of approval is a familiar phenomenon. It helps us to read the surrounding social structures almost at a glance. If it is described for us in a good story, our attention to emotional elements is stimulated, too, and we begin to see why it was that people did what they did. Among Athenians it was the value set on an ideal image that was at work – on the

117 Haidt (2001) 828 believes children's peer pressure is very important universally. He relies on Harris (1995); but as Harris makes clear, speaking of TV-watching, day-care, and other urban experiences, she looks only at Western children, evidently all or especially American and in the current generation; and she focuses on personality development and traits like timidity; so Haidt's proposed "social intuitionist model" has a very limited application.

118 Kelly (2006) 1 and 5–7 on "male power dressing"; passim, on Brummell's career.

119 Plutarch, *Life of Alcibiades* 5ff. (192d-f), my translation making *aulos* a plural, since this instrument was almost always played as a pair (shown in Daremberg and Saglio [1877] 5.309, s.v. *tibia*).

beauty of their young men and on a style of utter self-confidence in the bearing of all the highest classes. When appeal was made to these ideals it could change ideas about social accomplishments among the elite, and the elite in turn served to educate others beneath them. All society was in this way a school of values. As a sociologist puts it, "once opinion leaders adopt and begin telling others about an innovation, the number of adopters per unit of time takes off in an exponential curve" and significant change is established.[120]

When values are moral rather than aesthetic the same processes can be seen, at work on different points in our growing up.[121] At the adult level, inculcation through public expression of morality most obviously includes legislation, at least in developed societies; and by Plato, quoted earlier, we are reminded of the didactic role also of community art, rituals, and religion to reinforce accepted standards – on which, again, anthropology has much to say.[122] In less developed societies, private expressions by individuals insisting on their own rights and others' duties must take the place of law, for here in the world that anthropologists observe and take notes on, ethical systems are little articulated. People simply do what everyone else does and what their parents did before them; so "most ethnographies do not contain accounts of the motivational life of the people".[123] As Westermarck adds, "Society is the school in which men learn to distinguish between right and wrong. The headmaster is Custom" – and custom is hardly more than another word for culture.[124]

These various familiar means of socialization actually work. If they didn't, no people's survival would be possible, let alone anything so exalted as a way of life, a civilization. For such success, as philosophy insists, the obvious reason is reason. Behavior necessary to survive makes such very good sense that every member of whatever collectivity cannot help but subscribe, and, subscribing, must suit action to principle. So Justice with a capital letter will prevail, just as Rawls and Turiel and a million others have insisted. Yet strong as this bland insistence may have been in times past, and whatever defenders of it may still hold out, it is not often to be found in the social sciences. They more than tolerate theory or conjecture, but only to the

---

120 Rogers (2003) 300, quoted.

121 Stages in moral maturing, see, e.g., Kitayama et al. (2007) 136f., children learn from close family; also Emler (1987) 380, Damasio (1994) 174, Haidt (2001) 826f., Verbeek (2006) 429, or Fry (2006) 407; childhood inculcation of ideas and beliefs of all sorts, not just ethical, in Rokeach (1968) 8, Bem (1970) 6f., or Kim et al. (1994a) 8. For the views of anthropologists, see above, chap. 2 n. 50.

122 Above, chap. 2 at nn. 52–55.

123 Less analytic treatment is more usual, if any is offered at all, e.g., by Fortes and Evans-Pritchard (1940) 20, where rights and duties are contrasted to material interests; Feil (1988) 107, on ideals and duties in the *tee* system of the Enga; Lutz (1988) 82, 165, among the Ifaluk. Quoted on ethnographies, D'Andrade (1992) 23; cf. Aunger (2000) 445, 449, "This adult learning is usually ignored in socialization studies".

124 Westermarck (1906) 1.9; above, chap. 2 n. 62 on *habitus* and expectancies.

extent it chimes with (though it need not be demonstrated by) empirical data. Their data in fact, accumulating in the social sciences, instead assign an increasing role to the operation of affect in decision-making. As affect so nearly determines choices in behavior, whether directly or indirectly, and as behavior is the object always of moral judgment, so in the end morality cannot be seen as a rational construct. It is more naturally to be understood in purely cultural terms, as Westermarck and others since have maintained.

To examine this belief from the foundations, up: if codes and principles are not arrived at and obeyed through force of reason, then it is natural to ask where their initial energy comes from, to explain how and why they turn into action. If we not only believe in the priorities of the code but actually obey them, why is that? What is our motivation? Often the answer will be, emotions. Motivational force will be ascribed to them, which may be granted if nothing more is meant than the sensation of feeling (as we often do feel) that one choice of action is better than another, but not in any way that compels us to act. What is motivational in that latter sense doesn't amount to arousal.[125] A better, because deeper, answer lies in what are variously called, and endlessly defined and re-defined as, "urges" or "drives" or "instincts". Aggression, reproduction, and so forth impel us to respond to life around us by their more powerful claims. They are the ultimate determinants of both near-term action and long-term goals, toward which reason finds a path as a servant not a master.

But they lie all at the level of genetics, beneath culture and beyond our control; nor is it ever proposed, to the contrary, that Man is in charge of these forces (whatever they are called). They can only be left to the social sciences to be reviewed and arranged, if possible, into some order: to determine whether the Big Five Model of Hofstede, the Big Five of de Waal, or the Four of Haidt, most correctly carves up the innate into its essential sectors, or whether instead the sectors should be called dimensions or social axioms, and if so, in what number. The search for structure, together with the whole genetic realm, offers little of interest to historians; for historians have enough to do to understand what is man-made.

By exception, however, historians must take one instinct seriously: the social. It determines both motivation and what is man-made, namely custom or culture. The social instinct instills in us an emotional need for "the praise and blame of our fellow men," as Darwin wrote; and he goes on to say that in "the love of approbation and the dread of infamy" we can see "the development of the social virtues". "The need to

---

125 For the proposition that emotions are the proximate, motivating causes of most behavior including moral, see Frank (1988) 53, 255, 258; Haidt et al. (1993) 625, "emotions are cognitions invested with motivating force"; also Hirshleifer (1993) 185, emotions = impulses; Schwartz (2007) 170, it is goals that motivate people. But *contra*, see Atkinson (2009) 550, distinguishing between "motivational states such as hunger, thirst, and sex drive," and on the other hand, emotions = "appraisals"; also Schroeder (2010) 93, with evidence "that intrinsic desires [as opposed to moral judgments] are necessary to the production of motivation".

be approved and esteemed is a fundamental", in the words of the sociologists Talcott Parsons and Edward Shils.[126] They were quoted in an earlier chapter. It is in this way that instinct felt as emotion directs every school of values.

For whatever reason, perhaps because of the sheer familiarity of the subject, the study of the social instinct by biologists and psychologists has been slow in developing. It deserves a better place in explanations of motive; for "human beings may differ from other animals most dramatically, not in terms of their tendency to affiliate or interact, but rather in their efforts to be accepted by others".[127] Acceptance of course requires some degree of conformity. You must act and think as is expected by your family, first; then, by siblings, peers, neighbors, the village or tribe, church or labor union, nation or global industry to which you belong. Each has its rules, its expectations, its shared beliefs about right and wrong. Call them "values".[128] These are identified and summoned before our consciousness by emotions, as Damasio and others have shown, to indicate what will fit best within a given system of right and wrong at a given moment.

The entire range of other instincts beyond the social instinct demands expression in judgments and acts; but it is the social instinct that impels conformity. Acts of aggression, for example, are instinctual but take different forms and respond to different opportunities or inducements in different cultures. In America's southern states, testosterone levels go up in a man who is bumped into by a stranger on the street, and insulted for his awkwardness, while a Northerner sees it only as a sort of bad joke.[129] Or again, the urge to reproduce impels the search for a mate; but values will dictate within what boundaries, ruling out Capulets or deceased wife's sister. So it is also with all natural urges: culture determines the particular ways in which they will be satisfied.

As to such moral choices, they sometimes seems so natural, we can't say where they came from. The inner sensation, remarked on by Alan Fiske and others, especially characterizes "within-culture interactions [which] proceed effortlessly, even mindlessly... because enculturation has created 'sharedness', and [they] are less pro-

126 *Descent of Man* (1871) quoted in Verbeek (2006) 424; compare the statement of Parson and Shils quoted above, chap. 2 at n. 62, or Harris (1995) 465f., in the "older and deeper foundation" of group behavior, foremost is the predisposition toward group affiliation, i.e., the urge to belong; Smith et al. (2006) 131, quoting "the problems of achieving status and maintaining peer popularity are biologically mandated... The core of human nature consists of certain fixed, insistent, and largely unconscious biological motives... : (a) needs for social approval..."; or Newson et al. (2007) 454, "we are extremely social animals, and an overwhelming proportion of our behavior is socially learned", not innate.

127 Quoted, Leary and Allen (2011) 37.

128 Defining values, in a pioneer study often quoted, Rokeach (1968) 124f.; also Schwartz (1994) 20f. and (2007) 170f., Goodenough and Cheney (2008) xxvif., or Leung and Bond (2009) 1f.

129 Cohen (1997) 123f.; cf. Wyatt-Brown (1982) 34f., 43, 53.

blematic than across-culture interactions".[130] Jonathan Haidt and his associates likewise distinguish the virtually instantaneous character that marks much moral evaluation, and which may precede or make unnecessary any conscious sorting out of good and bad by cognitive processes. Instantaneity is possible, so it is suggested, because we are born with a capacity for sharing and reciprocity; but evaluations will be shaped by and conform to the surrounding ethical system. In whatever way it works, by intuition or cognition or, on occasion, both processes interacting, and whether it is best understood by Fiske or by Haidt or others along these lines, the result will be characteristic of one's culture.[131] That is the upshot. And it is important to historians.

The point is controversial. Can it really be the case that every people settles on its own moral ideas and turns them into rules, and is amazed that its neighbors should hit on any different code? That was the conclusion of early anthropology (early indeed: in Sophists and Herodotus 3.16 and 38); it was the conclusion also of not-quite-so-early social scientists like Herbert Spencer and other big names a century ago, preaching the philosophical acceptance of ethical differences.[132] For them, acceptance was a given; but for others then and since it was a scandal going by the name of relativity, by the lights of which one way of life, one ethical system, was quite as good as another. No one had to be told that such dangerous ideas must be nipped in the bud.[133] Rising to the challenge, the philosopher Turiel was instanced on an earlier page; or the philosopher John Rawls at one point in his argument stating flatly, "aristocratic and caste societies are unjust" – this, in the face of some hundreds of millions of persons in his

130 Quoted, Hofer and Bond (2008) 96f., on "automaticity"; Oyserman and Lee (2008) 259; de Waal (2008) 64, "automatic and intuitive" moral decisions. It is my own belief that the social instinct, in the form of attachment to persons around us (mother and all care-givers, closely held friends or teachers, and so on), invests moral preferences in affect at the time they are sensed or taught, and so gives them force. This general idea fits well with Fiske (1992) 690f., 693, 697–700, on the "communal sharing" relationship, one of the four types which determine how "people make moral judgments and take ideological positions".

131 Haidt (2001) 817, acknowledging both instant intuitive judgments and slow moral reasoning, and (824f.) finding both in Damasio's work; also Greene et al. (2004) 389, 397; briefly on the role of culture, Haidt (2001) 827f. and Haidt and Kesebir (2010) 798, 810; and Gazzaniga (2011) 165–68. But Greene and Haidt (2002) 517 (bare mention of "intuitions... shaped by cultural forces") and Cushman et al. (2010) 48f. and passim are concerned only with psychological processes, ignoring the origin of norms (67: "the origins of each system [intuitive or cognitive] of moral judgment is unknown").

132 Rawls (1971) 87, quoted; Spencer (1892) 468ff., in pungent pages; Westermarck (1906) 1.9 on custom quoted above in this chapter and more pointedly in his work (1932) on *Ethical Relativity*; and Bourdieu on *habitus*.

133 Kohlberg and Turiel (1971) 420; 461, the need to inculcate in the young especially "understanding and acceptance of the principles of justice which are the foundation of our constitutional democratic society". The problem as I see it is not our democratic ways but rather the belief in the religious foundations of morality, which is God-given; but Turiel and others of his school don't make this thought express.

and our own day, Indian, and untold more in times past who would quite shamelessly have disagreed.

From social scientists of that very sub-continent, a protest:

> Unfortunately the scientific psychology that emerged in the West has itself turned out to be another version of emic or culture-specific ethnopsychology, being heavily influenced by the cultural values and outlook of the Western world... Modern scientific psychology fails to account for all the variations of human behaviour across cultures and it is also limited in its scope and leaves out all those aspects of human nature and experience that do not fit the framework of scientific approach.[134]

All, quite true. Research has been described, above, in which universal consistencies and patterns were sought among test samples representing only Western researchers' own world.

Such ethnocentrism can't work for history; but it is challenged also by a growing body of social-scientific research. The characteristically Japanese *amae* is in common currency as an illustration of culture-specific emotions; interest is current, too, in contrasting the dominant values of America and Europe with the East Asian: specifically, individualism opposed to collectivism. The extent and permeation of these two value-structures into every corner of school and workplace, family and intergenerational relationships, has become a vital point of research in psychology.[135] The principal objective and the most logical, too, has been "the generalizability of psychological theories or constructs" – given the fact that ethnocentric boundaries invalidate broad conclusions and, as has been often brought out in previous chapters, above, broad conclusions are what a science aims at.[136] "Although understanding a specific culture or a certain group within a culture at a certain time and place may be interesting, parsimonious and predictive rather than detailed and descriptive modeling is the central goal of cultural and cross-cultural psychology".[137] Thus, while history is here described quite fairly, its practice can be dismissed and social research disciplines can be left unencumbered to pursue their own grander ambitions – with what success or failure, earlier chapters have indicated.

If success has been limited, consider what the challenge has been, to make sense, first, of mental processes some of which don't register on our consciousness but can

---

134 Kumar (2008) 19, continuing in technical language, "Its claim of universality is being viewed as 'imposed etic' rather than 'derived etic'" [i.e., universal, culture-free].

135 Above, chap. 1 n. 38; below, chap. 4 at nn. 59–63; Kim et al. (1994) 6f.; Harris (1995) 474; Iyengar and Lepper (1999) 349f., 363; Markus and Kitayama (2003) passim; Oyserman and Lee (2008) 238–41, this pair (collectivism/individualism) "has received the most attention"; and Kim and Park (2008) 500ff.

136 Hofer and Bond (2008) 104; and Gaddis (2002) 62, "without generalization historians would have nothing to say".

137 Quoted, Oyserman and Lee (2007) 255.

be known only from physical signs, while others instead register on all too many areas of the brain to allow of simple cause-and-effect conclusions. That human brain, by neuroscience, is shown to be an engine of response consisting of tens of billions of distinct operating units, most of which are linked to more than one other so as to produce some multiple of possible connections to each other and to a virtually infinite memory as well. All are served by electricity, very fast, but also by a variety of chemical messengers; the registration of external data (some still within the body, some from beyond the body) may show up at a great number of separate areas of activity. The fact is, we are too complicated for our own clear understanding. What the hard sciences aim at – verifiability, replication, parsimony, unified fields, laws – may be simply the wrong model for our study of ourselves.[138]

Consider the complexities in our mental operations, and multiply them beyond individuals to collectivities. Perhaps, then, we should expect no more from our analyses than did an appellate-court judge Posner speaking of reasonableness as common sense, a sociologist discounting quantifiability, or an anthropologist comparing success in one of the social sciences (ethnography) to medicine (diagnostics), dependent as much on flair as on facts; or again, a psychologist content with "predicting most of the people much of the time".[139] Let the social sciences strain after something better: a delusion, a will-o'-the-wisp. Approximations, not exact certainties, are after all what it is human to live with every day constituting thus our personal experience of history.

138 Quantifiable complexity of the brain, above, n. 74, and, for example, Greene and Haidt (2002) 518 on no less than eight known to respond to a question of moral preference; Schroeder et al. (2010) 88 on the many duties of the amygdala; Gazzaniga (2011) 69ff. and 102 on its diffuseness of organization; or Seung (2013) 184, "most mental functions require the cooperatioon of multiple cortical areas".

139 Posner, above, n. 29; Cameron, above in chap. 1 n. 14; Epstein, above in chap. 1 at n. 10; Tilly (2006) 410f. on the need of "cannily connecting art and science"; Gaddis (2002) 62f., accepting of partial accuracy in historical interpretations and the impossibilities in chaos (88f.), with constant revisions of once-accepted truths (104, 108); Appleby et al. (1994) 279, "most scientists and philosophers of science continue to... think that experimental methods and theoretical statements... capture enough about nature *to be close* to what is there" (italics added); and my own position spelt out (MacMullen 2011, chap. 9) through comparison of historical reasoning with "courtroom inquiry [which] may sometimes appear a sloppy business – certainly nothing like mathematics. No, it is much harder. Its difficulty lies in the number of variables that must so often be taken into account, and in their uncertain character that requires taking account also of still other variables, and so forth". Despite common sense, in the social sciences there are innumerable exercises in highly complex quantification where the data measured are themselves subjective (!), e.g., Jennings et al. (1982) 224. Codol (1984) 239 finds "too rigid... the requirement that they [analytical concepts] should denote quantifiable phenomena"; but this sort of demurral is very rare.

4 Culture as Cause

Wisdom has it that individuals amount to the sum of their general tendencies, which in the long run must shape their life's course. An entire people, too, may be characterized in this same way. It is a common belief, witness a recent piece in the *Times* finding a half dozen European nations and Americans, too, from the sixteenth century to the 1980s, defined and defining each other, mostly in unflattering terms.

Those stereotypes to which the man in the street reduced his neighbor states found no support in social science research, so it seems; and intellectuals didn't do much better. They spoke of national character in dreamy terms like *Geist*, *génie*, "essence", or "soul". Or worse: they might ask their readers to accept collective "genius" as a matter of "inherent hereditary traits of a biological and psychological nature", or similarly, "innate racial characteristic", according "to current assumptions" – this said in 1924.[1] Such ideas were a problem in the inter-war period, notoriously.

Thereafter, though stereotyping of nations continued unabated in the public media and popular discourse, there has been little serious history written in such terms. It could only be agreed that, at a more sophisticated level, differences among nations did and do exist, if perhaps exaggerated or misunderstood or "inaccurate" by some metric; and such differences are "cultural";[2] but beyond that, national character as a tool of historical study, at least in the usual terms, has enjoyed little favor.[3]

Instead, explanation for historical events and developments should be sought, not in an entire people's settled tendencies but rather in the operation of the external stimuli of the moment, in surrounding circumstances – "situationally" as psychologists would say. Circumstances and stimuli should be assessed calculatingly, cognitively, in defined settings. The process had a reassuring rigor about it. A passage drawn more or less at random from the hugely admired Fernand Braudel may serve in illustration:

> The fundamental characteristic of Philip II's empire was its Spanishness – or rather Castillianism – a fact which did not escape the contemporaries of the Prudent King, whether friend or foe: they saw him as a spider sitting motionless at the center of his web. But if Philip, after returning from Flanders in September, 1559, never again left the Peninsula, was it simply from

---

1 Ben Schott, "Vive la différence," *New York Times* 19 January 2011, A23, over fifty of such pithy characterizations in Robert Burton, Mark Twain, proverbs, and so on; but such stereotyping is most often mistaken, cf. the fullest study by questionnaire across dozens of countries, Terraciano et al. (2005), though with criticism of this study, above, chap. 1 nn. 34f. Hume's essay "On national characters" (1987) 197–213 is predictably full of sense; and on innate "national genius" and the like concepts, see Sapir (1924) 405f., quoted.

2 Laitin and Gordon (1998) 429, Robins (2005) 62, Smith et al. (2006) 56f. and 77, or Mesquita and Leu (2007) 738.

3 See, e.g., Wilterdink (1994) 43, Benthall (1997) 612, or Higgins et al. (2008) 162. Undeterred, I used national character as key to my understanding of ancient Rome, in MacMullen (2011).

> inclination, from a pronounced personal preference for things Spanish? Or might it not also have been largely dictated by necessity? We have seen how the states of Charles V, one after another, refused to support the expense of his campaigns. Their deficits... [and so forth].[4]

Braudel deliberates. Did the king and his subjects have a love or liking for one style of life over another, perhaps unreasonably? Philip was human, after all. We can try to read his face in his portrait in London or Madrid. But on reflection, it would be best for us to assume he was rather rational in his behavior, and in that assumption we should try to read his mind through the available statistics of international commerce, banking, population, and so forth.

Or here, a second example of method in another style but of the same generation. At school, my own introduction to history was a two-volume textbook approved in one edition after another for over half a century. On a quite typical page is an account of the U.S. reaction to waves of revolt among Spain's colonial possessions in the earlier 1800s. The Secretary of State under President Monroe, John Quincy Adams, informs a leader in Congress that, while he had wished the revolutionaries well, he saw no chance that U.S. support could work out for the nation. He contrasts what the revolutionaries have always had to submit to, with what they longed for: "Arbitrary power, military and ecclesiastical, was stamped upon their habits, and upon all their institutions. Civil dissension was infused into all their seminal principles... I had little expectation of any beneficial result to this country from any future connection with them, political or commercial." And "this passage," my textbook continues, "reveals the policy of Monroe's administration toward the Latin Americans. Their independence was desired as an additional bulwark for American isolation; but not with sufficient ardor to risk a European war."[5] The Secretary's words and train of thought are noted and his weighing of the most likely results of one policy over another: a "beneficial result" and consideration of factors "political" and "commercial". Here are calculation and cognition. The substance that the Secretary considered could at the time be observed and quantified: so many tons of imports, so many votes, and so forth. He was a calculating man, as was his President likewise.

What interests me is the preference demonstrated by the French historian and the two Americans for explanation in rational and situational terms. This they chose over attachments and passions, traditional values, attitudes, or collective self-image which they nevertheless acknowledge before turning away. Our natural human, more or less innocent post-facto rationalizing of our actions was noted in earlier chapters.[6] It infects historiography as well. And why not? About irrational factors, conclusions must remain uncertain, sometimes unreasonable because they can amount

---

4 Braudel (1972–73) 2.676, continuing (678) with a general recommendation to historians that they interpret political history by demography, ups and downs of commerce, and the like factors.

5 Morison and Commager (1942) 1.453f.; the book had its final edition in 1980.

6 See especially chap. 3 at n. 51.

to no more than guesswork about intangibles lying half-hidden behind what is observed and open to our five senses.

But the idea discarded by the historians – that collectivities are like individuals and have personalities, and it is traits that constitute both personality in individuals and culture in whole societies, shaping response in the decisions of the moment – this idea perhaps deserves a second hearing. In support I would cite the EVS (European Value Studies)/WVS (World Values Surveys), by now well known. They are the work of social scientists and theology scholars jointly at a Dutch and a Belgian university in 1981, growing out of some years of prior research and resulting in a questionnaire. It asks of each respondent how important family is, or religion, or leisure; which women's groups or sports associations they belong to; why one might or should do voluntary work; the significance of risk-taking in success; whether cheating on taxes is ever justified; how interested one is or should be in politics; and so on, in depth after depth. For its operations, large, randomly selected samples of respondents from among the fifteen countries of the European Union were polled face-to-face, and with minor improvements the process was subsequently repeated at several intervals to extend its reach almost everywhere around the globe.[7] The sixth repetition reached into 2012. For my purposes, what counts in this thirty-year effort is, first, the underlying belief in the distinct character of the Latvians, the French, and so forth, discernible in their commonly held beliefs, norms, and ethical standards, amounting to the validation of national character as a concept; and further, an underlying belief in the effect of all these many aspects of culture on collective institutions, including the economy.[8] The importance of economic behavior in my earlier chapters makes this aspect especially useful for my purposes; and both the EVS and WVS have from the start shown much interest in the norms and beliefs underlying prosperity.

"The idea that economic growth is partly shaped by cultural factors has encountered considerable resistance";[9] but in answer it could be pointed out that the problem lay in the false perception of all Germans as forever militaristic, Hispanic culture forever unfavorable to development, and similar stereotypes. They were wrong because (whether or not they had ever been justified) it could be shown by statistical evidence from the EVS/WVS, that cultures in recent decades in fact show change. Cultural history is dynamic, not static. There need be no claim that norms and beliefs entirely determined the course of economic development – only that these factors have a causal role along with the more familiar direct influence of raw mate-

7 On sampling technique, see Inglehart et al. (1998) 15, 467, 470ff., with hundreds of pages of the results of the 1990 WVS, showing the variety of the questions, while Halman et al. (2005) use over sixty maps to show national differences under some dozens of rubrics ("work ethos", "importance of God", etc.) across all of Europe.

8 Arts et al. (2003) 4 and, on economic values shaped by non-pecuniary preferences, 408 and Muffels (2003) 437.

9 Quoted, Granato et al. (1996) 624.

rials, political stability, technology, command of capital, and so forth. Here, value surveys permit multivariate analysis, if not demonstration: for example, through the measurement of the common emphasis on *thrift* and *determination* in children's upbringing, as against *obedience* and *religious faith*, in Korea as against Nigeria, and measurement of the value generally set on achievement in those two and many other societies, graphically represented.[10]

The analytical model of course brings to mind Max Weber, who is seen as a respected presence, indeed "a founding father of sociology", in the community that has supported the EVS/WVS; and Charles Tilly recently reminded his colleagues in that discipline that any general discussion taking off from a classical authority like Weber cannot go wrong.[11] It was in 1904/5 that Weber addressed national character, "Volkscharakter", in a work appearing as two halves in successive issues of a scholarly journal.[12] *The Protestant Ethic and the Spirit of Capitalism* was greeted with the greatest interest, and keen criticism, too, to which he responded when, fifteen years later, the two halves appeared in normal fashion as a book (1920). It may be called the first serious application of social science to the past, by a figure much in the public eye at the time as both an academic who straddled several fields and as a commentator on large questions of the day. He combined immense intellectual energy with an immensely wide embrace of facts and ideas, warranting the reception his book received and insuring for it a place in subsequent sociology and historiography to the present day.

He chose a straightforward title, indicating pretty well what he was about: an analysis of the theology of Lutheranism so far as it bore on salvation, and in turn, how such beliefs influenced or even dictated a certain course of life. He called them "culture", or sometimes "life-style" or "attitude", most often "spirit". Shortly after the book was published, when Weber was involved in replying to a critic, he also used the term "*habitus*".[13] Luther's reforms, as Weber argued, had been soon taken up by independent-minded followers, giving rise to Calvinism and derived sects like Mennonism. In these Weber discovered an explanation for important changes in economic behavior. As he saw it, these changes constituted the very building materials of

---

10 Granato (1996) 607, 613 (complementary causal roles); 624, European national character is dynamic in recent decades; 621 Fig. 2, showing the relation of achievement motivation to economic growth; and 611 and Inglehart et al. (2000) 24, inculcation of economically relevant values in childhood.

11 See, e.g.. Granato et al. (1996) 608–11 or Arts et al. (2003) 4; also Tilly (2003) 2f.

12 Weber (1920) 1.164, 194; (2008) 155, speaking loosely of any nation; 173, speaking of Britain. He puts the word "Volkscharakter" in quotation marks not to disavow it but to show its particular place in his argument, as he does with many other terms, e.g., (1920) 61, "Geist". Werner Sombart as Weber's contemporary was active in closely related questions but was never a match for Weber.

13 Weber (1920) 100, "Kultur"; 183, 191; or 203, "Lebensstil"; 202, "Gesinnung"; 12, similarly and close to traits, "Disposition der Menschen"; and *habitus* in 1922 used to explain Lebensstil, cf. Lehmann (2005) 14f.

modern capitalism, of which the seventeenth century was "the heroic age".[14] By the eighteenth, the patterns of behavior necessary for the spread and success of capitalism had been established even though religious inspiration had faded out of it. Such in brief is "the Weber thesis" – omitting, however, its genesis.

The attention of Weber himself and of others in the decades before he wrote had been attracted to a curious fact: that German Catholics quite noticeably preferred to send their sons to study the classics and humanistic subjects whereas Protestants sought to acquire science, mathematics, and skills useful in the real world.[15] Further, it was noticed that the Catholic population settled into traditional ways of earning a livelihood at a traditional pace and with traditional expectations, whereas Protestants more commonly occupied mid-level or high administrative positions in commerce or manufacture, giving themselves with tireless devotion and planning to their business so as to make it ever larger and better regulated. Their business was their calling, as God determined it, whether the most humble or the most rewarded; as God required, so his people must live out their sense of obligation. This was "absolutely central" to the making of capitalist man.[16]

In describing their common traits and goals Weber constantly uses the terms "rational" and "rationalization" or rough equivalents. Typically, a Protestant day like Protestant dress and Protestant furnishings at home must be thought-out, orderly, and controlled, where controlled meant also spare and self-denying, all directed "to the greater glory of God". Every moment's choice of conduct must reveal whether divine grace was at work and so whether one was among the Elect to be saved. To the observer, the life lived in this way could only seem strangely monastic, indeed "irrational". It is a "secular asceticism" in Weber's phrase, "which tried to enable a man to maintain and act upon his constant motives, especially those which it taught him itself, against the emotions. In this formal psychological sense of the term it tried to make him into a personality".[17]

Once established in various forms and sects in western Europe and, by emigration, in America, the personality-type proved itself in economic success even after its theological basis had faded. The habit or *habitus* to be seen in the rational inventory both of one's self, sometimes by a diary, and of one's business, served Protestants

14 Weber (2008) 166.

15 McClelland (1961) 320ff., confirming Weber with better statistics.

16 "The God of Calvinism demanded not single good works... but a life of good works combined into a unified system", and "it is an obligation which the individual is supposed to feel and does feel towards the content of his professional activity", Weber (2008) 117, "eine zum System gesteigerte Werkheilgkeit" ("a piety in work that rose to the level of a system") and 54, "der beruflichen Tätigket"; and "the sense of obligation was absolutely central", Weber (1920) 47.

17 "The ideal type" of capitalist "gets nothing out of his wealth for himself, except the irrational sense of having done his job well," in the words of Weber (2008) 71, (1920) 55. On "secular asceticism", "innerweltlich Askese", see Weber (1920) 84–163; quoted, Weber (2008) 119, (1920) 117.

well. It "is mentioned by all the moralists and theologians, while Benjamin Franklin's tabulated statistical book-keeping on his progress in the different virtues is a classic example."[18]

In the months in which Weber was composing the earlier half of his work America was much on his mind, and immediately after he finished correcting the proofs of his text he made a visit there to learn more of its ways. He had earlier read and in his book often cites Franklin's autobiography and provides extensive quotations also from Franklin as a "preacher" in his "sermons" – referring to two little booklets of advice for young men published in 1736 and 1748. Passages from them Weber had spotted in a German translation of 1855, and he used them to lead off his chapter on "the Spirit of Capitalism". In a brief, easily understandable form they illustrated what he calls "Americanism"; they revealed exactly that spirit which he proposed to set at the heart of the developed economy of the West.[19] Franklin thus was particularly well suited to Weber's argument – as to my own also.

In a characteristic page Franklin warns,

> Beware of thinking all your own that you possess, and of living accordingly. It is a mistake that many people who have credit fall into. To prevent this, keep an exact account for some time both of your expenses and your income. If you take the pains at first to mention particulars, it will have this good effect: you will discover how wonderfully small, trifling expenses mount up to large sums, and will discern what might have been, and may for the future, be saved, without occasioning any great inconvenience.[20]

The German historian of ideas, Richard van Dülmen, sums up: "As the analysis of Franklin's *habitus* makes clear, instanced by Weber as paradigmatic, the new spirit of capitalism could develop not out of a materialistic striving for gain that can be seen at all times and in all places, but rather from 'ethically colored maxims for conduct in life', as Weber wrote."[21]

The understanding of changes on an historical scale was certainly Weber's aim, but his handling of the historical discipline as it was understood more than a century

---

18 Weber (2008) 124.

19 The American trip, in Dülmen (1988) 90, Lehmann (2008) 6, or Barbalet (2008) 3; anecdotes and lessons from it, Weber (1991) 302–15; Swatos and Kivisto (2005) 128, quoting Sidney Hook, "An ideal illustration of the spirit of capitalism is furnished by the writings [n. b., not the person] of Franklin. Here we have a social morality which centers exclusively around the business of getting ahead in the world". On Franklin "preaching", cf. Weber (2008) 50f., (1920) 33; "sermon", (2008) 71, (1920) 55. Weber first met and then better translated the passages from Kürnberger (1890) 30ff. On "Americanism"/"Amerikanismus", see Weber (2005) 52; (1920) 35.

20 Weber (2008) 50.

21 Dülmen (1988) 91; Sidney Hook in exactly similar terms quoted in Swatos and Kivisto (2005) 128l; and Norris and Inglehart (2011) 160f.; the ethic, 162, "a materialistic value system" (!); and 317 for bibliography on the reception of the thesis.

ago doesn't show him at his best.[22] He was better at the "ethically colored" elements, for which read, "wrapped in affect". Such were the feelings of obligation and anxiety that possessed the Protestant. Though they constituted the motivational force behind the development of the capitalist personality, he has little to say about them in themselves, calling them correctly but clinically "the psychological motives that gave direction to one's conduct of life".[23] Living as he did in the midst of a capitalist society, he had no trouble with them; in his day empathic understanding reached its limit only when it encountered fanaticism, mysticism, or the like.[24] Protestant zeal and suppression of the natural man was indeed, in an instrumental sense, fully rational even when the vocation for its own sake governed decisions and lifelong efforts were continued beyond the point of attaining wealth. If instead the natural man was governed by passions, then suppression of them as the source of error made perfect sense. "Rationalism is an historical concept which covers a whole world of different things".[25] For "historical" we may read "cultural".

The personality-type mentioned above, or in Weber's term the "ideal-type", does suggest itself on many a page of *The Protestant Ethic*, changing somewhat over time, a figment useful in explaining complicated historical processes. Weber brought out the possibilities of such and similar concepts in other writings, too. They were not offered as objective science. He did not expect the individual driven by the Protestant ethic, in his own day or Franklin's or in earlier centuries still, to answer precisely to any real actor in history; nor did he think it necessary fully to understand such a person, intellectually, where empathy could be invoked to better effect.[26] Subjectivity was in fact inevitable. For his argument it was sufficient to sense a style of life in accordance with certain values as he had seen it in America or in his own

22 It would be easy to instance scholarly criticisms of Weber as a historian, as, e.g., in Furnham (1990) 2–7, Landes (1998) 176f. citing critics (but Landes himself, 177–81, is a defender of Weber) or Barbalet (2008) 7, 21, 24, etc.; but my own criticism might begin with his hopping in a few lines from the third century Roman empire to 19th century Prussia, to explain a certain phenomenon, as if the settings were comparable, or again from the first century Roman empire to 19th century Russia, to explain another, in the same fashion, Weber (1978) 476, 484f.; or again, with an absurd generalization about Christian marriage and barbarism, Weber (2008a) 117 (top).

23 Quoted, Weber (1920) 86 on "Antriebe", with a poor translation in Weber (2008) 97, "sanctions"; and emotions never given more than mere mention, e.g., Weber (2008) 112; (1920) 106, "Angstaffekte", though they are a continuous subtext.

24 Weber did not offer his readers insights which he would have said made no sense; he abjured intuition of that sort; but he did acknowledge a role for empathic understanding, cf. Weber (1978) 5f. Eliaeson (2000) 249 slightly misunderstands the question.

25 Emotions are to be suppressed, Barbalet (2008) 56, 76; quoted, Weber (2008) 78; (1920) 62; and cf. above, n. 17.

26 On ideal types, see Mommsen (1989) 127 and his chapter 8, passim; Tribe (1988) 7f.; further, Weber (1978) 5, ending in the statement, that "a lower degree of certainty" than when evaluating instrumental calculations and behavior "is, however, adequate for most purposes of explanation".

Germany, and as he had reported on it, emphasizing values as the driving force.[27] It was enough, too, if report could present a good approximation. Weber's interpretive model recalls Seymour Epstein's tolerance for "predicting most of the people much of the time".[28]

Much in the Weberian analysis has stood up pretty well. The consensus emerging in behavioral economics over the past generation supports, if quite timidly, the recognition of affect in decision-making; the proposal that rationality is relative to a given collectivity and with it, its value system – this notion no longer seems so alarming as it once did. That values or traits like conscientiousness may have cumulative long-term effects is a common view, too, and supporters (though also critics) of the idea of a modal personality characterizing each society are easily found, for example, in anthropology. The modal personality is not much different from Weber's "ideal type".[29] And of course the assumptions in the EVS/WVS underpin his thesis.

It is, however, in fitting his views into history that Weber showed the greatest ambition. Here some uncertainty appears. He speaks of "national character" in the West and specifically "Americanism" using comprehensive terms as if there were nothing to be seen or considered in these populations beyond capitalism and its ethic or values. In fact, however, the ethic he writes about nowhere governs more than a portion of society in a portion of life's values and pursuits. The vision may be too narrow for historians. If they wanted to explain the past through figments in Weberian fashion – that is, through ideal types – they would have to invent many others as well. Fairly to represent the entire tangle of historical cause and effect, they would need a landowning type or (which Weber did study at length) a bureaucratic type, a military type, and so forth. On the other hand, despite speaking of national character, his analysis disregards political boundaries quite confusedly to reach all over western Europe and the New World.

A good illustration of the methodological problems here lies in England, part Protestant, part Anglican. The latter through its catechism of 1662 taught the person who sought confirmation

---

27 Values supply the drive, cf. above, n. 18; Arts et al. (2003, p. 4) "following the ideas of Weber and Durkheim, [who] believed that values are prime guidelines in people's lives"; or Barbalet (2008) 36, "for Weber, values define human purposes and are the non-rational attributes of agency that sustain rationality".

28 Above, chap. 3 n. 139; "ethical Lebenstil", recalled in Tribe (1988) 30.

29 On affect in economic decisions, see, e.g., chap. 3 §1, above; on long-term trait-effects, cf. Mischel in chap. 1, above; on values and social relations, e.g., reciprocity or treatment of the unemployed, cf. above, chap. 3 and Levy et al. (2006) 96, where the Protestant work ethic is treated as a standard trait-cluster.

> To honour and obey the Queen, and all that are put in authority under her: To submit myself to all my governors, teachers, spiritual pastors and masters: To order myself lowly and reverently to all my betters... and to do my duty in that state of life which it shall please God to call me.[30]

In contrast was the Cromwellian side and, after the Restoration, John Bunyan and his contemporary, the very prolific and widely read theologian Richard Baxter. It was on these figures that Weber focused. The Protestant vision of social relations had been fixed by Calvin and his followers of every sect, who in Europe were encouraged or, more truly, were instructed by their doctrines to believe in "the Dignity of Labor and Predestination."

> A man could still demonstrate his inclusion in the ranks of the Elect through success in worldly affairs, especially commercial enterprises... There were still marked differences between the haves and have-nots. The old social categories remained: nobles, knights, merchants, and artisans. Yet now they were blurred. Nobody's status was irrevocably fixed by genealogy, for a man could rise legitimately by his own endeavor from rags to respectability, and even honor.[31]

National character in England was thus no single thing, as Weber would have it, but a mix of two churches and two social doctrines.

In the New World, this old world of haves and have-nots was at first replicated, though perhaps more in habits of mind than in realities. Forms of address in the traditional way defined *gentleman*, *esquire*, *mister*, and *master*; rules of decent behavior were interpreted in the light of status. Anglican prayer books taught children submissive acceptance of their place, the lesson unchanged since 1662, and Protestant preachers, too, like the Calvinist Jonathan Edwards in the 1730s, reminded all of "their appointed office, place and station, according to their several capacities and talents, and everyone keeps his place, and continues in his proper business".[32] But the American historian Gordon Wood points out, "The Puritan ethic was widely preached, but only for ordinary people, not for gentlemen".[33] Gentlemen and those of still higher status didn't have a proper business, or any at all, if business meant working not owning. Wood sets them at less than a tenth of the free population at the time when, near the mid-century, Benjamin Franklin established his claim to be one of them, withdrawing himself from all his former employments.[34] We can see two quite different worlds coexisting, one dominant in its leisure, traditions, lineage, wealth, education, manners, and the general respect; the other, supported only by *self*-respect and the Protestant spirit of possibilities.

---

30 Convenient in Hinde (2002) 98 or Mullin (1989) 8, the prayer book quoted, "My duty is to order myself lowly and reverently to all my betters".

31 Lawrence (1988) 76.

32 Above, n. 30, on the Anglican catechism; and on the Anglican church favored among the haves, Wood (1992) 201; 19, Edwards quoted.

33 Mullin (1989) 16; Wood (1992) 33.

34 Wood (1992) 30f. on proportions in the population.

However significant the workings of this latter spirit had been in Europe in its Heroic Age of the seventeenth century, they were still more marked, because less impeded by custom, in Franklin's new world of America. Here is a second population group, overlapping with Weber's, which can be used to show the relations between way of life and historical outcomes. In the British colonies changes were under way, not novel in character but in scale, which at an increasing rate simply transformed society even within the space of a single generation. Let us choose the years from 1745 to 1775 as illustration.

Visible and quantifiable changes are naturally the ones with which to begin an account. The rise in population is what might first strike the eye, a result of both a high birth rate and immigration at unprecedented levels from Ireland, Britain, and Germany. The majority of newcomers settled in the towns, where former customs of dependency and deference need not be re-established or were maintained only for a time under indenture. In this urban scene, economic opportunities along the eastern seaboard grew at a rate also unprecedented; small commercial and manufacturing enterprises proliferated. Here was freedom, here was opportunity. Behind the cities to the west, newly won territory opened up to purchase and settlement by the millions of acres, rewarding speculation and new fortunes as well as new farmsteads and riverside towns. The whole very vital, active picture is familiar in the textbooks.

In that one generation 1745–1775, what is most easily known because it left the most ample record in writing was the effect of change among the upper tenth. Benjamin Franklin supplies an illustration, convenient because of his appearance, above, as Weber's model. In his retirement from his printing house and rich from its proceeds, he involved himself repeatedly in the scramble for western land grants from the Crown, where the files are indeed very full of correspondence and of legal documents generated by individuals or most often by small groups of more or less wealthy, influential investors. They sought territory freed up through the extermination or hoodwinking of the Indian occupants in the Ohio valley and thereabouts. Two efforts of this sort were Franklin's, petitioning in 1756 for grants on both sides of the river. In the end, he was unsuccessful; but ten years later he joined the Illinois Company, which was asking for 1,200,000 acres in the Mississippi valley, and then also the Indiana Company in a third area; and in 1769 through the Grand Ohio Company he and associates with stupendous greed petitioned for twenty million acres. It would have been "the greatest speculative *coup* of the eighteenth century" – balked, however, by politics in London and the American colonies.[35]

Franklin's story in these years of speculation incidentally suggests a terminal point for Weber's thesis, with the transformation of the Protestant ethic into something very

35 Billington and Ridge (1982) 147, "extermination" of the Indian "vermin" proposed by the Indian affairs minister, through infecting them with smallpox; on land speculation, 146, 153, and 159 (quoted); on Franklin's, Labaree and Bell (1959–2011) vol. 31 (1995) 525–47.

remote from its Calvinist origins. Beyond that, however, the scale of the ambitions in which he was caught up shows how powerfully enticing were the possibilities opened up to the generation, 1745–1775. At its start and earlier still, land had been in short supply in the older colonies; younger sons who wanted marriage and independence were simply out of luck; but from mid-century on, the movement of new settlers from the more heavily farmed parts into unexploited regions in New York, northern Connecticut, Pennsylvania, or the Carolinas, increased at a remarkable rate. Of this rage for land, Franklin's speculation was only one early sign.[36]

Before the mid-eighteenth century those younger sons, and all but a small minority of the immigrant thousands, had known only a world where every square inch of land was bespoke. Anyone with little or none must live with the consequences – meaning submission and dependence in the face of patronage and control. What now, however, began to appear as the most consequential difference defining the New World was the great freedom of movement its society allowed and the closely related abundance of unoccupied land. There was more than enough room for that most extraordinary increase in the colonies' population, more than doubling in the one generation post-1745. In addition, coastal towns grew into cities and with them commerce picked up, joining them to inland agriculture and to maritime and overseas trade. Prosperity from the 1740s took hold and with it, rising expectations open to every rank and region. "The growth and movement of people strained and broke apart households, churches, and neighborhoods" – in sum, much of the fabric of place and obligation.[37]

To trace the consequences takes me among the ethical tendencies that shape a society, announced as a target of interest at the beginning of this chapter. They are to be seen as the eventual rather than the immediate consequence of interaction with changes in the economy, in population, or any such large causal factors. First, one takes advantage of material changes for material reasons; and on these, historians will fasten as the easiest thing to observe and quantify. They are rational. Only later, one might begin to feel that one's ideas of what was proper were in conflict with experience and should better reflect new realities. One's future decisions would thus be reconfigured, and on a more consequential scale, too, responsive to a general sense of what everyone around seemed to be doing. The effects would show in the prevailing code of behavior, the collective character.

The question whether or not to refuse obedience to one's king presents us with a test of such effects. At a juncture of dire need, Britain's treasury being worse than empty, its debts enormous after seven years of war only ending in 1763, the royal

36 Wood (1992) 50, 127ff.

37 On the demography, Wood (1992) 124–28; prosperity of 1740s-1750s, 133ff.; quoted, 129; but Hoerder (1977) 30 points out the rising land prices in New York which limited opportunity for escape from older family farms and townships.

government proposed to raise money from the colonies for their own defense. Hence, the Sugar Act of 1764, the Stamp Act of the next year, the Tea Party, and so on to Lexington. The path to that end has been traced a thousand times. What will ordinarily be offered to explain the colonists' disobedience are the surviving written expressions of protest or outrage. Commonly, they take the form of editorials or pamphlets embroidered with tags of a classical education and appeals to philosophy, above all, to John Locke and the logic, as it was seen, implicit in an imagined state of nature; almost as lofty, the recall of Magna Charta and the British origin and therefore British rights of the colonists. At greater length, follow fine points of law in the founding charters, the individual's proper rights and expectations, and, not least, the great money-losses to be suffered from parliament's exactions.[38] Written advocacy for the most part thus represented the upper classes who in addition to their education and perhaps added legal training drew their income from their various property rights and loans. All these must surely be affected by the king's demands. Their calculations, or in today's terms their business model, can sometimes be traced in detail.[39] Surely, too, the defiant reaction of the polemicists is rightly understood as a consequence of the attenuation of their ties to London, so far away, and their habituation to a great deal of self-government, so much a part of their lives. Their motivation was thus mixed. They had come to expect what had once been a novel and increasing degree of independence, now in jeopardy. They had been taught by their actual experience over the decades; and "expectations" are only another word for "rights". In the written record of the colonists' response, this latter word is their big gun. Violation of rights they declared insupportable. It was a moral matter, and nothing is more certain to produce anger among the wronged, whether or not any material injury also is felt.[40]

My understanding of the story told in these traditional terms is meant to bring out the causal links between the colonial leaders' experience in their setting, the effects of that setting on their ideas of right and wrong, and the irresistible urge to protest, even with force, that possessed them in the 1760s and 1770s. To my mind, not only is the causal chain here easily traced in the written evidence, but easily accepted. It makes sense. However, to repeat what was said earlier, there were within the population two different worlds, of which one was composed of leaders, the "haves". Now, these latter saw things in their own way, as has been seen. But there were also the "have-nots" who, except as their behavior is described for us by writers of the better

---

38 Thucydides, in Hopkins (1765) 6 or Bland (1766) 27; Brutus, in a 1770 public letter, Carp (2010) 84; Locke, e.g., in Otis (1764) 5, 22, and passim; 6, the state of nature as template proposed for the rise of civilized society; Bland (1766) 9, 11; or in Paine (1792) 8, 20; Miller (1949) 169ff.; Gilje (1987) 8; or Jared Ingersoll in 1764 on "natural and Constitutional rights", Middlekauff (2005) 76; Magna Charta recalled by the writer quoted in Countryman (1993) 132 or Paine (1792) 20; legal arguments, e.g., Bland (1766) 4ff., 8ff., or Hopkins (1765) 5f., 8ff.

39 Carp (2010) chapters 5–6 on Francis Rotch of Boston provides a good example.

40 Chap. 3, above, at nn. 100ff., 110f.

sort, hardly appear in the surviving record. They present a problem to our understanding which repays examination.

Clearly in pre-industrial times it is misleading to speak of classes. There were, however, plainly acknowledged distinctions. Dirk Hoerder's discussion of these seems the best, drawing as it does not only on a good deal of theoretical discussion, but also on a very full knowledge of the scene at least in Massachusetts. He accepts the style of contemporaries, denominating "the better sort" as those on top; and he accepts also real differences of which contemporaries were quite evidently aware, between the top and all those beneath them; but it was a matter not only of money but of entitlement as well. It was proper for gentlemen to be in charge. As illustration, there is John Adams insisting in the early years of the Revolution that

> there is one thing... that must be attempted and most sacredly observed, or we are all undone. There must be a decency and respect and veneration introduced for persons in authority of every rank, or we are undone. In a popular government, this is the only way of supporting order.[41]

I notice how "we" in Adams' statement sets him and his audience, all of them together "in authority", apart from "them" – who are everyone else.

Each of the two ranks in its own way made the Revolution, not only the be-wigged gentlemen so ready with their quill pens and elegant argumentation. Notoriously, crowds as well, some in the thousands, played a part. Indeed, as the dramatic and dynamic element necessary to the making of history on a grand scale, they attracted much notice at the time and since. Something is known about their composition. At different moments they embraced almost all socioeconomic levels: the respectable (perhaps disguised, and not including the most eminent) down to "boys and Negroes".[42] The motive that united them in action need not remain obscure, at least at a superficial level. They represented a demand for liberty. The colonists' most eloquent voice in Parliament had, in a speech of February 1765, described them as "the sons of liberty" – a familiar image, since Englishmen had long called themselves free and valued themselves in that quality against the French and other nationals who cowered under their kings. In the colonies, the claim of freedom was the same as the

---

41 Hoerder (1977) 7f. on John Adams; 38 and 71–77 on class; and 10, on "the middling interest" to indicate an intermediate stratum defined by its economic goals, but otherwise "difficult for the historian to trace"; so he generally sees a scene of the haves and have-nots (in my own simplifying terminology). Hoerder's tripartite division of society appears in Wood (2009) 28, noting that "Most people did not yet think explicitly in terms of modern 'classes'... that would become common forms of identity in the nineteenth century" (etc.); and 171, further on the ideas persisting into the late eighteenth century.
42 Crowds often described, e.g., by Miller (1949) 131, 143, 302, 371; Morgan and Morgan (1953) 181; Countryman (1981) 59; Gilje (1987) 83 and passim; Middlekauff (2005) 92f.; Carp (2010) 37, 131, 234–39, and passim; and especially Hoerder (1977) chapter 2. Adams in March 1770 describes the victims of the "Massacre" as "saucy boys, Negroes and Mulattoes, Iris Teagues, and outlandish Jack Tars", cf. Bourne (2006) 167; Gilje (1987) 12–14 uses the pair "patrician" and "plebeian".

claim of English derivation, and it was therefore natural for the honorific title to be taken up by the protesters in Boston, and soon elsewhere, to denominate local "Sons of Liberty" cooperating with each other.[43]

But this implied demand of theirs doesn't say what exactly they were to be free to do, or free not to do, or why and how they could wax so furious. The scourge of impressment by royal navy squads in seaports was a special separate affront, though it obviously involved the liberty of its victims;[44] but the greater part of the crowds gathered and angry or violent against the Sugar Act or the Stamp Act cannot have been hurt, or threatened with any material loss, by those measures.[45] Gordon Wood contends, rather, that "the Revolution brought respectability and even dominance to ordinary people long held in contempt and gave dignity to their menial labor in a manner unprecedented in history."[46] Revolution alone could elevate so ill-paid and little respected a thing as a cobbler to a position of authority, though it might be for no more than a moment at the head of some shouting throng of men in the streets. For such a person the reward in demonstrating seems to have been as Wood says, a claim on dignity.

The Boston cobbler Ebenezer MacIntosh, then in 1765 in his late twenties, a volunteer fireman, was approached by a small group of gentlemen to enlist his support and that of two elements in the population, the Northenders and the Southenders. They were known as "mobs", and they liked a scuffle. MacIntosh was the leader of the Southenders in the annual Pope's Day parade, the colonists' version of Guy Fawkes day, and was acceptable to represent both mobs united. The physical force he headed was to be aimed against one Andrew Oliver. This Oliver was prominent, wealthy, and hated as the royal agent for the collection of the stamp tax, along with all his equally detestable and profiteering agents and his far-from-popular brother-in-law, the lieutenant-governor himself. For a fortnight in August the mobs were front-page stuff. At least at the start their actions were generally approved, even blessed by the clergy. As the scene heated up, several houses were broken into and thoroughly trashed, their owners barely escaping.[47] On balance, however, the mobs seem to have ended on

43 Otis (1764) 69, fear to be "reduced from the character of free subjects to the miserable state of tributary slaves"; "Liberty" as opposed to slavery as the opening word of Hopkins (1765) 3.

44 Lemisch (1968) 390, 407, and passim; impressment at its worst in Boston and the 1740s, though much in the 1760s, too.

45 Morgan and Morgan (1953) 181, "Actually the lower classes probably had little to lose directly by the Stamp Act"; Miller (1949) 111, "the [Stamp Act] tax fell upon those best able to pay"; Kulikoff (1993) 93, the Stamp Act had little effect on the rural yeoman class; and Wood (1992) 169, "there was little evidence of those social conditions we often associate with revolution (and some historians have sought to find): no mass poverty, no seething social discontent, no grinding oppression".

46 Quoted, Wood (1992) 8.

47 Hoerder (1977) 96, 101, clergy, and 112f., MacIntosh arrested but quickly released; Middlekauff (2005) 93–97; Carp (2010) 32, 36, 43 (a teenage kinsman a victim in the Massacre).

the winning side, whatever may have been thought about the violence they showed to property.

Not only in Boston but in many other cities, New York in chief, and in small townships in rural New York as well, demonstrations were not an uncommon feature of life throughout the eighteenth century. They came in all sizes and in every temperature, from warm to boiling. In European history from Antiquity on, in one city or another at one time or another, those who were ruled could express their wishes without a formal vote but by collective noise and speech, and were really listened to by their rulers, in what can only be called democracy (though the modern age reserves the term for a narrow part of the possibilities). The Southend cobbler, MacIntosh, was in this radical sense a democratic leader without being a radical. The better sort acknowledged the distinction and accepted – indeed they invited – his role on behalf of the entire city, so far as it was anti-tax. They needed him and his men. The "dignity" of which Gordon Wood speaks was thus his reward and may be fairly taken as his motive and, in a less intense way, the motive of his following as well. He had been elevated to equality with the better sort, if only briefly and by their leave. He and his following were to act out this honorable part before the whole city as their audience.

As the first day, the good day, degenerated into more violence, vandalism, and drunkenness, the full spectrum of common crowd behavior was illustrated, and the reaction to it of those uninvolved on the sidelines. They could approve a demonstration, they could even accept one as "constitutional", so long as it was well behaved and called attention to real public concerns. They were used to that.[48] On the other hand, they feared and condemned the threat to order, if it was also a threat to life and property. What they perhaps understood was that – in the view of the populace, not of the better sort – the gap between the ordinary man in the street and the very wealthy was in itself a public concern; and this was evident in the pattern of vandalism and destruction of property (not theft). It was directed at profiteers and show-offs, people seen and detested in the streets for their costly coaches and jewelry, their silver cane-handles, shoe-buckles and buttons, on their way to some glittering theater performance. A matching luxury and display when their grand homes were burst into was sure to provoke the mob's outrage at the gap, as unfair; and so much of such high style was imported from England, too![49] Hence, more justified anger; for, as an anthropologist says in generalizing terms about all societies known to his science,

48 Gilje (1987) 8, 17, 23; Middlekauff (2005) 104, "rioting had a long and apparently honorable history in Newport"; Hoerder (1977) 80, quotations to show gingerly acceptance of legitimacy of demonstrations, as "constitutional"; 84, "riots were recognized as part of the contemporary social and political institutions"; and 117, "the public good" at stake.

49 On the finery as detestably British, Miller (1949) 149f.; Hoerder (1977) 74f.; or Countryman (1981) 48f., 59f.; on anger at wealth, see Gilje (1987) 44, 50f.

"injustice, unfairness, and lack of reciprocity often motivate human aggression and indignation." The subject was discussed above.[50]

Lastly, on the essence of the gap: it represented inequality in violation of plain ordinary justice. It took on historical significance on a grand scale, as Paul Gilje pointed out:[51]

> The repeated use of crowd politics, expressed in traditional plebeian ritual [such as Pope's Day], had some unexpected consequences as the innate sense of fair play implicit in that ritual gave way to incipient egalitarianism. This politicization of the common man, clearly linked to the heavy dependence on crowd activity from 1765 to 1776, pushed the Revolutionary leaders to reformulate their own conception of good government... laborers, seamen, and mechanics assumed they had a voice...

And Gordon Wood again adds that, "once invoked, the idea of equality could not be stopped, and it tore through American society and culture with awesome power."[52]

Another cobbler like MacIntosh was a little short man (an inch over five feet) with a long name, George Robert Twelve Hewes. He spent his whole life in and out of destitution. It was this unlikely hero who stepped forward to tend to a dying man at the scene of the Boston Massacre in March of 1770 and was present again as a volunteer and assault-party captain with the Tea Party patriots three years later. On the day after the Massacre he testified in court:

> On his way back to the Town House with his cane he had a defiant exchange with Sergeant Chambers of the Twenty-Ninth Regiment and eight or nine soldiers, 'all with very large clubs or cutlasses.' A soldier, Dobson, 'ask'd him how he far'd; he told him very badly to see his townsmen shot in such a manner, and asked him if he did not think it was a dreadful thing.' Dobson swore 'it was fine thing' and 'you shall see more of it.' Chambers 'seized and forced' the cane from Hewes, 'saying I had no right to carry it. I told him I had as good a right to carry a cane as they had to carry clubs'.[53]

It was in encounters like this that the relaxing of patronage and dependency at work in the generation leading up to 1775 could be seen – and not only in the better reported cities but in rural townships as well, among small farmers and tenants.[54] Contem-

---

50 Above, chap. 3 n. 113.
51 Gilje (1987) 42, quoted.
52 Wood (1992) 232.
53 Young (1999) 39; for an exactly similar situation and behavior, involving a ropemaker, see Countryman (2000) 155.
54 Countryman (1981) 24, 40, 48ff., especially 71, that "crowd action stretched and rent the fabric of New York [up-state] society" in the period 1750–1775, and "nearly continuous rioting in one place or another built up a tradition of rural protest". Similarly, Young (1993) 324 on Robert Hewes (with some exaggeration), that "the experience of participating in the Boston Massacre, the Boston Tea Party, and countless other events of resistance enabled him to cast off deference".

poraries noticed the rising freedom of demeanor and speech among the have-nots, among whom cobblers and rope-makers and agricultural tenants were most obviously numbered and yet, being so humble, were proud and prickly beyond all expectation.[55] The assertion of individual rights and independence, whether in the face of a local elite or of an imperial government and its military, had evidently become more acceptable or at least less risky in the New World than in the Old. So much is clear. Experience reinforced it as it gained acceptance; and it was an ungovernable spirit. At the end, "the conflict that tore the British empire apart between 1754 and 1783 drew upon the deepest moral passion of Americans of virtually every sort and status."[56]

If among Americans the ungentlemanly nine tenths have left so little in print to explain the change in moral culture, Tom Paine may speak for them at the turn of 1776, "not inflaming or exaggerating matters," as he says, "but trying them by those feelings and affections which nature justifies, and without which we should be incapable of discharging the social duties of life or enjoying the felicities of it."[57] *Common-Sense* sales of half a million within a year show how his words resonated even among the masses, and give weight to his view that it was popular feelings that drove events, or moral *passions* to repeat the term used above.

Paine's view fits well with the approach taken to historical causation in the present chapter and in the preceding one as well. Beliefs about right and wrong may change for all sorts of causes, external as well as internal, but the new like the old will be acted out at the urge of associated feelings. Emotion supplies motive force. Whole populations like individuals act in characteristic ways, too, which when observed in an individual would be called "traits" comprising personality. Similarly, in a population, traits may be called "collective character", whether of a nation or a class of people. Character determines the general direction of conduct if not, certainly, each twist and turn.

In the demographic and territorial environment that the colonists in part created, over the generation 1745–1775, and in part found ready waiting for them, it is tempting to see the heart of Frederick Jackson Turner's famous thesis. This, and its elaboration by its author and his students, may serve as a third illustration of how culture as cause can be treated on a grand scale. In shaping the discussion of the American narrative, Turner's ideas enjoyed an influence unmatched in the twentieth century. He sought to explain "how European life entered the continent and how America modified and

---

55 Woods (1992) 145 draws on Charles Carroll of Maryland in 1765 to generalize, that "in all the colonies... any mark of superiority, any pretension of aristocracy, was 'sure to entail a general ill-will and dislike upon the owner'. Threats and anger were becoming more common than mutual respect and deference".

56 Middlekauff (2005) 30f.

57 Paine (1792) 15f. Eustace (2008) 3 and 440 stresses "Paine's emotional tone" but focuses not on how it worked on readers and made history, but rather on the propriety of feeling and expressing emotions, as discussed among the Colonial elite (4ff., 121, and passim; 393, "genteel sensibilities").

developed that life and reacted on Europe" – and by "life" of course he meant "way of life" or culture, not simply biological existence. "Our early history," he continues, "is the study of the germs developing in an American environment." To the early period, in our first two hundred years, he gave little attention. What rather interested him was "the really American part of our history", meaning the settler's world of the untamed fringes and what such regions gave rise to: a personality "strong in selfishness and individualism", as he says, most evident after 1815 or 1820. "The frontier is productive of individualism… [and] frontier individualism has from the beginning promoted democracy". These twin processes were the two legs on which his thesis stood.[58]

It was the underlying assumption here that a group or collectivity of whatever sort will have a personality that will in some degree reflect surrounding conditions. The proposition so broadly stated seems unobjectionable, just short of banal. It underlies my own outline, above, of the urges and values characterizing the have-nots of 1745–1775. Turner's thesis nevertheless provoked a welter of critical discussion. One of his students who was also an admirer and who made an honorable place for himself in the same line of studies, Ray Billington, was dismissive of American individualism as "fiction", "myth", "folklore", and "legend" except in pursuit of material profits, while Gordon Wood pronounced American society as the most individualist in the Western world – but he mentions Turner only once, to find fault with him.[59] How well the thesis has survived all such scholarly back-and-forth is, however, of less interest to me than one feature of Turner's style. He does not shrink from involving both himself and his readers in the affective aspects of the scenes he describes – as, for example, in an essay of 1903. Here he directs attention to the rise of "democratic influence" in America of the period 1800–1820, at which "the established classes in New England and the South began to take alarm. Perhaps no better illustration of the old-time Federal conservative" can be found, he says, than in a passage drawn from a travel book of 1822/3 by the Yale College president Timothy Dwight:[60]

---

58 Quoted from the original essay of 1893, Turner (1920b) 3, 32 ("selfishness"), 30 ("productive of individualism"); and his concluding long paragraph is given to the resulting "common traits" of Americans, including "that dominant individualism"; also Turner (1961) 68f. or Turner (1920) 320 of 1911, or Turner (1920a) 254, "the unchecked development of the individual was the significant product of this frontier democracy"; (1920b) 4, "the really American part". On the "two legs", in slightly different words ("concepts"), see Billington (1966) 139.

59 Much criticism, e.g., Berkhofer (1981) 43f.; Cronon (1991) 90f.; Billington (1966) 142f., 146, and 148, echoed by Brown (2009) 40, 48, "mythmaking", "dream world", "myth"; but cf. Billington and Ridge (1982) 687, on "the distinctive form of individualism that Europeans still associate with those reared in America. To the pioneer, every person was a self-dependent individual". Similarly, Wood (1992) 230, "by the early nineteenth century America had already emerged as the most egalitarian, most materialistic, most individualistic… society"; but, 311, Turner is faulted for leaving out too many causal factors; and his name is conspicuously absent in Wood (2009).

60 Turner (1920a) 251f., with no specific reference and slightly misquoting the first half-dozen words (the passage is in Dwight [1969] 4.321f.); and 261 ("Western democracy", quoted).

> The class of pioneers cannot live in a regular society. They are too idle, too talkative, too passionate, too prodigal, and too shiftless to acquire either property or character. They are impatient of the restraints of law, religion, and morality, and grumble about the taxes by which Rulers, Ministers, and Schoolmasters are supported... After exposing the injustice of the community in neglecting to invest persons of such superior merit [as themselves] in public offices, in many an eloquent harangue uttered by many a kitchen fire, in every blacksmith shop, in every corner of the streets, and finding all their efforts vain, they become at length discouraged, and under the pressure of poverty, the fear of gaol, and consciousness of public contempt, leave their native places and betake themselves to the wilderness.

The passage is well chosen to discredit Dwight's views, with which Turner diametrically disagreed. The Yale president is shown at his most unpleasant. A century after the publication of the passage quoted, in Turner's own day – to say nothing of our present times – the man's cruel caricature could only repel readers and provoke their dissent. In contrast a few pages later, Turner instead offered a strikingly different characterization:

> Western democracy has been from the time of its birth idealistic. The very fact of the wilderness appealed to men as a fair, blank page on which to write a new chapter in the story of man's struggle for a higher type of society. The Western wilds, from the Alleghenies to the Pacific, constituted the richest free gift that was ever spread out before civilized man. To the peasant and artisan of the Old World, bound by the chain of social class, as old as custom and as inevitable as fate, the West offered an exit into a free life... The existence of this land of opportunity has made America the goal of idealists from the days of the Pilgrim Fathers. With all the materialism of the pioneer movement, this idealistic conception of the vacant lands as an opportunity for a new order of things is unmistakably present.

– and Turner follows this up with a long passage of romantic poetry and lyric bits of prose not from common settlers but from Roger Williams and William Penn.

In another passage often offered to show both his magic and his method, he expatiates on

> That coarseness and strength combined with acuteness and inquisitiveness; that practical inventive turn of mind, quick to find expedients; that masterful grasp of material things, lacking in the artistic but powerful to effect great ends; that restless, nervous energy; that dominant individualism, working for good and evil, and withal that buoyancy and exuberance which comes with freedom – these are the traits of the frontier, or traits called out elsewhere because of the existence of the frontier.[61]

Such fine writing as Turner's has, or it once did have, its place and audience, certainly; but then, so did Timothy Dwight's in its time; and if one is to take science as the model for historical analysis, the stylists are equally at fault. They are too obviously

---

61 Quoted in Cronon (1991) 84; 83, he "articulated his thesis as a catalogue of 'character traits' that were the results of American evolution".

subjective. Instead, the sources need to be opened up as if to a jury, emphasizing the observation of signs of motivation as well as overt acts as they are reported by eyewitnesses; characterizing the witnesses by status and point of view; and taking care not to select only data that fit one's ends. None of these rules of argument, at which my own treatment of the "have-nots" aimed, is observed by either Dwight or Turner; so there is no good way to choose between them. Readers have only their own equally subjective reactions to go on, in believing the one or the other. It is indeed by just this everyday process that the historical profession arrives at its consensus, and declares one or another interpretation of events to be right.

Turner, however, engaging his imagination in the scenes he describes, evidently believed he could empathetically discern the feelings that explained behavior and, further, that those certain feelings typically animated the group he was interested in. Feelings shaped life and revealed prevailing values; and values are "the mediating variable of interest that connects to culture".[62] This, as Turner showed, is a fact that bears on choices made in the preferred form of government – government, among other things. Should it be authoritarian, or democratic? In this question and all its implications, historians have an obvious interest.

At the center of Turner's thesis was a personality of a certain sort that found increasing acceptance among historians. Over time and in a way he could not have been foreseen back in 1893, the key element in that American personality was also identified by an entirely different discipline, cross-cultural psychology, as the preceding chapter explained.[63] *Individualism* was Turner's very word; and individualism without any consciousness of his thesis was what psychologists beginning in the 1970s focused on more and more in their own way. It was a big part of their favorite subject, namely, Americans, increasingly seen in comparison with personality-types dominant in other societies. The comparison has occupied the EVS and WVS; and personality types as a concept could be fitted into the idea of modal personalities, familiar in anthropology.[64]

---

62 Bond (1994) 74, quoted; Yu and Yang (1994) 246, "society prescribes... goals... individual goals must conform with the values of the in-group" which thus give direction to achievement, cf. also 250; and Helwig (2006) 198, 202f.

63 Above, chap. 1 at n. 39 and elsewhere; chap. 3 at n. 134.

64 On "modal" personality in anthropology, see above, chap. 2 at nn. 37f. Smith et al. (2006) 46, 51, and 142, argue that "the values of an average person will give only a weak indication of the context within which that person is operating. We will do better if we know more about the way that an overall average set of values is distributed among the population... [C]haracterizing a whole nation as individualist or collectivist is at best a convenient shorthand... [I]t is individuals, not nations who possess these types of qualities [such as Assertiveness, Human-heartedness, Loyal Involvement]... Their mean values [of the "Big Five" personality traits] do not, of course, characterize each individual, but they do provide a sense of the typical personality...". On "the Big Five" traits, see above, chap. 1 at n. 28; on individualism/collectivism and Confucianism, and prevailing work ethic in EVS/WVS, see Halman et al. (2005) 54.

Contrast was first and most fully drawn with Japan and its collectivist society. To all the resulting research there could be no better introduction than an article co-authored by two veterans of cross-cultural psychology, Hazel Markus and Shinobu Kitayama. In their opening pages before taking up more technical matters, they recall how one of them left her home to teach in Osaka, while the other left his, for advanced study in Ann Arbor.[65] They had each been astonished at "finding ourselves in worlds that did not make sense with people who were behaving in strange and unfamiliar ways". Markus had never expected, in response to her lectures and still after many weeks into the term, that no student "said anything – nothing – no questions, no comments… Where were the arguments, the debates, and the signs of critical thinking? And moreover, if you asked somebody a completely straightforward question such as, 'Where is the best noodle shop?' why was the answer invariably an audible intake of air followed by the response, 'It depends'". On the other hand, Kitayama couldn't understand students continually interrupting each other and talking over even the professor; and the high level of emotions and competition was strange, and the professors' trick of starting a lecture with a joke, and the behavior of students and faculty alike at restaurants.

There were endless things to notice, fascinating to these two trained observers – especially the "dynamic interdependencies between psychological tendencies and the sociocultural, sociostructural, and sociohistorical situations and contexts in which these tendencies occur" (descriptive phrases that Turner might have approved, hearing his own core ideas compressed into the latest techno-speak). The authors go on to support with their findings the pairing most familiar in their field, individualism vs. collectivism, as personality types shaped by culture. Where the types differ, it shouldn't be seen as a matter of cognitive content. Indeed, as they say, "meanings and values may not be cognized and stored in memory at all. Instead, they may be so deeply ingrained in the everyday mundane practices of the culture that they are 'lived' rather than being 'known' or 'cognized'". These very findings in studies without cultural connections appeared (it may be recalled) in the preceding chapter.[66]

As to a cultural background, collectivism in Asian societies has been most often associated with Confucianism (a conclusion on which Weber in his turn might have smiled, seeing in Confucianism the same formative role he assigns to Calvinism). It teaches subordination of self to family, to age, even to those departed, that is, tradition. It marks the wish not to stand out; to be a team-player in one's place of work; to defer to the common will and established authority. Individualism on the other hand shows itself in a willingness to act on one's own even unsupported by one's group; in the preference for authority that will recognize one's right to be different and inde-

---

65 Markus and Kitayama (2003) 278f.

66 Markus and Kitayama (2003) 277, 280, 283; also Markus and Hamedani (2007) 12. On unconscious responses, see also above, chap. 3 at nn. 62 and 112.

pendent, and the equal claim of every person to be heard; in tolerance of rivalry, novelty, and disregard of convention. While the contrast between the two cultural tendencies is usually discussed in East-West and contemporary contexts, and with an eye to practical applications, African and other examples receive social-scientific attention, too.[67]

The recollections of Shinobu Kitayama and Hazel Markus, and individualism vs. collectivism, and comparison of cultures – all these together serve my interest in culture as a cause of historical events and developments. Returning now to that focus, three points stand out, of which the first is perhaps the most obvious: that national character is simply a given among modern psychologists, whether cross-cultural or not. They assume its existence without need to support their assumption; and, for that matter, so do the anthropologists seen in my second chapter dealing with collectivities not as large as nations, and the sociologists conducting their values surveys. As a reminder of the deep roots of these views in the social sciences, here is the sociologist, anthropologist, and historical linguist, Edward Sapir, speaking of the French nearly a century ago:[68]

> No one who has even superficially concerned himself with French culture can have failed to be impressed by the qualities of clarity, lucid systematization, balance, care in choice or means, and good taste, that permeate so many aspects of the national civilization. These qualities have their weaker side. We are familiar with the overmechanization, the emotional timidity or shallowness,... that are revealed in some of the manifestations of the French spirit. Those elements of French civilization that give characteristic evidence of the qualities of its genius may be said, in our present limited sense, to constitute the culture of France.

As a second point equally clear, national character is seen to control national behavior on what may be called an historical scale – at least (but not least interesting) in the achieving of economic success. The favored explanation for this is sought in the comparison of Confucianism with Calvinism. Both these thought-systems serve the businessman but not at all in the same way.[69] If one wished, too, the effects of

67 On collectivism contrasted with individualism, see especially Triandis (1995) passim and the volume with many articles edited by Kim et al. (1994); also, e.g., Fiske (1992) 697f., Matsumoto (1994) 119, or Oishi et al. (2008) 307; on Confucianism as a business ethic, Kim et al. (1994a) 6f., Yu and Yang (1994) 240ff. and 245ff., Triandis (1995) 26, Helwig (2006) 199ff., Kim and Park (2008) 500f., or Khilji et al. (2011) passim.

68 Sapir (1924) 407, quoted.

69 Economic effects of philosophic/religious factors extend beyond Weber to research in contemporary Asian countries, cf. Yu and Yang (1994) 241 or McCleary (2007) 49 emphasizing values such as honesty and frugality; Furnham (1990) 19 and Landes (1998) 391, 487f., on "the Japanese economic miracle" explained by collectivism and the competition of groups not individuals; and Franke et al. (1991) rating economic performance across 20 nations and concluding that "performance seems facilitated by Confucian dynamism" (meaning, p. 167, acceptance of hierarchy, thrift, perseverance),

national character could be shown in the preference for one political system over another, authoritarian and doctrinaire as opposed to pragmatic and empiricist, thus to be studied on the lines of Turner's thesis and its links with American democracy. And so forth.

But as a third point to notice: in contrast to historical treatments, social-scientific studies are generally synchronic. They don't pursue a train of development within a population, traced from some external stimulus to a widespread consciousness of it, and so to action at the urging of responsive instincts or strong feelings, at the end producing a change in values and traits. All this is cinema, not still photography; and the variables necessarily attendant on such diachronic treatment, in their infinite unpredictability, simply cannot be contained within the laboratory. They don't lend themselves to study in a decently scientific way.

At best, the effect of a thought-system or physical environment on some whole population, so as to shape its character, may be conjectured as a matter of theory not confined to a period of time: for example, by identifying prevailing moral values through research among college students of one nation or another, and suggesting in Weberian fashion how these values must constitute a representative personality that particularly serves, let us say, gainful activity.

But to go further and demonstrate exactly how it so serves has always been the proper business of historians, as Katherine Verdery explains in a recent volume:

> For individual members of a nation to experience the world in terms of a self that is national requires bringing together the sense of self and the sense of one's group: self and group must be experienced simultaneously, as constitutive of the person. The notion of a national character establishes precisely such a link. "Character," whether it is taken to be something inborn or something molded by experience, is a notion that can apply equally to persons and collectivities: much as one might explain an individual's trajectory through life in terms of his being of a rigid, uncompromising character or supple and adaptable...[70]

Her closing thought, that the dominant traits of a single person or of an entire population equally determine a general narrative, is supported by a great deal of social science reviewed in my pages. It directs attention to what is implied by the comparison or equating of person with population; and it invites our use of certain quite familiar means of sizing up our fellow creatures. We use our eyes, yes, and the recall of what we have noticed before, but also and most important, our powers of empathy. We have seen Joachim or Joanna in action as neighbors or co-workers and out of our life's experience and affective powers, asking ourselves how would we ourselves feel

---

whereas "cultural individualism seems a liability, while the propensity for work in cohesive groups is an asset".

70 Verdery (1995) xxv, "'national character', a subject now reemerging after a number of years in the shade" (cf. above, n. 3); and quoted, xvif.

if we behaved similarly, we can draw our conclusions. We can do this, we believe, even more certainly than from judging whatever they have said. Their actions reveal tendencies. Tendencies reveal choices, and choices reveal moral values. "Values are beliefs that are linked inextricably to affect... when values are activated they become infused with feeling." It is of course a social scientist quoted.[71]

Right and wrong, feelings about them, and the motive behind actions are surely best explained in diachronic fashion – that is, historically. The method is undeniably unscientific in any usual sense. Properly, individual behavior should be observed and described within a given setting, that is (in the term of art) "situationally".[72] Historians, however, choose to follow their subject through a succession of situations constantly changing, since change is their concern. As a result, their observations become increasingly approximate. True – but what is lost in accuracy is gained in insight into cause and effect. "Y" can be seen following from "X"; from cause and effect, it is possible to reason to motive, and by this means to control the actors' own explanations if any are offered. Commonly, of course, these do indeed turn up in surviving records; and all these routines of historical understanding are, as Katherine Verdery says, as valid for collectivities as for individuals. They allow the analyst to get inside the scene and its operations as into a novel, which is by no means the worst way to learn about humanity.

---

71 Schwartz (2007) 170.

72 As illustration of the rules of good analysis, see the back-and-forth in which Walter Mischel and Seymour Epstein engaged, with other researchers in the same area (above, chap. 1).

5 Conclusions

In the Preface, after spelling out my general objective, I drew attention to the social sciences' "ways of thinking about humankind that are infinitely rich," and "the certainty of profiting from them". I went on in the chapters that followed to notice promising points of intersection between history and these disciplines, despite their various differences, and I recall some of those points at the end of the present chapter to illustrate the possibilities.

First, however, the differences: historical findings, unlike those of social science research, can be characterized as *diachronic, consequential*, and *approximate*. There are limits to what historians can borrow and apply.

As to the first of these rubrics, it is true that psychologists undertake studies of change over time, witness Walter Mischel (in chap. 1) and many others earlier and later; but, though they look as if they were doing history, that's not really the case. They choose as subject a child of a certain trait at the age of four, let us say, who is likely ten years later to be of such-and-such attainments, to be measured, and again at a still later age, and to differ from other children of different tendencies. Surely all this helps to explain *why we do what we do*, the question I asked at the outset. But the object of study is the trait, objectified in realist fashion, and not the child's biography, seen in a given social context; and the same is true where adults and their business performances are measured by Hofstede and others (also in chap. 1), to determine whether or not some particular philosophy or thought-system serves the respondents in their careers.

As to *consequentiality*, it is a given in scientific research that all knowledge is desirable because no one knows where some little fact may some day lead. Its effects in the real world of a given moment, whether great or none at all, are irrelevant. *Applied* science is of course more focused on things that matter in a practical sense than on those that don't, so as to reach out beyond the laboratory and stimulate both general interest and funding; but it hasn't the prestige of pure science. The aim of this latter is rather the discovery of universals and rules that will support a general theory. Such is the ambition of psychologists, anthropologists, and economists explicitly and often. Some have been quoted in earlier pages. Certainly social science prefers targets of study that are consequential in the sense of having causal ties into many and widely connected behavioral traits; and these traits could be called major or fundamental. But their elaboration into networks and across time is not commonly pursued in any way like a historian's.

And as to *approximation*: to the contrary, in the sciences exactness is everything. Research results are supposed to be right, meaning that they can be quantified, replicated, and verified or falsified. If a small sample isn't adequate, then a larger can be attempted and an approach through aggregation, producing a list of twenty thousand English trait-words for study, as we saw in chap. 1, or a hundred thousand questionnaires about job-satisfaction, or cross-cultural comparisons in forty or fifty different populations. The large size of a sample is needed for a nearer approach to exactness where more parsimonious perfection is despaired of. When, however, account is taken of different cultures as well as the behavior of different individuals in different situations, and all the variables are considered, exact measurement becomes impossible. Rational patterns even in the pursuit of material benefits can no longer be taken for granted, nor the accuracy of tightly focused testing on small samples of respondents. Hints of something like despair appear in the search for universal truths within social science. The whole effort is seen to be at a dead end.[1]

I notice these differences from history not because they are important to my purpose in themselves but to show why historians for their own ends cannot simply download everything that social scientists publish. The disciplines compared are too differently formed.

The fact appears at the very commencement of a research project. In social science, the choice of what to study can be controlled very simply through what goes into tests and samples or, in anthropology and sociology, through what observers have the opportunity to observe within physical limits. For historians, however, defining their inquiry in any exclusive way is a trickier proposition. They must choose a period – but not at random. It must be in some way significant, and significance requires *diachronic* comparison of some Before, and an After; for, without such comparison, among all the data about our past, how can one identify topics that will prove rewarding, that is, consequential?

To recognize this quality when one comes upon it, imagine some scandal of long ago, announced like a headline as INCEST AND SERIAL RAPE. The subject has an irresistible horrible attraction: someone fathered children on his thirty-years-younger deceased wife's sister (actually, half-sister), which counts in some faiths as incest and is certainly shocking. To this is added the fact that the father in question owned the girl as a slave, for whom free consent to sex was therefore not a reality. Yet the story falls short of history if it is set in a slave-owning society a couple of centuries in the past; it falls short, since it intimately and clearly disturbs the lives of only two people. It falls short, until the father is identified as Thomas Jefferson![2] Then on the instant everything becomes important. We have headlines indeed. They have given rise to a great quantity of research and publication of the usual scholarly sort (and some, not).

What is it that made the difference between this human interest tale, no matter how striking, and anything we would call history? It is evidently not the direct effect of acts by which little may have changed beyond the immediate circle of the actors,

1 On quantification, see Cameron, above, chap. 1 at n. 14, and from a totally different point of view, the protest against fancy mathematics by Leontief (1982) 104f.; further, Novick (1988) 588ff., holding up his hands in dismay at the mathematical excesses of argument among historians of the cliometric school; on too-narrow sampling, above, chap. 1 at n. 35; and on the "dead-end", chap. 1 at n. 7.

2 Gordon-Reed (2008) 590, 652f., 718f., and passim.

but rather the outspreading network of influence and publicity in question, at the very center of which one of the actors lived out his life, touching and being touched by many others and thus giving significance to everything he did. *Consequentiality* guides historians' choice of what to study and what to disregard. It narrows their focus. In contrast, social sciences in their search for universals only expand their samples to make them more and more comprehensive.

Historians identifying a promising causal network may see that it ties into others, and so on almost *ad infinitum*. In the understanding of this vision all clarity must soon be lost. The contemplation of it is appalling even to the hardiest veterans of the discipline.[3] How then should they proceed? They must narrow their choice. They must fix not only on a certain time-period but on some finite population as well. An illustration is identifiable at the dawn of history. As far back as ancient Greece there were ethnicities and city-states that knew each other as discrete entities. Alcibiades in an anecdote quoted earlier illustrates how people in his day might grasp and think about one such entity, speaking with a sneer about the Thebans. While he and his fellow Athenians were never at a loss for words, Thebans were everywhere ridiculed as inarticulate dunderheads, along with the inhabitants of all Boeotia around them. The stereotype and others similar were in common circulation at the time. Their match can be found much later attached to the regions of medieval France or in use today to distinguish Scots from the incontestably inferior Sassenachs. With these as the objects of study we are certainly doing history, and drawing closer to group conduct and narratives.

The subject of national character therefore arises naturally. It has been explored (chaps. 3 and 4) in different ways which can be recognized by their focus on a most-typical personality, or alternatively, on institutions, rituals and celebrations, narrative myths, social representations such as proverbs, and a host of other constructs that seem to have some integral quality – in a word, a genius, a spirit.[4] The two approaches, through both people and things, may be pursued together as (for example) in asking what the English reveal about themselves in their devotion to cricket, or what both the tattered traditions and the newer mores among Romans of the later centuries BC can tell us about the personality – the tendencies – of their ancestors much earlier.[5] Like an individual's life story, the narrative of a people can show who they are across time.

And national character as a reality to be studied, quite aside from its existence as a fixture in the common mind, has recently returned to favor after a half-century

3 The amazingly prolific president of the historical association wrote of the "continuum" of past data, a continuum in time and change, within which "each event is harnessed to another", all "one vast *un*enclosure", and so forth (Taylor [1928] 248f.).

4 Spain (1982) 175 and passim.

5 Cf. my book with the subtitle "A Character Sketch" (*The Earliest Romans*, 2011).

of disrepute.[6] Whatever may explain this favor, certainly some support for it can be found in psychology, where a quite random population sample can be compared with a cadre of some defined tendency, as, for example, marked conscientiousness, and this group can be shown to behave differently and across time to produce a corresponding history. In my first chapter much evidence for this was cited, and the fact was again emphasized in my second chapter, in anthropological findings.

Beyond that, it is now intellectually respectable for psychologists to canvass scores of distinct large population groups, most of them politically bounded and therefore *nations* in the common sense of the word, asking in dozens of languages, "how likely it is that the typical member of a culture is anxious, nervous, and worrying versus at ease, calm, and relaxed" or, in surveys of a different method, even discovering genetically different dispositions (e.g., toward anxiety and depression, the Japanese allele-count contrasted with the Caucasian).[7]

Historians surely may learn from these research developments. A given culture can be told from others by what its members are likely to do in given situations. The social scientist and the historian alike are prompted to ask what that connection may be, between culture and behavior. It is accepted that there is no useful distinction to be drawn between the tendencies discoverable in a given group and in its most typical or modal individuals.[8] To bring out the relevance of the fact, it may be added that "a *settled* tendency at work continuously over any length of time need not be a *marked* tendency, in order to produce differences of significant historical magnitude".[9] This is the assumption underlying the choice of individualism, for example, as a particular target of social-scientific study since the 1970s. The trait is seen as making a good businessman, recognized in elaborate cross-cultural research; measured also to identify business potential in little Nigerian villages.[10] It will produce predictable results over the course of time. It is consequential. Historians can study it or any other trait with the help of social science.

But results of such study can only be *approximate* (the third rubric of difference that I noted at the outset of this chapter). They can't be predicted with complete

6 Mandler (2006) 2 notes how the two approaches, popular and scholarly, may flow together; 187, that the acceptance of national character as a usefully descriptive idea peaked in the West toward the mid-twentieth century; cf. above, chap. 4 nn. 2f.; and for essays on the phenomenon in the interwar period, see Lass (1995) 42 on Czechoslovakia; also Verdery (1995a) 104 and 110, showing the view even post-WWII that a people (Romania) possesses a collective personality, "unitary in essence".

7 Quoted, Terraciano (2005) 97f., measuring self-appraisal by cultures seen in college students; the problems of sampling, above, chap. 1 nn. 34f.; the assumption of cultural variation, above, chap. 1 at nn. 25f. and 55f.; chap. 2 at nn. 32f.; chap. 3 at n. 101 (*amae*); chap. 4 passim; and Chiao and Ambady (2007) 245 or Gazzaniga (2011) 184f. on cross-cultural allele-measurement.

8 Above, chap. 1 at n. 2.

9 Quoted (only as the best way I can think of to say it) from MacMullen (1990) 18 (originally, 1980).

10 Above, chap. 4 at nn. 59 and 62; on Nigerian villages, chap. 2 at n. 32.

accuracy because of the problem noted, where one causal network touches an infinity of others in domino fashion. In the evaluation not of group tendencies but of individuals', a situationalist answer is possible: many individuals can be subjected to many repetitions of a test on different days and in different circumstances. How they respond can then be aggregated to define a modal personality, which provides a starting point for prediction. Even such an approximate understanding of cause and effect is, however, beyond the capability of historians. They can only make an informed guess about causal probabilities in a manner quite obviously inexact; and in fact the ambition among them, or among some of them, to rise to a higher level of accuracy and generalization, in the opening and early twentieth century, had been abandoned by the 1940s.[11] Thereafter "science" in history was limited to the use of such statistics as happened to turn up, bearing on exports, demography, and the like, and exploited for example in Braudel's work of the 1950s to 1970s and the *Annales* of those years and later. The French journal announced as its mission to encompass social sciences, economies, societies, civilizations, and history. The counting of the things that could be counted had many admirers in the U.S., without their necessarily admiring the *Annales*. Witness Morison and Commager in their survey volumes or Robert Fogel in the 1980s (in chap. 4).

No-nonsense, factually detailed history will always have a special appeal. That midnight ride inspiring the American Revolution at a certain crucial moment somehow has less reality in it and seems less true than a map of the area aroused by Paul Revere with all its known patriot households and networks of sympathizers plotted on it. Or again: those dark scenes of the French Revolution envisioned by Thomas Carlyle in 1837, inviting their novelistic use by Dickens, could never hold out a century later against the quite different parsing of class and interest by Lucien Febvre.[12] The best historical evidence – so the argument for rational decision-making would insist – should be sought among people's thought-out choices of actions, not their passions; in material benefits, not dreams and drama; and nowhere with more promise of truth than in economic history, where Fogel could find, as he insisted, "'scientific' reinterpretations". If older authorities like Keynes or Marc Bloch reserved some role for non-rational factors, the lapse could be disregarded.[13]

Rational utility, however, as the preferred heuristic in economic history, faced a challenge beginning in the 1970s. Psychological research directed attention to the

---

11 On the ambition for "scientific" history, cf. Beard (1934) 223ff.; also Bourguière (1982) 424ff., mostly in Europe; and many attempts to assert history's claim to the title, e.g., Gaddis (2002) 66 and chaps. 5–8, asking what is historical knowledge, is it true, etc., making his case through special definitions in good (or misguided) realist fashion.

12 On Revere, see Fischer (1994) 141–48, abjuring any "romantic idea" of the scene and laying out the network-explanation, "a fact of vital importance" and "profoundly different from the popular image of a solitary hero-figure". L. Febvre's work on the coming of the French Revolution appeared in 1939.

13 On Keynes, writing in 1935, and Bloch, cf. above, chap. 3 nn. 1 and 19.

tricks that our minds play on us in decision-making where "the illusion of validity" takes over or "the psychophysics of hedonic experience". Even cool professionals in the market could be discovered in the grip of herd instinct and anxiety. No-one wanted the eighteenth-century Man of Feeling to displace *Homo economicus* (chap. 3), but psychologists did see what was implied in two linked propositions: *first*, that an overwhelming majority of our mental operations somehow connect us with other human beings, undeniably, since after all most of us communicate in one way or another with our fellows, actually or in imagination, at some point in every hour of the waking day, and moreover, as we do so, undeniably, we experience some feeling. In all of the evaluations of this social sort there is an affective element. Moreover, *second*, this social element is accompanied by a sensation we would describe as thinking. A newfangled Siamese term, then, *thought-feeling*, seemed necessary to describe this and other aspects of what has been called "the affective revolution".[14]

There is evidence, furthermore, suggesting that such an intimate mix as the "Siamese" metaphor implies can be found even in mental processes that have no social character at all. We would call them entirely intellectual or mathematical.[15] If this possibility needs more discussion, historians needn't be concerned. Mental activity that they see as significant because it governs decisions, not the mere choice of instruments, is what can be shown to be most certainly associated with emotions. The fact points to the need to consider the emotional side of events and developments whether in the most remote past or in the most recent, and whether in the narrative of individuals or of collectivities, quite as much as any logical calculating of profit.

In fact, in my earlier chapters I showed social scientists commenting on the all-too-human preference for rational explanations of what we do, especially (but by no means only) in explanations for our own decisions and even when rationality is clearly not the real story. Self-deception or misrepresentation has been noticed in all sorts of circumstances as the common tribute we pay to reason.[16] But at least in social interaction, regarding choices that in some way have to do with our fellow beings around us, what is *rational* has itself become less and less clear. Much of my third chapter, above, was given to the term itself. In English, the Latinate word and the easier *reasonable* ought to be synonymous. In fact, however, the two are not quite the same. *Rational* is a little more scientific, asking for more nearly perfect logic and consistency, whereas to *be reasonable* is something we ask even of a child. It describes a sort of *approximation*. And when evidence for this latitude is assembled out of a sample of authorities – and I instanced a famous judge, a famous a philosopher, a psychologist, an anthropologist – what is best supported is a contingent definition.

14 Zajonc (1980) 153; the term *thought-feeling* invented by Strauss (1992) 2; "the affective revolution" in Haidt and Kesebir (2010) 801; the fact if not the term in Loewenstein et al. (2001) 268.

15 Above, chap. 3 n. 82.

16 Cf. above, chap. 3 at nn. 28, 50f., and passim.

We are all quite used to it. *Reasonable* is no more than what most of the people around us think; it cannot be exact, only *approximate*; and it is what most American historians are quite ready to accept, too. They prefer it, at least, when the alternative is that forever-unresolved debate among their more philosophically inclined colleagues, asking with Pontius Pilate, *What is truth*?[17]

As applied to choices in real life rather than in metaphysics or in matters like weather prediction, reason therefore differs according to cultures. Cultural variation is increasingly accepted as a fact. At the same time, the world has grown smaller. Social-scientific studies have extended their focus beyond the U.S. with its relative homogeneity and parochial research interests. As a result, psychological and sociological concepts like anger or timidity, once familiar, are redefined in as many ways as there are countries to be studied. Rationality itself loses some of its home-grown meaning. As the anthropologist Michelle Rosaldo reminds us, "Once upon a time, the world was simple. People knew that thought was not the same as feeling. Cognition could be readily opposed to affect, explicit to implicit" (and here exactly is "the affective revolution referred to", above). "But," she continues, "recognition of the fact that thought is always culturally patterned and infused with feelings, which themselves reflect a culturally ordered past, suggests that just as thought does not exist in isolation from affective life, so affect is culturally ordered."[18] Relativity is thus accounted for, at least and most obviously in social, i.e., moral, decision-making; explanation that assumes uncomplicated logicality in motivation will only mislead. At best, then, we may hope only to explain "most of the people much of the time", in Seymour Epstein's warning.[19]

By this path I return to that new-fangled Siamese term, *thought-feeling*. Its usefulness has been often and dramatically shown through the study of brain-lesions. They have been best explained to the non-specialist by Antonio Damasio in the 1990s. Destruction of a particular part of the frontal lobe, long of interest to neuroscience, was known to produce results of a particular sort resembling sociopathy and autism. It incapacitated the victim in relationships with others, and the same brain part was also known to be the seat of social affect. Hence it was argued, and is now widely accepted, that getting along with our fellow employees, our family and everyone else in a normal life with normal choices of behavior is somehow dependent on feelings not only about those individuals but also about how to behave. The ability to sort out right and wrong is acquired in childhood and later reinforced and refined by persons around us who mean something to us. Sorting makes use of the resulting aversive or

---

17 On Posner, Rawls, Kahneman, and Malinowski, see above, chap. 3; on the common wisdom, Novik (1988) 593: "Michael Kammen described in the 1980s the utter indifference of the overwhelming majority of American historians to issues of epistemology or philosophy of history".
18 Quoted, Rosaldo (1984) 137.
19 Epstein (1979) 1098.

appetitive signals attached to life's choices. By feelings as identifiers, individuals are guided, often so instantaneously that they have no consciousness of what's happening, and act in characteristic ways that will be commonly labeled as their *traits*. All traits together constitute their personality.[20]

It is accepted also that traits are, if not entirely shaped by socialization, i.e., by one's culture, they are at least largely so formed. Collective personality can't be known by the same methods as individual personality, but the latter will resemble the former if it is aggregated; and both will be predictive to a significant degree. As an example, take the settled belligerence of a people across time: it can be shown statistically in both the remote past, by a sociologist, and in the more recent past, in the 1940s and 1950s, by an anthropologist. In just the same way, the relation between economic development and prevailing values like honesty and respect for hard work has been examined by Weber and others of his discipline down to this day, as illustrations in my chap. 4 made plain.[21]

In socialization, the coloring imparted to values by feelings has long been accepted in the social sciences.[22] This process has affect at its center, as recent science has further explained; and affect is central to other research areas touched on, too, in the preceding few pages. The new directions opening up in research together make an interesting series including, as they do, economic decision-making; further, the term "thought-feeling"; also rationality contrasted with irrationality; cross-cultural research in traits and values; "the affective revolution", as Rosaldo termed it; and the neuroscience of social behavior especially in studies by Damasio – which brings us back to socialization. All these new targets of study, taken together, testify to a very striking consensus. It can be reduced to summary statement, that motivation and decision-making are ruled by feeling where reason was once thought to hold sway.

If this is another lesson historians can learn from social science, I wonder just how they should apply it to their own use. To the extent motivation is not innate and instinctual, they need not treat it in any novel way, and existential facts like life expectancy under the age of five, or the cost in labor of a day's staple food, must still be considered in the familiar instrumental terms. On the other hand, if there is evidently more of feeling than of calculation in common decision-making, it is a different game. Decisions need to be revisited to see what the fact implies and how to handle it.

---

20 I lay out some of the relevant findings for this outline of socialization in chap. 1 at nn. 57–70 and chap. 2 at nn. 50–63.

21 Belligerence is measured among the ancient Romans by the sociologist turned historian, Keith Hopkins, cf. MacMullen (1990) 17, and among an Amazonian people by Napoleon Chagnon, above, chap. 2 at n. 30; on measurement of economic traits by, e.g., Weber, see chap. 4 and Norris and Inglehart (2011) 178.

22 Above at chap. 1 nn. 69f; at chap. 2 n. 38, "the strongly affective nature of most cultural learning", and at nn. 50ff.; and in chap. 3 at nn. 123 and 128ff.

We are interested only in what has consequences, as for example the rebellious actions of the cobbler Hewes (chap. 4) – and this, despite the fact that such a person as Hewes was perfectly ordinary and unimportant. All the better to represent the impulses of the general population! But our direct evidence tells us only *what* he and others like him did, not *why*. It can only be shown that their motivation had nothing to do with material advantage or profit. Of equal interest is the matter of celebrity status. Here is something else of consequence but in a quite different form, where someone by no means ordinary is able to change the manners and customs of his society – someone like Alcibiades or "Beau" Brummel, also appearing in chap. 4. In the two cases illustrative of political history through Hewes and cultural history through the two trend-setters, it is relations with other people that are illuminated – hostile relations where Hewes is concerned, or admiring relations in Alcibiades's circle or Brummel's.

Exactly what animated the people involved can only be guessed at, not really known; for, in the interpreting of motivation and decision-making, in history exactly as in a criminal trial, there can be no such thing as proof, strictly speaking. There can only be advocates – historians or lawyers – trying to arouse in others, whether readers or jurors, those same feelings that they sense in themselves when they consider people's actions empathetically, so as to infer motivation.

How else can historians think beyond "What?" to the "Why?" of past behavior?[23] But the question is not often confronted.

One report opens an interesting window on the process of inference. "For the first time in history," says the psychologist Keith Oatley, "there is now scientific evidence that reading fiction really does have psychological benefits... people's social skills improve when they spend time reading fiction"; and, beyond that, it helps them to "understand not just characters in books but human character in general".[24] What

---

23 This was the argument in MacMullen (2003). In opposition, it has been argued by academics especially from the 1970s that no historical knowledge at all is possible, where "knowledge" is explicitly or implicitly taken as incontrovertible and verifiable; and William Harris asserts the impossibility particularly in identifying motivation. See his 2008 lecture, "History, empathy, and emotion" ("forthcoming", but for the moment at http://weblearn.ox.ac.uk/access/content/group/wolfson/Podcasts/Harris%20_2008_.mp3). He declares his own inability to enter into the emotional world of anyone not of his own time and class, because of the problem of "otherness'; and if he can't do it, then he says that historians, historical novelists, or writers of any sort of fiction claiming more for themselves must simply be deceiving themselves. His opinion, lacking support, is not helpful. Rather (summarizing what is suggested elsewhere in these pages), the attempt at empathy may produce, and humans are most often satisfied with, insights (though only approximate), to be validated (only provisionally) by consensus, as, e.g., in a jury trial.

24 Oatley (2008) 42, comparing the exercise of the mind to simulator-training for pilots; See also www.the psychologist.org.uk vol. 21 (2008) 1030–32 and Oatley (2011) 64f., with 63 quoted, "understand" and "improve your ability to take another person's point of view"; or a historian, Demos (1998) 1529, in a short piece on the usefulness of historical detail for fiction-writing, concluding *vice versa*,

Oatley has found seems to me not only readily intuited but reassuring to historians, since surely they are drawn, more than most people, to Tolstoy, Dickens, Flaubert, and other novelists that offer tableaus of different times and social values as well as individual story-lines. The three novelists named are, incidentally, among those whose creative efforts so involved them emotionally, they were reduced to tears and sobs as they wrote.[25] Recall of one's own emotional experiences as an aid in interpreting how someone else feels in a given situation is of course the most familiar of our mental operations, here put to work by dramatic writers creatively. They stimulate in their readers an answering, identical response. It is empathetic but may be used equally well analytically. So close is the affinity between fiction and history; so very instructive is the empathetic reading of a novel side by side with a factual account – let us say, a documentary version of a maddened mob, or of a daughter-father relationship, compared with a quite imaginary but affecting equivalent.[26]

The fact may be applied to such a large subject as the nineteenth-century American abolitionist movement, whose proponents had become involved through dearly held moral convictions and who responded emotionally to *Uncle Tom's Cabin.* The scale of the response to that work was quite extraordinary, later prompting Lincoln's greeting to the author when they met, "So this is the little lady who started this great war". His joking words, and even more clearly her book-sales, testify to the role of affect in decision-making on a historic scale. Contemporaries had no need to be reminded of the great strength of feelings aroused in those who read about the ordeals of Tom, Eliza, and the rest of Harriet Beecher Stowe's *dramatis personae.*[27]

It may still be asked what was the motivation of abolitionists. To say they disapproved of slavery is descriptive but not explanatory, since of course people disapprove of all sorts of things without taking action, let alone taking up arms. Conventional answers to the question asked will most naturally look first at what was in print in the decades preceding 1862, so as to learn what moral views prevailed at the time, what picture of slavery was widely available, and how the northern public would most likely see it. A study of Stowe's words that could be thought to "turn people on", as we

"Should we [historians] continue to leave the most basic, universal, and personally significant parts of our lives to novelists, poets, philosophers, religious leaders, and their like? I hope not".

25 MacMullen (2003) 132.

26 Compare a Paris newspaper report of 1610, Tilly (1981) 4, with Tolstoy's *War and Peace,* vol. 3, part 3, chap. 25; or the New York letter-collection of 1828–32, MacMullen (2001a), with Henry James' *Washington Square* (*The Heiress*) (1880).

27 As a demonstration-piece of historical narrative focused on affect, using the abolitionist movement in the North, see MacMullen (2003) 110–28, more than matched in the third volume of Robert Caro's biography of Lyndon Johnson (chap. 30, civil rights in the ,50s). On Lincoln's remark, see Stowe (1911) 203 – attested only some time subsequently, and so sometimes dismissed as an invention, but without asking if the reporters were of the sort to pass off fiction as fact. See recently Goldfield (2011) 79.

would say, and comparison with the emotive vocabulary of publications meant for a large readership would help, too.

Alternatively, however, one could begin at a deeper level, as I suggested in the Preface, among our innate prosocial tendencies, matched and illustrated in the reaction of a rat to the unhappy condition of another rat deprived of its freedom. The lab experiments were mentioned earlier (chap. 3). From these, which indicate the bedrock of explanation, interpretation may proceed to the analysis of values and traits by which instinct is shaped by culture, noting especially the differential between the white populations of the North and South in seeing African-Americans as cospecifics.[28]

For another example of historic book sales, we have Thomas Paine's well known *Common Sense*. Relative to the size of the adult market, it won an even more spectacular success than had Stowe's work. It too induced action among its readers. Its effects registered more obviously and most consequentially among the non-elite nine tenths of the population.[29] Beyond any other event, its publication aroused a rebellion.

And what was the motivation for this? To simplify very greatly, the answer may be sought in the public testimony of an already rebellious cobbler, Hewes, whose cane was snatched away by one of the king's troops: "I told him I had as good a right to carry a cane as they had to carry clubs".[30] The words show the cobbler was angry, and no need to say why. The court that heard him knew without his telling.

Nothing serves illustration, or one may fairly say nothing serves *demonstration*, better than an anecdote like this, a little moment, rightly distinguished, that can point only in one direction and from which much can be inferred. Historians may then go on to confirm their intuitions with social science findings; they may point out that it was a question of rights, on which *Common Sense* insists, and that rights meant expectancies within the terms of the prevailing ethic, at least as Hewes and his like understood it. Rights had to be observed by all. Such was the law; this was fairness, this was *reciprocity* in the term that psychologists and anthropologists use to explain what is a cross-cultural and "biological" urge, linking emotional reaction to moral values. At a still deeper level will lie the instinct for fairness.[31]

---

28 Above, chap. 3 at n. 110: Bartal et al. (2011) 1427 on "empathic concern" in humans and in rodents, with "biological roots", as an aspect of general prosocial behavior.

29 Sales in the first year (1776) between 150,000 and 500, 000, cf. Paine's own estimate of 150,000 in Hawke (1974) 47; larger sales, Kamiski (2002) 10 or Hitchens (2006) 37; a range, in Ferguson (2012) 180 and note.

30 Chap. 4 at n. 53.

31 Above, chap. 3 n. 100, on anger; Trivers (1971) 43–48 passim; Brown (1986) 575; Fry (2006) 399, on "resentment" and (399f.) "reciprocity the foundation-stone of morality" as a cross-cultural phenomenon; and Verbeek (2006) 424 (quoted, "biological link") and 439 with primatological comparisons. For the fairness instinct, see chap. 3 nn. 100ff.

Even when conclusions of this sort seem to fit so well with layman intuitions, these latter may be pursued a little differently, and with more confidence, if historians look for further understanding to the social sciences, and with their help, "touch on instincts that will be found in any social animal," as I suggested in the Preface. "Instincts are as far as the search for motivation can go."

Bibliography

Aken and Asendorpf (1996) – Aken, M. A. G. van, and J. B. Asendorpf, "Continuity of the prototypes of social competence and shyness over the life span and across life transitions," *Journal of Adult Development* 3 (1996) 205–16

Akerlof and Shiller (2009) – Akerlof, G. A., and R. J. Shiller, *Animal Spirits. How Human Psychology Drives the Economy, and Why It Matters for Global Capitalism* (Princeton)

Allport (1954) – Allport, G. W., "The historical background of modern social psychology," *The Handbook of Social Psychology*, ed. 2 (Reading MA) 1.1–80

Ames (1995) – Ames, K. M., "Chiefly power and household production in the Northwest coast," *Foundations of Social Inequality*, eds. T. D. Price and G. M. Feinman (New York/London) 155–87

Anderson et al. (1999) – Anderson, S. W., et al., "Impairment of social and moral behavior related to early damage in prefrontal cortex," *Nature Neuroscience* 2 (1999) 1032–38

Appleby et al. (1994) – Appleby, J., et al., *Telling the Truth About History* (New York/London)

Arts et al. (2003) – Arts, W., et al., eds., *The Cultural Diversity of European Unity. Findings, Explanations and Reflections from the European Values Study* (Leiden)

Arsenio et al. (2006) – Arsenio, W. F. et al., "Children's conceptions and displays of moral emotions," *Handbook of Moral Development*, eds. M. Killen and J. G. Smetana (Mahwah NJ/London) 581–609

Asendorpf (1999) – Asendorpf, J. B., "Social-personality development," *Individual Development from 3 to 12. Findings From the Munich Longitudinal Studies*, eds. F. E. Weinert and W. Schneide (Cambridge UK) 227–42

Asendorpf and Aken (1999) – Asendorpf, J. B., and M. A. G. van Aken, "Resilient, overcontrolled, and uncontrolled personality prototypes in childhood: replicability, predictive power, and the trait-type issue," *Journal of Personality and Social Psychology* 77 (1999) 815–32

Asendorpf and Weinert (1990) – Asendorpf, J. B., and F. E. Weinert,"Stability of patterns and patterns of stability in personality development," *Data Quality in Longitudinal Research*, eds. D. Magnusson and L. R. Bergman (Cambridge UK) 181–97

Atkinson (2009) – Atkinson, A. P., "Emotion," *Routledge Companion to Philosophy of Psychology*, eds. J. Symons and P. Calvo (London/New York) 543–55 Aunger (2000) – Aunger, R., "The life history of culture. Learning in a face-to-face society," *Ethos* 28 (2000) 445–81

Baldwin (2004) – Baldwin, P., "Comparing and generalizing: why all history is comparative, yet no history is sociological," *Comparison and*

History. Europe in Cross-National Perspective, eds. D. Cohen and M. O'Connor (New York/London) 1–22

Bandura and Mischel (1965) – Bandura, A., and W. Mischel, "Modification of self-imposed delay of reward through exposure to live and symbolic models," *Journal of Personality and Social Psychology* 2 (1965) 698–705

Barbalet (2008) – Barbalet, J., *Weber, Passion, and Profits. 'The Protestant Ethic and the Spirit of Capitalism' in Context* (Cambridge UK)

Barclay (1971) – Barclay, H. B., "Is there a theme of equality in the Arab rural community?" *Themes in Culture (Essays in Honor of Morris E. Opler)*, eds. M. D. Zamora et al. (Quezon City, Philippines) 285–306

Barkow et al. (1992) – Barkow, J. H., et al., eds., *The Adapted Mind. Evolutionary Psychology and the Generation of Culture* (New York/Oxford)

Barnes (1980) – Barnes, R. H., "Concordance, structure, and variation: considerations of alliance in Kédang," *The Flow of Life: Essays on Eastern Indonesia*, ed. J. J. Fox (Cambridge 1980) 68–97

Barnett (2007) – Barnett, M. A., "Moral development," *Encyclopedia of Social Psychology*, eds. R. Baumeister and K. D. Vohs (Thousand Oaks CA) 1.586–87

Barnouw (1985) – Barnouw, V., *Culture and Personality*, ed. 4 (Homewood IL)
Barraza and Zak (2009) – Barraza, J. A., and P. J. Zak, "Empathy toward strangers triggers release and subsequent generosity," *Values, Empathy, and Fairness Across Social Barriers*, eds. O. Villaroya et al. New York) 182–89
Bartal et al. (2011) – Bartal, B.-A., et al., "Empathy and pro-social behavior in rats," *Science* 334 (2011) 1427–30
Bateson (1936) – *Naven. A Survey of the Problems Suggested By a Composite Picture of the Culture of a New Guinea Tribe Drawn From Three Points of View*, ed. 2 (Stanford 1958 [1936])
Baumeister and Vohs (2003) – Baumeister, R. F., and K. D. Vohs, "Willpower, choice, and self-control," *Time and Decision. Economic and Psychological Perspectives on Intertemporal Choice*, eds. G. Loewenstein et al. (New York) 201–16
Beard (1934) – Beard, C. A., "Written history as an act of faith," *American Historical Review* 39 (1934) 219–31
Bechara and Damasio (2005) – Bechara, A., and A. Damasio, "The somatic marker hypothesis: a neural theory of economic decision," *Games and Economic Behavior* 52 (2005) 336–72
Bedford (1986) – Bedford, E., "Emotions and statements about them," *The Social Construction of Emotions*, ed. R. Harré (Oxford) 15–31
Beik (2007) – Beik, W., "The violence of the French crowd from charivari to revolution," *Past & Present* 197 (2007) 75–110
Bem (1970) – Bem, D. J., *Beliefs, Attitudes, and Human Affairs* (Belmont CA)
Benartzi and Thaler (2000) – Benartzi, S., and R. H. Thaler, "Myopic loss aversion and the equity premium puzzle," *Choices, Values, and Frames*, eds. D. Kahneman and A.Tversky (Cambridge UK) 301–16
Benedict (1934) – Benedict, R., *Patterns of Culture, with a New Preface by Margaret Mead* (Boston 1989 [1934])
Bennett (1999) – Bennett, J. W., "Classic anthropology," *American Anthropologist* 100 (1999) 951–56
Benthall (1997) – Benthall, J., "Inkeles, Alex and others, *National Character*" [review], *Journal of the Royal Anthropological Institute* 3 (1997) 612–13
Bercé (1990) – Bercé, *History of Peasant Revolts. The Social Origins of Rebellion in Early Modern France*, trans. A. Whitmore (Cambridge UK)
Bergman and Magnusson (1990) – Bergman, L. R., and D. Magnusson, "General issues about data quality in longitudinal research," *Data Quality in Longitudinal Research*, eds. D. Magnusson and L. R. Bergman (Cambridge UK) 1–31
Bergman et al. (2003) – Bergman, L., et al., *Studying Individual Development in an Interindividual Context: A Person-Oriented Approach* (Mahwah NJ)
Bergmüller and Taborsky (2010) – Bergmüller, R., and M. Taborsky, "Animal personality due to social niche specialisation," *Trends in Ecology and Evolution* 25 (2010) 504–11
Berkhofer (1981) – Berkhofer, R. F., "The North American frontier as process and context," *The Frontier in History. North America and Southern Africa Compared*, eds. H. Lamar and L. Thompson (New Haven) 43–75
Bermúdez (2009) – Bermúdez, J. L., *Decision Theory and Rationality* (Oxford)
Bernard (1945) –Bernard, J., "Observation and generalization in cultural anthropology," *Theory in Anthropology. A Sourcebook*, eds. R. A. Manners and D. Kaplan (Chicago/New York 1968 [1945]) 175–80
Berry et al. (2002) – Berry, J. W., et al., *Cross-Cultural Psychology. Research and Applications*, ed. 2 (Cambridge UK)
Bickart et al. (2010) – Bickart, K. C., et al., "Amygdala volume and social network size in humans," *Nature Neuroscience* 14 (2010) 163–64
Billington (1966) – Billington, R. A., *America's Frontier Heritage* (New York)

Billington and Ridge (1982) – Billington, R. A., and M. Ridge, *Westward Expansion. A History of the American Frontier*, ed. 5 (New York/London)
Bintliff (1991) – Bintliff, J., "The contribution of an *Annaliste*/structural historical approach to archaeology," *The* Annales *School and Archaeology*, ed. J. Bintliff (Leicester UK) 1–33
Bland (1766) – Bland, R., *An Inquiry into the Rights of the British Colonies* (Williamsburg, reprint Richmond VA 1922, ed. E. G. Swem)
Blanton (1995) – Blanton, R. E., "The cultural foundation of inequality in households," *Foundations of Social Inequality*, eds. T. D. Price and G. M. Feinman (New York/London) 105–27
Blascovich et al. (1999) – Blascovich, J., et al., "Social 'facilitation' as challenge and threat," *Journal of Personality and Social Psychology* 77 (1999) 68–77
Blossfeld (1996) – Blossfeld, H.-P., "Macro-sociology, rational choice theory, and time: a theoretical perspective on the empirical analysis of social processes," *European Sociological Review* 12 (1996) 181–206
Boas (1936) – Boas, F., "Die Individualität primitiven Kulturen," *Reine und angewandte Soziologie. Eine Festgabe für Ferdinand Tönnies* (Leipzig) 263–67
Boehm (1999) – Boehm, C., *Hierarchy in the Forest. The Evolution of Egalitarian Behavior* (Cambridge)
Bolyanatz (2004) – Bolyanatz, A. H., *Pacific Romanticism. Tahiti and the European Imagination* (Westport CT)
Boldizzoni (2011) – Boldizzoni, F., *The Poverty of Clio: Resurrecting Economic History* (Princeton)
Bond (1994) – Bond, M. H., "Into the heart of collectivism. Toward a new formulation," *Individualism and Collectivism. Theory, Method, and Applications*, eds. U. Kim et al. (Thousand Oaks CA) 66–76
Borofsky (2005) – Borofsky, R., *Yanomani. The Fierce Controversy and What We can Learn From It* (Berkeley)
Bourdieu (1977) – Bourdieu, P., *Outline of a Theory of Practice*, trans. R. Nice (Cambridge UK)
Bourguière (1982) – Bourguière, A., "The fate of the history of *mentalités* in the *Annales*," *Comparative Studies in Social History* 24 (1982) 424–37
Bourne (2006) – Bourne, R., *Cradle of Violence. How Boston's Waterfront Mobs Ignited the American Revolution* (Hoboken NJ)
Bovenberg (2003) – Bovenberg, L., "Unity produces diversity: the economics of Europe's social capital," *The Cultural Diversity of European Unity. Findings, Explanations and Reflections from the European Values Study*, eds. W. Arts et al. (Leiden) 403–19
Braudel (1972–1973) – Braudel, F., *The Mediterranean and the Mediterranean World in the Age of Philip II*, trans. S. Reynolds, 2 vols. (New York [Fr. original 1949])
Briggs (1970) – Briggs, J. L., *Never in Anger. Portrait of an Eskimo Family* (Cambridge)
Brody (1994) – Brody, N., "Traits," *Encyclopedia of Human Behavior*, ed. V. S. Ramachandran (San Diego) 4.419–25
Brosnan (2006) – Brosnan, S. F., "Nonhuman species' reactions to inequity and their implications for fairness," *Social Justice Research* 19 (2006) 153–85
Brown (2009) – Brown, D. S., *Beyond the Frontier. The Midwestern Voice in American Historical Writing* (Chicago)
Brown (1965) – Brown, R., *Social Psychology* (New York/London)
Brown (1986) – Brown, R., *Social Psychology. The Second Edition* (New York/London)
Brubaker (2004) – Brubaker, R., *Ethnicity without Groups* (Cambridge)
Buc (2001) – Buc, P., *The Danger of Ritual: Between Early Medieval Texts and Social Scientific Theory* (Princeton)
Buchanan et al. (2009) – Buchanan, T., et al., "The human amygdala in social function," *The Human Amygdala*, eds. P. J. Whalen and E. A. Phelps (New York/London) 289–318

Burguière (1982) – Burguière, A., "The fate of the history of *mentalités* in the *Annales*," *Comparative Studies in Society and History* 24 (1982) 424–37

Burke (1986) – Burke, P., "Strengths and weaknesses of the history of mentalities," *History of European Ideas* 7 (1986) 439–51

Calaresu et al. (2010) – Calaresu, M., et al., "Introduction. Peter Burke and the history of cultural history," *Exploring Cultural History. Essays in Honour of Peter Burke* (Farnham UK/Burlington VT) 1–28

Camerer et al. (2005) – Camerer, C., et al., "Neuroeconomics: how neuroscience can inform economics," *Journal of Economic Literature* 43 (2005) 9–64

Cameron (1963) – Cameron, W. B., *Informal Sociology. A Casual Introduction to Sociological Thinking* (New York)

Carp (2010) – Carp, B. L., *Defiance of the Patriots. The Boston Tea Party & the Making of America* (New Haven/London)

Caspi (1998) – Caspi, A., "Personality development across the life course," *Handbook of Child Psychology*, ed. W. Damon, ed. 5 (New York) 311–88

Chagnon (1997) – Chagnon, N. A., *Yanomamö*, ed. 5 (Ft. Worth TX 1997)

Chiao and Ambady (2007) – Chiao, J. Y., and N. Ambady, "Cultural neuroscience. Parsing universality and diversity across levels of analysis," *Handbook of Cultural Psychology*, eds. S. Kitayama and D.

Cohen (New York/London) 237–54

Coates (2012) – Coates, J., *The Hour Between Dog and Wolf. Risk Taking, Gut Feelings and the Biology of Boom and Bust* (New York)

Codere (1956) – Codere, H., "The amiable side of Kwakiutl life: the potlatch and the play potlatch," *American Anthropologist* 58 (1956) 334–51

Codol (1984) – Codol, J. P., "On the system of representations in an artificial social situation," *Social Representations*, eds. R. M. Farr and S. Moscovici (Cambridge UK) 239–53

Cohen (1997) – Cohen, D., "*Ifs* and *thens* in cultural psychology," *The Automaticity of Everyday Life*, ed. R. S. Wyer (Mahwah NJ) 121–31

Coleman (1987) – Coleman, J. S., "Norms as social capital," *Economic Imperialism. The Economic Approach Applied Outside the Fields of Economics*, eds. G. Radnitzky and P. Bernholz (New York) 133–55

Coleman (1991) – Coleman, J. S., "Comments on 'Taking interests seriously'," *Rationality and Society* 3 (1991) 500–03

Cosmides and Tooby (1992) – Cosmides, L., and J. Tooby, "Cognitive adaptations for social exchange," *The Adapted Mind. Evolutionary Psychology and the Generation of Culture*, eds. J. H. Barkow et al. (New York/Oxford) 163–228

Costa and McCrae (2008) – Costa, P. T., and R. R. McCrae, "The revised NEO personality inventory (NEO-PI-R)," *The Sage Handbook of Personality Theory and Assessment*, eds. G. J. Boyle et al. (Los Angeles) 2.179–98

Costa and McCrae (2009) – Costa, P. T., and R. R. McCrae, "The five-factor model and the NEO inventories," *Oxford Handbook of Personality Assessment*, ed. J. N. Butcher (Oxford) 298–322

Cote et al. (2012) – Cote, J., et al., "Individual sociability and choosiness between shoal types," *Animal Behaviour* 83, 6 (2012) 1469–76

Countryman (1981) – Countryman, E., *A People in Revolution: the American Revolution and Political Society in New York, 1760–1790* (Baltimore)

Countryman (1993) – Countryman, E., "'To secure the blessings of liberty'. Language, the Revolution, and American capitalism," *Beyond the American Revolution. Explorations in the History of American Radicalism*, ed. A. F. Young (De Kalb NE) 123–48

Countryman (2000) – Countryman, E., “Moral economy, political economy and the American bourgeois revolution,” *Moral Economy and Popular Protest. Crowds, Conflict and Authority*, eds. A. Randall and A. Charlesworth (New York) 146–65

Cranach (1998) – Cranach, M. von, “The knowledge of social systems,” trans. R. Morris, *The Psychology of the Social*, ed. U. Flick [*Psychologie des Sozialen*, 1995] (Cambridge UK) 15–40

Crespo (1986) – Crespo, E., “A regional variation: emotions in Spain,” *The Social Construction of Emotions*, ed. R. Harré (Oxford) 209–17

Cronon (1991) – Cronon, W., “Turner's first stand: the significance of significance in American history,” *Writing Western History. Essays on Major Western Historians*, ed. R. W. Etulain (Albuquerque) 73–101

Crook (2007) – Crook, T., *Anthropological Knowledge, Secrecy, and Bolivip, Papua New Guinea: Exchanging Skin* (Oxford)

Cushman et al. (2010) – Cushman, F., et al., “Multi-system moral psychology,” *Handbook of Moral Psychology*, eds. John Doris et al. (Oxford) 47–71

Damasio (1990) – Damasio, A. [R.], “Individuals with sociopathic behavior caused by frontal damage fail to respond autonomically to social stimuli,” *Behavioral Brain Research* (41 (1990) 81–94

Damasio (1994) – Damasio, A. [R.], *Descartes' Error. Emotion, Reason, and the Human Brain* (New York)

D'Andrade (1992) – D'Andrade, P. G., “Schemas and motivation,” *Human Motives and Cultural Models*, eds. P. G. D'Andrade and C. Strauss (Cambridge UK) 23–44

Daremberg and Saglio (1877) – Daremberg, C., and E. Saglio, *Dictionnaire des antiquités grecques et romaines d'après les textes et les monuments*, 6 vols. (Paris)

Darnton (1985) – Darnton, R., *The Great Cat Massacre and Other Episodes in French Cultural History* (New York)

Davidson (1984) – Davidson, R. J., “Affect, cognition, and hemispheric specialization,” *Emotions, Cognition, and Behavior*, eds. C. E. Izard et al. (Cambridge UK) 320–65

Davidson (2003) – Davidson, R. J., “Darwin and the neural bases of emotion and affective style,” *Annals of the New York Academy of Science* 1000 (2003) 316–36

Davis (1988) – Davis, N. [Z.], “On the lame,” *American Historical Review* 93 (1988) 572–603

Dawkins (2005) – Dawkins, R., “The science of religion. The religion of science,” *Tanner Lectures on Human Values* 25, ed. G. B. Peterson (Salt Lake City UT) 43–76

Demos (1998) – Demos, J., “In search of reasons for historians to read novels,” *American Historical Review* 103 (1998) 1526–29

Demsetz (1996) – Demsetz, H., “Rationality, evolution and acquisitiveness,” *Economic Inquiry* 34 (1996) 484–95

Devine (2012) – Devine, D. J., *Jury Decision Making. The State of the Science* (New York/London) de Waal, see Waal, F. M. B. de Diaz-Guerrero and Diaz-Loving (1994) – Diaz-Guerrero, R., and R. Diaz-Loving, “Personality across cultures,” *Cross-Cultural Topics in Psychology*, eds. L. L. Adler and U. P. Gielen (Westport CT) 125–38

Dienstbier (1984) – Dienstbier, R. A., “The role of emotion in moral socialization,” *Emotions, Cognition, and Behavior*, eds. C. E. Izard et al. (Cambridge UK) 483–514

Dirlik (1996) – Dirlik, A., “The past as legacy and project: postcolonial criticism in the perspective of indigenous historicism,” *American Indian Culture and Research Journal* 20, 2 (1996) 1–31

Dolan (1999) – Dolan, R. J., “On the neurology of morals,” *Nature Neuroscience* 2 (1999) 927–29

Donnellan (2009) – Donnellan, M. B., “Introduction to personality assessment at age 40: reflections on the legacy of the person-situation debate and the future of person-situation integration,” *Journal of Research in Personality* 43 (2009) 117–19

Dülmen (1988) – Dülmen, R. van, “Protestantismus und Kapitalismus. Max Webers These im Licht der neueren Sozialgeschichte,” *Max Weber. Ein Symposium*, eds. C. Gneuss and C. Kocka (München) 88–101

Durkheim (1982) – Durkheim, E., *The Rules of Sociological Method*, ed. S. Lukes, trans. W. D. Halls (New York)

Dwight (1969) – Dwight, T., *Travels in New England and New York*, ed. B. M. Solomon, 4 vols. (Cambridge)

Eagley (2007) – Eagley, A. H., "The advantages of an inclusive definition of attitude," *Social Cognition* 25 (2007) 582–602

Eatwell et al. (1987) – Eatwell, J., et al., eds., *The New Palgrave. A Dictionary of Economics*, 4 vols. (London)

Eggan (1954) – Eggan, F., "Social anthropology and the method of controlled comparison," *Theory in Anthropology. A Sourcebook*, eds. R. A. Manners and D. Kaplan (Chicago/New York 1968 [1954]) 54–66

Ehrlich (2000) – Ehrlich, P. R., *Human Natures: Genes, Culture, and the Human Prospect* (Washington DC)

Ekman (1992) – Ekman, P., "Facial expressions of emotion. New findings, new questions," *Psychological Science* 3 (1992) 34–38

Eliaeson (2000) – Eliaeson, S., "Max Weber's methodology: an ideal-type," *Journal of the History of Behavioral Sciences* 36 (2000) 241–63

Ellsworth (1994) – Ellsworth, P. C., "Sense, culture, and sensibility," *Emotion and Culture. Empirical Studies of Mutual Influence*, eds. S. Kitayama and H. R. Markus (Washington DC) 23–50

Elster (1999) – Elster, J., *Strong Feelings. Emotions, Addiction, and Human Behavior* (Cambridge UK)

Elster (1999a) – Elster, J., *Alchemies of the Mind. Rationality and the Emotions* (Cambridge UK)

Emler (1987) – Emler, N., "Socio-moral development from the perspective of social representations," *Journal of the Theory of Social Behaviour* 17 (1987) 371–88

Epstein (1979) – Epstein, S., "The stability of behavior: I, On predicting most of the people much of the time," *Journal of Personality and Social Psychology* 37 (1979) 1097–1126

Epstein (1980) – Epstein, S., "The stability of behavior: II, Implications for psychological research," *American Psychologist* 35 (1980) 790–806

Epstein (1984) – Epstein, S., "The stability of behavior across time and situations," *Personality and the Prediction of Behavior*, eds. R. A. Zucker et al. (Orlando FL) 209–68

Epstein (1994) – Epstein, S., "Integration of the cognitive and the psychodynamic unconscious," *American Psychologist* 49 (1994) 709–24

Eustace (2008) – Eustace, N., *Passion Is the Gale. Emotion, Power, and the Coming of the American Revolution* (Chapel Hill)

Evans-Pritchard (1940) – Evans-Pritchard, E. E., *The Nuer. A Description of the Modes of Livelihood and Political Institutions of a Nilotic People* (Oxford).

Evans-Pritchard (1962) – Evans-Pritchard, E. E., "Social anthropology: past and present," *Theory in Anthropology. A Sourcebook*, eds. R. A. Manners and D. Kaplan (Chicago/New York 1968 [1962]) 46–54

Farr (1984) – Farr, R. M., "Social representations: their role in the design and execution of laboratory experiments," *Social Representations*, eds. R. M. Farr and S. Moscovici (Cambridge UK) 125–47

Farr (1987) – Farr, R. [M.], "Social representations: a French tradition of research," *Journal of the Theory of Social Behaviour* 17 (1987) 343–69

Febvre (1973) – Febvre, L., *A new Kind of History from the Writings of Febvre*, ed. P. Burke, trans. K. Folca (New York)

Feil (1988) – Feil, D. K., "The morality of exchange," *Choice and Morality in Anthropological Perspective. Essays in Honor of Derek Freeman*, eds. G. N. Appell and T. N. Madan (Albany) 99–109

Ferguson (2012) – Ferguson, R. A., "The commonalities of *Common Sense*," *Thomas Paine,* Common Sense *and Other Writings*, ed. J. M. Opal (New York/ London) 179–218

Fernández-Armesto (2009) – Fernández-Armesto, F., "History beyond history: new adventurers on the frontiers of traditional historiography. A review essay," *Comparative Studies in Society and History* 51 (2009) 212–19

Festugière (1970) – Festugière, A.-J., *Vie de Théodore de Sykéon*, 2 vols. (Brussels)

Finlay (1988) – Finlay, R., "The refashioning of Martin Guerre," *American Historical Review* 93 (1988) 553–71

Fischer (1994) – Fischer, D. H., *Paul Revere's Ride* (New York/Oxford)

Fish (2000) – Fish, J. M., "What anthropology can do for psychology: facing physics envy, ethnocentrism, and a belief in 'race'," *American Anthropologist* 102 (2000) 552–63

Fisher (1936) – Fisher, H. A. L., *A History of Europe* (London)

Fiske (1992) – Fiske, A. P., "The four elementary forms of sociality: framework for a unified theory of social relations," *Psychological Review* 99 (1992) 689–723

Fleisher (2000) – "Kuria cattle raiding: capitalist transformation, commoditization, and crime formation among an East African agro-pastoral people," *Comparative Studies in Society and History* 42 (2000) 745–69

Fogel (1989) – Fogel, R. W., *Without Consent or Contract. The Rise and Fall of American Slavery* (New York/London)

Fogel (2003) – Fogel, R. W., *The Slavery Debates, 1952–1990. A Retrospective* (Baton Rouge LA)Fogel and Engerman (1974) – Fogel, R. W., and S. L. Engerman, *Time on the Cross. The Economics of American Negro Slavery* (Boston/Toronto)

Fogel and Engerman (1974a) – Fogel, R. W., and S. L. Engerman, *Time on the Cross. Evidence and Methods – A Supplement* (Boston/Toronto)

Forgas (1995) – Forgas, J. P., "Mood and judgment: the affect infusion model (AIM)," *Psychological Bulletin* 117 (1995) 39–66

Forgas (2001) – Forgas, J. P., "Introduction: affect and social cognition," *Handbook of Affect and Social Cognition*, ed. J. P. Forgas (Mahwah NJ) 1–24

Fortes and Evans-Pritchard (1940) – Fortes, M., and E. E. Evans-Pritchard, "Introduction," *African Political Systems*, eds. M. Fortes and E. E. Evans-Pritchard (Oxford) 1–23

Frank (1988) – Frank, R. H., *Passions Within Reason. The Strategic Role of the Emotions* (New York/London)

Franke et al. (1991) – Franke, R. H., et al., "Cultural roots of economic performance: a research note," *Strategic Management Journal* 12 (1991) 163–73

Frazer (1935) – Frazer, J. G., *The Golden Bough*, ed. 3, 12 vols (New York)

Frazer (1959) – Frazer, J. G., *The New Golden Bough. An Abridgement of the Classic Work*, ed. T. H. Gaster (New York)

Freeman (1983) – Freeman, D., *Margaret Mead and Samoa. The Making and Unmaking of an Anthropological Myth* (Cambridge)

Freidin and Kacelnik (2011) – Freidin, E., and A. Kacelnik, "Rational choice, context dependence, and the value of information in European starlings," *Science* 334 (2011) 1000–02

Friedman and Martin (2011) – Friedman, H. S., and I. R. Martin, *The Longevity Project* (New York)

Fry (2006) – Fry, D. P., "Reciprocity: the foundation stone of morality," *Handbook of Moral Development*, eds. M. Killen and J. G. Smetana (Mahwah NJ/London) 399–423

Furnham (1990) – Furnham, A., *The Protestant Work Ethic. The Psychology of Work-related Beliefs and Behaviours* (London/New York)

Gaddis (2002) – Gaddis, J. L., *The Landscape of History. How Historians Map the Past* (Oxford)

Gammage (2011) – Gammage, B., *The Biggest Estate on Earth. How Aborigines Made Australia* (Sydney)

Gazzaniga (2011) – Gazzaniga, M. S., *Who's In Charge? Freee Will and the Science of the Brain* (New York)

Geen (1995) – Geen, R. G., "Social motivation," *Emotion and Motivation*, eds. B. Parkinson and A. M. Colman (London/New York) 38–56

Geertz (1960) – Geertz, C., *The Religion of Java* (London)

Genovese (1989) – Genovese, E. D., *The Political Economy of Slavery. Studies in the Economy & Society of the Slave South*, ed. 2 (Middletown CT)

Gilje (1987) – Gilje, P. A., *The Road to Mobocracy. Popular Disorder in New York City, 1763–1834* (Chapel Hill NC)

Giordano (2005) – Giordano, C., "The past in the present. Actualized history in the social construction of reality," *Critical Junctions. Anthropology and History Beyond the Cultural Turn*, eds. D. Kalb and H. Tak (New York/ Oxford) 53–71

Gluckman (1965) – Gluckman, M., *Politics, Law and Ritual in Tribal Society* (Chicago)

Goldfield (2011) – Goldfield, D., *America Aflame. How the Civil War Created a Nation* (New York/ Berlin)

Goodenough and Cheney (2008) – Goodenough, O., and M. G. Cheney, "Preface," *Moral Markets. The Critical Role of Values in the Economy* (Princeton) xxiii-xxx

Goodman (2003) – Goodman, J. E., "The proverbial Bourdieu: habitus and the polictics of representation in the ethnography of Kabylia," *American Anthropologist* 105 (2003) 782–93

Goody (1991) – Goody, E. [N.], "The learning of prosocial behaviour in small-scale egalitarian societies: an anthropological view," *Cooperation and Prosocial Behaviour*, eds. R. A. Hinde and G. Groebel (Cambridge UK) 106–28

Goody (1992) – Goody, E. N., *Parenthood and Social Reproduction. Fostering and Occupational Roles in West Africa* (Cambridge UK)

Goody (2006) – Goody, J., *The Theft of History* (Cambridge UK)

Gordon (2004) – Gordon, D. M., "The cultural politics of a traditional ceremony: Mutomboko and the performance of history on the Luapula (Zambia)," *Comparative Studies in Society and History* 46 (2004) 63–83

Gordon-Reed (2008) – Gordon-Reed, A., *The Hemingses of Monticello. An American Family* (New York/London)

Gottlieb (2000) – Gottlieb, A., "Luring your child into this life. A Beng path for infant care," *A World of Babies. Imagined Childcare Guides for Seven Societies*, eds. J. S. De Loche and A. Gottlieb (Cambridge UK) 55–89

Gouldner and Peterson (1962) – Gouldner, A. W., and R. A. Peterson, *Technology and the Moral Order* (Indianapolis/New York)

Granato et al. (1996) – Granato, J., et al., "The effect of cultural values on economic development: theory, hypotheses, and some empirical tests," *American Journal of Political Science* 40 (1996) 607–31

Grant (1952) – Grant, R. M., *Miracle and Natural Law in Graeco-Roman and Early Christian Thought* (Amsterdam)

Gray (1987) – Gray, J. [N.], "The economic approach to human behavior: its prospects and limitations," *Economic Imperialism. The Economic Approach Applied Outside the Fields of Economics*, eds. G. Radnitzky and P. Bernholz (New York) 33–49

Greene and Haidt (2002) – Greene, J., and J. Haidt, "How (and where?) does moral judgment work?" *Trends in Cognitive Sciences* 6 (2002) 517–323

Greene et al. (2004) – Greene, J. D., et al. "The neural bases of cognitive conflict and control in moral judgment," *Neuron* 44 (2004) 389–400

Greenspan (2013) – Greenspan, A., *The Map and the Territory. Risk, Human Nature, and the Future of Forecasting* (New York)

Gregor and Gross (2004) – Gregor, Thomas A., and Daniel R Gross, "Guilt by Association: The Culture of Accusation and The American Anthropological Association's Investigation of *Darkness in El Dorado*," *American Anthropologist* 106 (2004) 687–98

Grize et al. (1987) – Grize, J.-B., et al., *Salariés face aux nouvelles technologies* (Paris)
Guimelli (1999) – Guimelli, C., *La pensée sociale* (Paris)
Gulliver (1963) – Gulliver, P. H., *Social Control in an African Society: A Study of the Arusha: Agricultural Masai of Northern Tanganyika* (Boston)
Gutman (1975) – Gutman, H. G., *Slavery and the Numbers Game: A critique of Time on the Cross* (Urbana IL)
Haidt (2001) – Haidt, J., "The emotional dog and its rational tail: a social intuitionist approach to moral judgment," *Psychology Review* 108 (2001) 814–34
Haidt (2012) – Haidt, J., *The Righteous Mind. Why Good People Are Divided by Politics and Religion* (New York)
Haidt and Kesebir (2010) – Haidt, J., and S. Kesebir, "Morality," *Handbook of Social Psychology*, ed. 5, eds. S. Fiske et al. (Hoboken NJ) 797–832
Haidt et al. (1993) – Haidt, J., et al., "Affect, culture, and morality, or is it wrong to eat your dog?" *Journal of Personality and Social Psychology* 65 (1993) 613–28
Hall and Farkas (2011) – Hall, M., and Farkas, G., "Adolescent cognitive skills, attitudinal/behavioral traits and career wages," *Social Forces* 89 (2011) 1261–85
Hallowell (1955) – Hallowell, A. I., *Culture and Experience* (Philadelphia)
Halman et al. (2005) – Halman, L., et al., *Atlas of European Values* (Leiden)
Harbaugh et al. (2007) – Harbaugh, W. T., et al., "Neural responses to taxation and voluntary giving reveal motives for charitable donations," *Science* 316 (2007) 1622–25
Hare and Tomasello (2005) – Hare, B., and M. Tomasello, "Human-like social skills in dogs?" *Trends in Cognitive Science* 9 (2005) 439–44
Harré (1986) – Harré, R., "An outline of the social constructionist viewpoint," *The Social Construction of Emotions*, ed. R. Harré (Oxford) 2–14
Harris (1995) – Harris, J. R., "Where is the child's environment? A group socialization theory of development," *Psychological Review* 102 (1995) 458–89
Harris (1984) – Harris, M., "A cultural materialist theory of band and village warfare: the Yanomamo test," *Warfare, Culture, and Environment*, ed. R. B. Ferguson (Orlando FL) 111–40
Hastie (1993) – Hastie, R., "Introduction," *Inside the Juror. The Psychology of Juror Decision Making*, ed. R. Hastie (Cambridge UK) 3–41
Hastings et al. (2006) – Hastings, P. D., et al., "We are, by nature, moral creatures: biological bases of concern for others," *Handbook of Moral Development*, eds. M. Killen and J. G. Smetana (Mahwah NJ/London) 483–516
Hawke (1974) – Hawke, D. F., *Paine* (New York)
Hayden (1995) – Hayden, B., "Pathways to power. Principles for creating socioeconomic inequality," *Foundations of Social Inequality*, eds. T. D. Price and G. M. Feinman (New York/London) 15–86
Helbling (2006) – Helbling, J., *Tribale Kriege. Konflikte im Gesellschaften ohne Zentralgewalt* (Frankfurt/New York)
Helmstaedter (2013) – Helmstaedter, M., "Cellular-resolution connectomics: challenges of dense neural circuit reconstruction," *Nature Methods* 10, 6 (2013) 501–07
Helwig (2006) – Helwig, C. C., "Rights, civil liberties, and democracy across cultures," *Handbook of Moral Development*, eds. M. Killen and J. G. Smetana (Mahwah NJ/London) 185–210
Henrich (2005) – Henrich, J., "'Economic man' in cross-cultural perspective: behavioral experiments in 15 small-scale societies," *Behavioral and Brain Sciences* 28 (2005) 795–814
Henry (1994) – Henry, R. M., "The fetters of continuity: a critique of Bourdieu and Giddens," *Anthropology UCLA* 21 (1994) 89–105
Hermann (1995) – Hermann, E., *Emotionen und Historizität. Der emotionalen Diskurs über die Yal-Bewegung in einer Dorfgemeinschaft der Ngaing, Papua New Guinea* (Berlin)
Hertwig and Herzog (2009) – Hertwig, R., and S. M. Herzog, "Fast and frugal heuristics: tools of social rationality," *Social Cognition* 27 (2009) 661–98

Higgins et al. (2008) – Higgins, E. T., et al., "Re-thinking culture and personality: how self-regulatory universals create cross-cultural differences," *Handbook of Motivation and Cognition Across Cultures*, eds. R. M. Sorrentino and S. Yamaguchi (San Diego) 161–90

Hill (1961) – Hill, J. E. C., "Notes and comments," *Past & Present* 20 (1961) 3–5

Hill and Lapsley (2009) – Hill, P. L., and D. K. Lapsley, "Persons and situations in the moral domain," *Journal of Research in Personality* 43 (2009) 245–46

Himmelfarb (2004) – Himmelfarb, G., *The New History and the Old: Critical Essays and Reappraisals*, ed.2 revised (Cambridge)

Hinde (1996) – Hinde, R. A., "The interpenetration of biology and culture," *The Lifespan Development of Individuals: Behavioral, Neurobiological, and Psychosocial Perspectives*, ed. D. Magnusson (Cambridge UK) 359–75

Hinde (2002) – Hinde, R. A., *Why Good is Good. The Sources of Morality* (London/New York)

Hirshleifer (1993) – Hirshleifer, J., "The affections and the passions," *Rationality and Society* 5 (1993) 185–202

Hitchens (2006) – Hitchens, C., *Thomas Paine's* Rights of Man. *Biography* (New York)

Hoerder (1977) – Hoerder, D., *Crowd Action in Revolutionary Massachusetts 1765–1780* (New York/ London)

Hofer and Bond (2008) – Hofer, J., and M. H. Bond, "Do implicit motives add to our understanding of psychological and behavioral outcomes within and across cultures?" *Handbook of Motivation and Cognition Across Cultures*, eds. R. M. Sorrentino and S. Yamaguchi (San Diego) 95–118

Hofstede (1994) – Hofstede, G., "Foreword," *Individualism and Collectivism. Theory, Method, and Applications*, eds. U. Kim et al. (Thousand Oaks CA) ix-xiii

Hofstede (2002) – Hofstede, G., "Culture does not exist," *Center for Intercultural Learning Magazine* 2002 no. 3, www.interculturals.gc.ca

Hofstede (2002a) – Hofstede. G., "Dimensions do not exist: a reply to Brendan McSweeney," *Human Relations* 55 (2002) 1355–61

Hogan (2009) – Hogan, R., "Much ado about nothing: the person-situation debate," *Journal of Research in Personality* 43 (2009) 249.

Hogbin (1970) – Hogbin, H. I., *Experiment in Civilization. The Effects of European Culture on a Native Community of the Solomon Islands* (New York)

Hollan (1988) – Hollan, D., "Staying 'cool' in Toraja: informal strategies for the management of anger and hostility in a nonviolent society," *Ethos* 16 (1988) 52–72

Holt (2012) – Holt, M. P., "Religious violence in sixteenth-century France: moving beyond pollution and purification," *Rites and Ritual, Past & Present* 214 *Supplement* 7 (2012) 52–74

Hopkins (1765) – Hopkins, S., *The Rights of Colonies Examined* (Providence RI)

Hume (1987) – Hume, D., *Essays Moral, Political, and Literary*, ed. E. F. Miller, revised ed. (Indianapolis IN)

Hunt (1989) – Hunt, L. [A.], "Introduction: history, culture, and text," *The New Cultural History*, ed. L. Hunt (Berkeley) 1–24

Inbar et al. (2009) – Inbar, Y., et al., "Conservatives are more easily disgusted than liberals," *Cognition and Emotion* 23 (2009) 714–25

Inglehart et al. (1998) – Inglehart, R., et al., *Human Values and Beliefs: A Cross-cultural Sourcebook. Political, Religious, Sexual, and Economic Norms in 43 Societies: Findings from the 1990–1993 World Values Survey* (Ann Arbor MI)

Inglehart et al. (2000) – Inglehart, R., et al.,*World Values Surveys and European Values Surveys, 1981–1984, 1990–1993, and 1995–1997* (Ann Arbor MI) [computer file]

Iyengar and Lepper (1999) – Iyengar, S. S., and M. R. Lepper, "Rethinking the value of choice: a cultural perspective on intrinsic motivation," *Journal of Personality and Social Psychology* 76 (1999) 349–66

Izard (1984) – Izard, C. E., "Emotion-cognition relationships and human development," *Emotions, Cognition, and Behavior*, eds. C. E. Izard et al. (Cambridge UK) 17–37

Izard et al. (1984) – Izard, C. E., et al., "Introduction," *Emotions, Cognition, and Behavior*, eds. C. E. Izard et al. (Cambridge UK) 1–14

Jackson (2006) – Jackson, M., "Personality traits and occupational attainment," *European Sociological Review* 22 (2006) 187–99

Jennings et al. (1982) – Jennings, D. L., et al., "Informal covariation assessment: data-based versus theory-based judgments," *Judgement Under Uncertainty: Heuristics and Biases*, eds. D. Kahneman and A. Tversky (Cambridge UK) 212–30

Jodelet (1991) – Jodelet, D., *Madness and Social Representations*, trans. T. Pownell (New York/ London 1991 [1989])

Jones (1971) – Jones, G. I., "Councils among the central Ibo," *Councils in Action*, eds. A. Richards and A. Kuper (Cambridge UK) 63–79

Just (1991) – Just, P., "Going through the emotions: passion, violence, and 'other'-control among the Dou-Donggo," *Ethos* 19 (1991) 288–312

Kahneman (2000) – Kahneman, D., "New challenges to the rationality assumption," *Choices, Values, and Frames*, eds. D. Kahneman and A. Tversky (Cambridge UK) 758–74

Kahneman (2002) – Kahneman, D., "Maps of bounded rationality: a perspective on intuitive judgment and choice," *The Sveriges Rijksbank Prize in Economic Sciences in Memory of Alfred Nobel [Prize Lecture] in the Proceedings of the Award*, 449–89

Kahneman (2011) – Kahneman, D., *Thinking, Fast and Slow* (New York)

Kahneman and Tversky (1973) – Kahneman, D., and A. Tversky, "On the psychology of prediction," *Psychological Review* 80 (1973) 237–51

Kahneman and Tversky (1974) – Kahneman, D., and A. Tversky, "Judgment under uncertainty; heuristics and biases," *Science* 185 (1974) 1124–31

Kahneman and Tversky (1979) – Kahneman, D., and A. Tversky, "Prospect theory: an analysis of decision under risk," *Econometrica* 47 (1979) 263–81

Kahneman and Tversky (1982) – Kahneman, D., and A. Tversky, "The psychology of preferences. When people make risky choices, they often do not do so objectively. Experimental surveys indicate that such departures from objectivity tend to follow regular patterns that can be described mathematically," *Scientific American* 246 (1982) 160–171

Kahneman and Tversky (1982a) – Kahneman, D., and A. Tversky, "The simulation heuristic," *Judgment Under Uncertainty: Heuristics and Biases*, eds. D. Kahneman et al. (Cambridge UK) 201–08

Kahneman et al. (2000) – Kahneman, D., et al., "Fairness as a constraint on profit seeking entitlement in the market," *Choices, Values, and Frames*, eds. D. Kahneman and A. Tversky (Cambridge UK) 317–34

Kamiski (2002) – Kamiski, J. P., ed., *Citizen Paine. Thomas Paines' Thoughts on Man, Government, Society, and Religion* (Lanham MD)

Kapferer (2002) – "Ethnicity, nationalism and the culture of the state," *Suomen Antropologi* 2 (2002) 4–25

Kaplan (1954) – Kaplan, B., "Personality and social structure," *Theory in Anthropology. A Sourcebook*, eds. R. A. Manners and D. Kaplan (Chicago/New York 1968 [1954]) 318–42

Kashima and Kashima (2003) – Kashima, Y., and E. S. Kashima, "Individualism, GNP, climate, and pronoun drop. Is individualism deteremined by affluence and climate, or does language play a role?" *Journal of Cross-Cultural Psychology* 34 (2003) 125–34

Keith (2011) – Keith, K. D., "Ethnocentrism: seeing the world from where we stand," *Cross-Cultural Psychology. Contemporary Themes and Perspectives*, ed. K. D. Keith (Malden MA) 20–33

Kelly (2006) – Kelly, I., *Beau Brummell the Ultimate Man of Style* (New York/London)

Kemper (1978) – Kemper, T. D., *A Social Interactional Theory of Emotions* (New York)

Kenrick et al. (2009) – Kenrick, D. T., *et al.*, "Deep rationality: the evolutionary economics of decision makiing," *Social Cognition* 27 (2009) 764–85

Keynes (1973) – Keynes, J. M., *The Collected Writings of John Maynard Keynes*, vol. VII: *The General Theory of Employment Interest and Money* (Cambridge UK)

Khilji et al. (2011) – Khilji, S. E., et al. "Maintaining the 'Single Samsung' spirit: new challenges in a changing environment," *Business Case Study 8 July 2011* (Iveycases.com, Richard Ivey Publishing, London ON CA)

Killen et al. (2006) – Killen, M., et al., "Morality in the context of intergroup relationships," *Handbook of Moral Development*, eds. M. Killen and J. G. Smetana (Mahwah NJ/London) 155–83

Kim and Park (2008) – Kim, U., and Y.-S. Park, "Cognitive, relational and social basis of academic achievement in Confucian cultures: psychological, indigenous, and cultural perspectives," *Handbook of Motivation and Cognition Across Cultures*, eds. R. M. Sorrentino and S. Yamaguchi (San Diego) 491–515

Kim et al. (1994) – Kim, U., et al., eds., *Individualism and Collectivism. Theory, Method, and Applications* (Thousand Oaks CA)

Kim et al. (1994a) – Kim, U., et al., "Introduction", *Individualism and Collectivism. Theory, Method, and Applications,* eds. U. Kim et al. (Thousand Oaks CA) 1–16

Kitayama et al. (2000) – Kitayama, S., et al., "Culture, emotion, and well-being: good feelings in Japan and the U.S.," *Cognition and Emotion* 14 (2000) 93–124

Kitayama et al. (2007) – Kitayama, S., et al., "Self as cultural mode of being," *Handbook of Cultural Psychology*, eds. S. Kitayama and D. Cohen (New York/London) 136–74

Kitcher (1995) – Kitcher, P., "The hypothalmic imperative," *Issues in Evolutionary Ethics*, ed. P. Thompson (Albany) 203–23

Kluckhohn and Strodtbeck (1961) – Kluckhohn, F. R., and F. L. Strodtbeck, *Variations in Value Orientations* (Chicago)

Knauft (1985) – Knauft, B. M., *Good Company and Violence. Sorcery and Social Action in a Lowland New Guinea Society* (Berkeley)

Knauft (1987) – Knauft, B. M., "Reconsidering violence in simple human societies. Homicide among the Gebusi of New Guinea," *Current Anthropology* 28 (1987) 457–82, 493–500; Comments and Reply, 482–493

Kohlberg and Turiel (1971) – Kohlberg, L., and E. Turiel, "Moral development and moral education," *Psychology and Educational Practice*, ed. G. Lesser (Glenview IL/London) 410–65

Kopcke et al. (2004) – Kopcke, R. W., et al., "How humans behave: implications for economics and economic policy," *New England Economic Review* 2004, 1–31

Kosfeld et al. (2005) – Kosfeld, M., et al., "Oxytocin increases trust in humans," *Nature* 435 (2005) 673–676

Kottak (1983) – Kottak, C. P., *Assault on Paradise. Social Change in a Brazilian Village* (New York)

Kousser (1980) – Kousser, J. M., "Quantitative social-scientific history," *The Past Before Us. Contemporary Historical Writing in the United States*, ed. M. Kammen (Ithaca/London) 433–56

Kousser (1993) – Kousser, J. M., "Ignoble intentions and noble dreams: on relativism and history with a purpose," *The Public Historian* 15, 3 (1993) 15–28

Kousser (1999) – Kousser, J. M., *Colorblind Injustice. Minority Voting Rights and the Undoing of the Second Reconstruction* (Chapel Hill NC)

Kroeber and Kluckhohn (1952) – Kroeber, A. L., and C. Kluckhohn, *Culture. A Critical Review of Concepts and Definitions* (Cambridge)

Krueger (2009) – Krueger, J. I., "Rationality restored: an introduction to the special issue," *Social Cognition* 27, 5 (2009) 635–38

Kruglanski and Orehek (2009) – Kruglanski, A. W., and E. Orehek, "Toward a relativity theory of rationality," *Social Cognition* 27 (2009) 639–60

Kürnberger (1890) – Kürnberger, F., *Der Amerikamüde* (Leipzig 1890 [1855])

Kulikoff (1993) – Kulikoff, A., "The American Revolution, capitalism, and the formation of the yeoman class," *Beyond the American Revolution. Explorations in the History of American Radicalism*, ed. A. F. Young (De Kalb NE) 80–119

Kumar (2008) – Kumar, S. K. K., "Indian thought and tradition: a psychohistorical perspective," *Handbook of Indian Psychology*, eds. K. K. Rao et al. (Delhi) 19–52

Kuper (1996) – Kuper, A., *Anthropology and Anthropologists. The Modern British School*, ed. 3 (London/New York)

Labaree and Bell (1959–2011) – Labaree, L. W., and W. J. Bell, *The Papers of Benjamin Franklin* (New Haven)

Laitin and Gordon (1998) – Laitin, D. D., and S. M. Gordon, "National Character: A Psychosocial Perspective. By Alex Inkeles," *Journal of Interdisciplinary History* 3 (1998) 429–31

Landes (1998) – Landes, D. S., *The Wealth and Poverty of Nations. Why Some Are So Rich and Some So Poor* (New York/London)

Lang (1984) – Lang, P. J., "Cognition in emotion: concept and action," *Emotions, Cognition, and Behavior*, eds. C. E. Izard et al. (Cambridge UK) 192–226

Lapsley (2006) – Lapsley, D. K., "Moral stage theory," *Handbook of Moral Development*, eds. M. Killen and J. G. Smetana (Mahwah NJ/London) 37–66

Lass (1995) –Lass, A., "'What are we like?' National character and the aesthetics of distinction in interwar Czechoslovakia," *National Character and National Ideology in Interwar Eastern Europe*, eds. I. Banac and K. Verdery (New Haven) 39–64

Lawrence (1988) – Lawrence, P., "Corpus morale collectivum: social anthropology without tears?" *Choice and Morality in Anthropological Perspective. Essays in Honor of Derek Freeman*, eds. G. N. Appell and T. N. Maden (Albany NY) 69–98

Leary and Allen (2011) – Leary, M. R., and A. B. Allen, "Belonging motivation: establishing, maintaining, and repairing relational value," *Social Motivation*, ed. D. Dunning (New York/London) 37–55

Lehman et al. (2004) – Lehman, D. R., et al., "Psychology and culture," *American Review of Psychology* 55 (2004) 689–714

Lehman and Witty (1946) – Lehman, H. C., and P. A. Witty, "Faculty psychology and personality traits," *American Journal of Psychology* 34 (1946) 486–500

Lehmann (2005) – Lehmann, H., "Friends and foes. The formation and consolidation of the *Protestant Ethic* thesis," *The Protestant Ethic Turns 100. Essays on the Centenary of the Weber Thesis*, eds. W. H. Swatos and L. Kaelber (Boulder CO/London) 1–22

Lehrer (2009) – Lehrer, J., "Don't! The secret of self-control," *The New Yorker* May 18, 2009, 26–32

Lemisch (1968) – Lemisch, J., "Jack Tar in the streets: merchant seamen in the politics of revolutionary America," *William and Mary Quarterly* 25 (1968) 371–407

Leonardo (2003) – Leonardo, M. di, "Margaret Mead and the culture of forgetting in anthropology: a response to Paul Roscoe," *American Anthropologist* 105 (2003) 592–95

Leontief (1982) – Leontief, W., "Academic economics," *Science* 217 (1982) 104–05

Leung and Bond (2009) – Leung, K., and M. H. Bond, "Introduction," *Psychological Aspects of Social Axioms. Understanding Global Belief Systems*, eds. K. Leung and M. H. Bond (New York) 1–9

Levenson (1992) – Levenson, R. W., "Autonomic nervous system differences among emotions," *Psychological Science* 3 (1992) 23–27

Levine (2003) – Levine, B., "Introduction to the 2003 paperback. Horatio Alger in the cotton fields? Herbert Gutman and the debate over slave consciousness," in Gutman, H. G., *Slavery and the Numbers Game: A critique of Time on the Cross* (reprint [Urbana IL 1975]) xi-xx

LeVine (1984) – LeVine, R. A., "Properties of culture. An ethnographic view," *Culture Theory. Essays on Mind, Self, and Emotion*, eds. R. A. Shweder and R. A. LeVine (Cambridge UK) 67–87

Levy et al. (2006) – Levy, S., et al., "The Protestant work ethic: a lay theory with dual intergroup implications," *Group Processes & Intergroup Relations* 9 (2006) 95–115

Lévy-Bruhl (1985) – L. Lévy-Bruhl, *How Natives Think*, trans. L. A. Clare (Princeton)

Liem et al. (2009) – Liem, A. D., et al., "Do general beliefs predict specific behavioral intentions in Indonesia? The role of social axioms within the theory of planned behavior," *Psychological Aspects of Social Axioms. Understanding Global Belief Systems*, eds. K. Leung and M. H. Bond (New York) 217–38

Littleton (1985) – Littleton, C. S., "Introduction," in L. Lévy-Bruhl, *How Natives Think*, trans. L. A. Clare (Princeton) v-lviii

Lloyd (1990) – Lloyd, G. E. R., *Demystifying Mentalities* (Cambridge UK)

Lo Monaco (2009) – Lo Monaco, G., *Les représentations sociales du vin* (Lille)

Loewenstein et al. (2001) – Loewenstein, G. F., et al., "Risk as feelings," *Psychological Bulletin* 127 (2001) 267–86

Löckenhoff and Costa (2007) – Löckenhoff, C. E., and P. T. Costa, "Big Five personality traits," *Encyclopedia of Social Psychology*, eds. R. E. Baumeister and K. D. Vohs (Thousand Oaks CA) 1.115–17

Lüdtke (1986) – Lüdtke, A., "Cash, coffee-breaks, horseplay: Eigensinn and politics among factory workers in Germany circa 1900," *Confrontation, Class Consciousness, and the Labor Process. Studies in Proletarian Class Formation*, eds. M. Hanagan and C. Stephenson (Westport CT) 65–95

Lutz (1985) – Lutz, C., "Ethnopsychology compared to what? Explaining behavior and consciousness among the Ifaluk," *Person, Self, and Experience. Exploring Pacific Ethnopsychologies*, eds. G. M. White and J. Kirkpatrick (Berkeley) 35–79

Lutz (1988) – Lutz, C. A., *Unnatural Emotions. Everyday Sentiments on a Micronesian Atoll & Their Challenge to Western Theory* (Chicago)

MacMullen (1990) – MacMullen, R., *Changes in the Roman Empire. Essays in the Ordinary* (Princeton)

MacMullen (1997) – MacMullen, R., *Christianity and Paganism in the Fourth to Eighth Centuries* (New Haven; e-book 2012)

MacMullen (1997a) – MacMullen, R., *Sisters of the Brush. Their Family, Art, Life and Letters* (New Haven; e-book 2012) MacMullen (2001) – MacMullen, R., "Punctuation and voice in expository prose," *Literary Imagination* 3 (2001) 1–17

MacMullen (2003) – MacMullen, R., *Feelings in History, Ancient and Modern* (Claremont CA; e-book 2012)

MacMullen (2003a) – MacMullen, R., "Historiens, attention: motivation = émotion," *Diogène* 2003, 3 (2003) 23–31

MacMullen (2006) – MacMullen, R., *Voting About God in the Early Church Councils* (New Haven; e-book 2012)

MacMullen (2011) – MacMullen, R., *The Earliest Romans. A Character Sketch* (Ann Arbor MI)

MacMullen (2014) – MacMullen, R., "The end of ancestor worship: affect and class," *Historia* 63 (2014)

Magnusson (1988) – Magnusson, D., *Individual Development from an Interactional Perspective: A Longitudinal Study* (Hillsdale NJ)

Malinowski (1922) – Malinowski, B., *Argonauts of the Western Pacific. An Account of Native Enterprise and Adventure in the Archipelagoes of Melanesian New Guinea* (London/New York)

Malinowski (1947) – Malinowski, B., *Freedom and Civilization* (London)

Malinowski (1979) – Malinowski, B., *The Ethnography of Malinowski: The Trobriand Islands 1915–18*, ed. M. W. Young (London)

Malle (2008) – Malle, B. F., "The fundamental tools, and possibly universals, of human social cognition," *Handbook of Motivation and Cognition Across Cultures*, eds. R. M. Sorrentino and S. Yamaguchi (San Diego) 267–96

Malle and Dickert (2007) – Malle, B. F., and S. Dickert, "Value," *Encyclopedia of Social Psychology*, eds. R. E. Baumeister and K. D. Vohs (Thousand Oaks CA) 2.1011–13

Malnic (1998) – Malnic, J., *Kula. Myth and Magic in the Trobriand Islands* (Wahroonga AU)

Mandler (2006) – Mandler, P., *The English National Character. The History of an Idea from Edmund Burke to Tony Blair* (New Haven)

Manners (1956) – Manners, R. A., "Functionalism, realpolitik, and anthropology in underdeveloped areas," *Theory in Anthropology. A Sourcebook*, eds. R. A. Manners and D. Kaplan (Chicago/New York 1968 [1956]) 156–68

Manson (1988) – Manson, W. C., *The Psychodynamics of Culture. Abram Kardiner and Neo-Freudian Anthropology* (New York)

Manuck et al. (2003) – Manuck, S. B., et al., "A neurobiology of intertemporal choice," *Time and Decision. Economic and Psychological Perspectives on Intertemporal Choice*, eds. G. Loewenstein et al. (New York) 139–72

Marcus (2004) – Marcus, G. [F.], *The Birth of the Mind. How a Tiny Number of Genes Creates the Complexities of Human Thought* (New York)

Marcus and Fischer (1986) – Marcus, G. E., and M. M. J. Fischer, *Anthropology as Cultural Critique. An Experimental Moment in the Human Sciences* (Chicago)

Markus and Hamedani (2007) – Markus, H. R., and M. G. Hamedani, "Sociocultural psychology. The dynamic interdependence among self systems and social systems," *Handbook of Cultural Psychology*, eds. S. Kitayama and D. Cohen (New York/London) 3–39

Markus and Kitayama (2003) – Markus, H. R., and S. Kitayama, "Culture, self, and the reality of the social," *Psychological Inquiry* 14 (2003) 277–83

Mathews (1992) – Mathews, H. F., "The directive force of morality tales in a Mexican community," *Human Motives and Cultural Models*, eds. R. Andrade and C. Strauss (Cambridge UK) 127–62

Matsumoto (1994) – Matsumoto, D., "Culture and emotion", *Cross-Cultural Topics in Psychology*, eds. L. L. Adler and U. P. Gielen (Westport CT) 115–24

McCleary (2007) – McCleary, R. M., "Salvation, damnation, and economic incentives," *Journal of Contemporary Religion* 22 (2007) 49–74 McClelland (1961) – McClelland, D. C., *The Achieving Society* (Princeton)

McCrae and Terracciano (2005) – McCrae, R. R., and A. Terracciano, "Universal features of personality traits from the observer's perspective: data from 50 cultures," *Journal of Personality and Social Psychology* 88 (2005) 547–61

McMillan (1994) – McMillan, J. F., "Social history, 'new cultural history', and the rediscovery of politics: some recent work on modern France," *Journal of Modern History* 66 (1994) 755–72

McSweeney (2002) – McSweeney, B., "Hofstede's model of national cultural differences and their consequences. A triumph of faith – a failure of analysis," *Human Relations* 55 (2002) 80–118

McSweeney (2002a) – McSweeney, B., "The essentials of scholarship: a reply to Geert Hofstede," *Human Relations* 55 (2002) 1363–72 Meek (1937) – Meek, C. K., *Law and Authority in a Nigerian Tribe. A Study in Indirect Rule* (London/New York)

Mehta and Josephs (2011) – Mehta, P. J., and R. A. Josephs, , "Social endocrinology: hormones and social motivation," *Social Motivation*, ed. D. Dunning (New York/London) 171–89

Mendes (2007) – Mendes, W. B., "Social facilitation," *Encyclopedia of Social Psychology*, eds. R. E. Baumeister and K. D. Vohs (Thousand Oaks CA) 2.897–901

Mendoza-Denton and Mischel (2007) – Mendoza-Denton, R., and W. Mischel, "Integrating system approaches to culture and personality. The cultural-cognitive-affective processing system," *Handbook of Cultural Psychology*, eds. S. Kitayama and D. Cohen (New York/London) 175–95

Mesquita and Leu (2007) – Mesquita, B., and J. Leu, "The cultural psychology of emotion," *Handbook of Cultural Psychology*, eds. S. Kitayama and D. Cohen (New York/ London) 734–59

Metcalf and Mischel (1999) – Metcalf, J., and W. Mischel, "A hot cool-system analysis of delay of gratification: dynamics of willpower," *Psychological Review* 106 (1999) 3–19

Middlekauff (2005) – Middlekauff, R., *The Glorious Cause. The American Revolution 1763–1789*, revised and expanded ed. (Oxford) Middleton (1965) – Middleton, J., *The Lugbara of Uganda* (New York)

Miller (1949) – Miller, J. C., *Origins of the American Revolution* (Boston)

Miller and Cohen (2001) – Miller, E. K., and J. D. Cohen, "An integrative theory of prefrontal cortex function," *Annual Review of Neuroscience* 24 (2001) 167–202

Miller et al. (1990) – Miller, J. G., et al., "Perceptions of social responsibilities in India and in the U.S.", *Journal of Personality and Social Psychology* 58, 1 (1990) 33–47

Mischel (1968) – Mischel, W., *Personality and Assessment* (Mahwah NJ)

Mischel (1984) – Mischel, W., "On the predictability of behavior and the structure of personality," *Personality and the Prediction of Behavior*, eds. R. A. Zucker et al. (Orlando FL) 209–68

Mischel (2004) – Mischel, W., "Toward an integrative science of the person," *Annual Review of Psychology* 55 (2004) 1–22

Mischel (2007) – Mischel, W., "Toward a science of the individual. Past, present, future?" *Persons in Context. Building a Science of the Individual*, eds. Y. Shoda et al. (New York) 263–77

Mischel and Gilligan (1964) – Mischel, W., and C. Gilligan, "Delay of gratification, motivation for the prohibited gratification, and responses to temptation," *Journal of Abnormal and Social Psychology* 69 (1964) 411–17

Mischel and Shoda (1995) – Mischel, W., and Y. Shoda, "A cognitive-affective system theory of personality: reconceptualizing situations, dispositions, dynamics, and invariance in personality structure," *Psychological Review* 102 (1995) 246–68

Mischel et al. (1988) – Mischel, W., et al., "The nature of adolescent competencies predicted by preschool delay of gratification," *Journal of Personality and Social Psychology* 54 (1988) 687–96

Mischel et al. (1989) – Mischel, W., et al., "Delay of gratification in children," *Science* 244 (1989) 933–38

Mischel et al. (2011) – Mischel, W., et al., "'Willpower' over the life span: decomposing self-regulation," *Social, Cognitive and Affective Neuroscience* 6 (2011) 252–56

Mishra (1994) – Mishra, R. C., "Individualist and collectivist orientations across generations," *Individualism and Collectivism. Theory, Method, and Applications*, eds. U. Kim et al. (Thousand Oaks CA) 224–38

Moffit et al. (2011) – Moffit, T. E., et al., "A gradient of childhood self-
control predicts health, wealth, and public safety," *Proceedings of the National Academy of Sciences* 108 (2011) 2693–98

Molitor and Hsu (2011) – Molitor, A., and H.-C. Hsu, "Child development across cultures," *Cross-Cultural Psychology. Contemporary Themes and Perspectives*, ed. K. D. Keith (Malden MA) 75–109

Mommsen (1989) – Mommsen, W. J., *The Political and Social Theory of Max Weber. Collected Essays* (Chicago)

Morgan and Morgan (1953) – Morgan, E. S., and H. M. Morgan, *The Stamp Act Crisis. Prologue to the Revolution* (Chapel Hill NC)

Morison and Commager (1942) – Morison, S. E., and H. S. Commager, *The Growth of the American Republic*, ed. 3, 2 vols. (New York/London) Morren (1984) – Morren, G. E. B., "Warfare on the Highland Fringe of New Guinea: the case of the Mountain Ok," *Warfare, Culture, and Environment*, ed. R. B. Ferguson (Orlando FL) 169–207

Moscovici (1984) – Moscovici, S., "The phenomenon of social representations," *Social Representations*, eds. R. M. Farr and S. Moscovici (Cambridge UK) 3–69

Moscovici (1985) – Moscovici, S., *L'âge des foules. Un traité historique de psychologie des masses*, ed. 2 (Paris)

Moscovici (1987) – Moscovici, S., "Answers and questions," *Journal of the Theory of Social Behaviour* 17, 4 (1987) 513–29

Moscovici (1998) – Moscovici, S., "The history and actuality of social representations," trans. G. Duveen, *The Psychology of the Social*, ed. U. Flick (Cambridge UK [Ger. 1995]) 209–73

Muffels (2003) – Muffels, R., "One European world of welfare or many: the role of values, behavior, and institutions," *The Cultural Diversity of European Unity. Findings, Explanations and Reflections from the European Values Study*, eds. W. Arts et al. (Leiden) 433–48

Mullin (1989) – Mullin, R. B., ed., *Moneygripe's Apprentice. The Personal Narratve of Samuel Seabury III* (New Haven)

Munn (1986) – Munn, N. D., *The Fame of Gawa. A Symbolic Study of Value Transformation in a Massim (Papua New Guinea) Society* (Cambridge UK)

Munslow (2007) – Munslow, A., *Narrative and History* (Houndmills UK/New York)

Munslow (2010) – Munslow, A., *The Future of History* (Houndmills UK/ New York) Murray (1951) – Murray, H. A., "Toward a classification of interactions," *Toward a General Theory of Action*, eds. T. Parsons and E. A. Shils (Cambridge) 434–64

Murty and Vyas (2006) – Murty, K. S., and A. G. Vyas, "Cultural constraints," *Encyclopedia of Anthropology*, ed. H. J. Birx (Thousand Oaks CA) 2.626–27

Nadel (1940) – Nadel, S. F., "The Kede: a riverain state in northern Nigeria," *African Political Systems*, eds. M. Fortes and E. E. Evans-Pritchard (Oxford) 164–95

Nader (1990) – Nader, L., *Harmony and Ideology. Justice and Control in a Zapotec Mountain Village* (Stanford)

Nado et al. (2009) – Nado, J., et al., "Moral judgment," *Routledge Companion to Philosophy of Psychology*, eds. J. Symons and P. Calvo (London/New York) 621–33

Newcomb (1950) – Newcomb, W. W., "A re-examination of the causes of Plains warfare," *American Anthropologist* 52 (1950) 317–31

Newson et al. (2007) – Newson, L., et al., "Cultural evolution and the shaping of cultural diversity," *Handbook of Cultural Psychology*, eds. S. Kitayama and D. Cohen (New York/ London) 454–76

Nisbett (1990) – Nisbett, R. E., "Evolutionary psychology, biology, and cultural evolution," *Motivation and Emotion* 14 (1990) 255–63

Nohria et al. (2008) – Nohria, N., et al., "Employee motivation. A powerful new model," *Harvard Business Review* 86 (2008) 78–84

Norris and Inglehart (2011) – Norris, P., and R. Inglehart, *Sacred and Secular. Religion and Politics Worldwide*, ed. 2 (Cambridge UK)

Novick (1988) – Novick, P., *That Noble Dream. The "Objectivity Question" and the American Historical Profession* (Cambridge UK)

Nozick (1993) – Nozick, R., *The Nature of Rationality* (Princeton) Nunner-Winkler (1999) – Nunner-Winkler, G., "Development of moral understanding and moral motivation," *Individual Development from 3 to 12. Findings From the Munich Longitudinal Studies*, eds. F. E. Weinert and W. Schneider (Cambridge UK) 253–90

Oakley (1992) – Oakley, J., *Morality and the Emotions* (London)

Oatley (2008) – Oatley, K., "The science of fiction," *New Scientist* 25 (2008) 42–43

Oatley (2011) – Oatley, K., "In the minds of others. Reading fiction can strengthen your social ties and even change your personality," *Scientific American.com/Mind* Nov./Dec 2011, 63–67

Obeyesekere (1997) – Obeyesekere, G., *The Apotheosis of Captain Cook. European Mythmaking in the Pacific, with an Afterword by the Author* (Princeton [1992])

Oelze (1991) – Oelze, B., *Wilhelm Wundt. Die Konzeption der Völkerpsychologie* (Münter/New York)

Oishi et al. (2008) – Oishi, S., et al., "Culture, interpersonal perceptions, and happiness in social interactions," *Personality and Social Psychology Bulletin* 34 (2008) 307–20

Okazaki et al. (2009) – Okazaki, S., et al., "Clinical personality assessment with Asian Americans," *Oxford Handbook of Personality Assessment*, ed. J. N. Butcher (Oxford) 377–95

Ortner (1984) – Ortner, S. B., "Theory in anthropology since the sixties," *Comparative Studies in Society and History* 26 (1984) 126–66
Ortner (1989) – Ortner, S. B., *High Religion: a Cultural and Political History of Sherpa Buddhism* (Princeton)
Otis (1764) – Otis, J., *The Rights of the British Colonies Asserted and Proved* (Boston)
Oyserman and Lee (2007) – Oyserman, D., and S. W.-S. Lee, "Priming 'culture'. Culture as situated cognition," *Handbook of Cultural Psychology*, eds. S. Kitayama and D. Cohen (New York/London) 255–79
Oyserman and Lee (2008) – Oyserman, D., and S. W.-S. Lee, "A situated cognition perspective on culture: effects of priming culture syndromes on cognition and motivation," *Handbook of Motivation and Cognition Across Cultures*, eds. R. M. Sorrentino and S. Yamaguchi (San Diego) 237–65
Ozer and Benet-Martínez (2006) – Ozer, D. A., and V. Benet-Martínez, "Personality and the prediction of consequential outcomes," *Annual Review of Psychology* 57 (2006) 401–21
Paine (1776) – Paine, T., *Common Sense Addressed to the Inhabitants of America*, 2nd ed. (London)
Parson and Shils (1962) – Parsons, T., and E. A. Shils, eds., *Toward a General Theory of Action* (New York [1951])
Pervin (1994) – Pervin, L. A., "A critical analysis of current trait theory," *Psychological Inquiry* 5 (1994) 103–13
Peters and Slovic (2000) – Peters, E., and P. Slovic, "The springs of action: affective and analytical information processing in choice," *Personality and Social Psychology Bulletin* 26 (2000) 1465–75
Peters et al. (2006) – Peters, E., et al., "Affect and decision making: a 'hot' topic," *Journal of Behavioral Decision Making* 19 (2006) 79–85
Peterson (1993) – Peterson, N., "Demand sharing: reciprocity and the pressure for generosity among foragers," *American Anthropologist* 95 (1993) 861–74
Pink (2009) – Pink, D. H., *Drive. The Surprising Truth About What Motivates Us* (New York)
Pinker (2002) – Pinker, S., *The Blank Slate. The Modern Denial of Human Nature* (New York/London)
Pizarro (2007) – Pizarro, D. A., "Moral emotions," *Encyclopedia of Social Psychology*, eds. R. E. Baumeister and K. D. Vohs (Thousand Oaks CA) 1.587–89
Plog (1995) – Plog, S., "Equality and hierarchy. Holistic approaches to understanding social dynamics in the Pueblo Southwest," *Foundations of Social Inequality*, eds. T. D. Price and G. M. Feinman (New York/London) 189–206
Popper (1962) – Popper, K. R., *The Open Society and Its Enemies*, 2 vols. (New York)
Quinlan and Quinlan (2007) – Quinlan, R. J., and M. B. Quinlan, "Parenting and cultures of risk: a comparative analysis of infidelity, aggression, and witchcraft," *American Anthropologist* 109 (2007) 164–79
Radcliffe-Brown (1940) – Radcliffe-Brown, A. R., "Preface," *African Political Systems*, eds. M. Fortes and E. E. Evans-Pritchard (Oxford) xi-xxii
Rawls (1971) – Rawls, J., *A Theory of Justice*, ed. 2 (Cambridge)
Reiser (1987) – Reiser, M., "Commonsense science and public opinion," *Journal of the Theory of Social Behaviour* 17, 4 (1987) 411–33
Ritter (1955) – Ritter, E. A., *Shaka Zulu. The Rise of the Zulu Empire* (London/New York)
Roberson et al. (2000) – Roberson, D., et al., "Color categories are not universal: replication and new evidence from a Stone-Age culture," *Journal of Experimental Psychology: General* 129 (2000) 369–98
Roberts (2009) – Roberts, B. W., "Back to the future: *Personality and Assessment* and personality development," *Journal of Research in Personality* 43 (2009) 137–45
Robins (2005) – Robins, R. W., "The nature of personality: genes, culture, and national character," *Science* 310 (2005) 62–63

Rogers (2003) – Rogers, E. M., *Diffusion of Innovations*, ed. 5 (New York/London)
Rogers (2011) – Rogers, D. T., *The Age of Fracture* (Cambridge)
Rohan (2007) – Rohan, M. J., "Value priorities," *Encyclopedia of Social Psychology*, eds. R. E. Baumeister and K. D. Vohs, (Thousand Oaks CA) 2.1009–11
Rokeach (1968) – Rokeach, M., *Beliefs, Attitudes and Values. A Theory of Organization and Change* (San Francisco)
Rosaldo (1980) – Rosaldo, M. Z., *Knowledge and Passion: Ilongot Notions of Self and Social Life* (Cambridge UK)
Rosaldo (1984) – Rosaldo, M. Z., "Toward an anthropology of self and feeling," *Culture Theory. Essays on Mind, Self, and Emotion*, eds. R. A. S. LeVine and R. A. LeVine (Cambridge UK) 137–57
Roscoe (2003) – Roscoe, P., "Margaret Mead, Reo Fortune, and mountain Arapesh warfare," *American Anthropologist* 105 (2003) 581–91
Ross (1984) – Ross, J. B., "Effects of contact on revenge hostilities among the Achuara Jivaro," *Warfare, Culture, and Environment*, ed. R. B. Ferguson (Orlando FL) 83–109
Roulin et al. (2012) – Roulin, A., et al., "Dominant nestlings displaying female-like melanin coloration behave altruistically in the barn owl," *Animal Behavior* 84 (2012) 1229–1236
Rousseau (2006) – Rousseau, J., *Rethinking Social Evolution. The Perspective from Middle-Range Societies* (Montreal)
Rudé (1959) – Rudé, G., *The Crowd in the French Revolution* (Oxford)
Sahlins (1972) – Sahlins, M.[D.], *Stone Age Economics* (New York)
Sahlins (1995) – Sahlins, M. D., *How Natives Think about Captain Cook, for Example* (Chicago)
Sahlins (2004) – Sahlins, M. [D.], *Apologies to Thucydides. Understanding History as Culture and Vice Versa* (Chicago)
Salzman (2000) – Salzman, P. C., "Hierarchical image and reality: the construction of a tribal chiefship," *Comparative Studies in Society and History* 42 (2000) 49–66
Sanderson (1941) – Sanderson, I. T., *Living Treasure* (New York)
Sapir (1924) – Sapir, E., "Culture, genuine and spurious," *American Journal of Sociology* 29 (1924) 401–29
Sapir (2010) – Sapir, E., *The Psychology of Culture: a Course of Lectures*, ed. J. T. Irvine (Berlin/New York)
Saucier (2009) – Saucier, G., "Recurrent personality dimensions in inclusive lexical studies: indications for a Big Six structure," *Journal of Personality* 77 (2009) 1577–1614
Saucier and Goldberg (2006) – Saucier, G., and L.-R. Goldberg, "Personalité, caractère et tempérament: la structure translinguistique des traits," *Psychologie française* 51 (2006) 265–84
Schroeder et al. (2010) – Schroeder, T., et al., "Moral motivation," *The Moral Psychology Handbook*, ed J. M. Doris et al. (Oxford) 72–110
Schütz and Vater (2007) – Schütz, A., and A. Vater, "Traits," *Encyclopedia of Social Psychology*, eds. R. E. Baumeister and K. D. Vohs (Thousand Oaks CA) 2.994–95
Schwartz (1980) – Schwartz, R. D., "Mores and the law: taking Sumner seriously," *Behavior Science Research* 15 (1980) 159–80
Schwartz (1994) – Schwartz, S. H., "Are there universal aspects in the structure and contents of human values?" *Journal of Social Issues* 50, 4 (1994) 19–45
Schwartz (2007) – Schwartz, S. H., "Value orientations: measurement, antecedents and consequences across nations," *Measuring Attitudes Cross-Nationally. Lessons from the European Social Survey*, eds. R. Jowell et al. (Los Angeles/London) 169–203
Segal (2012) – Segal, C., "Working when no one is watching: motivation, test-scores, and economic success," *Management Science* 58 (2012) 1438–57
Segall (2011) – Segall, E., "The court: a talk with Judge Richard Posner," *New York Review of Books*, September 29, 2011, 47

Seung (2013) – Seung, S., *Connectome. How the Brain's Wiring Makes Us Who We Are* (Boston/New York)

Shack (1985) – Shack, W. A., *The Kula. A Bronislaw Malinowski Centennial Exhibition* (Berkeley)

Shafer (1988) – Shafer G., "Savage revisited," *Decision Making. Descriptive, Normative, and Prescriptive Interactions*, eds. D. E. Bell et al. (Cambridge UK) 193–234

Shiller (1989) – Shiller, R. J., *Market Volatility* (Cambridge)

Shiller (2000) – Shiller, R. J., *Irrational Exuberance* (Princeton)

Shiner (2011) – Shiner, R. L., "Persons and situations act together to shape the course of human lives," *Social, Cognitive, and Affective Neuroscience* 6 (2011) 270–71

Shweder (1977) – "Likeness and likelihood in everyday thought: magical thinking in judgments about personality," *Current Anthropology* 18, 4 (1977) 637–48

Shweder (1984) – Shweder, R. A., "Anthropology's romantic rebellion against the enlightenment, or there's more to thinking than reason and evidence," *Culture Theory. Essays on Mind, Self, and Emotion*, eds. R. A. Shweder and R. A. LeVine (Cambridge UK) 27–66

Shweder and Bourne (1984) – Shweder, R. A., and E. J. Bourne, "Does the concept of the person vary cross-culturally?" *Culture Theory. Essays on Mind, Self, and Emotion*, eds. R. A. Shweder and R. A. LeVine (Cambridge UK) 158–199

Shweder and Sullivan (1993) – Shweder, R. A., and M. A. Sullivan, "Cultural psychology: who needs it?" *Annual Review of Psychology* 44 (1993) 497–523

Sider (2005) – Sider, G., "Anthropology and history: opening points for a new synthesis," *Critical Junctions. Anthropology and History Beyond the Cultural Turn*, eds. D. Kalb and H. Tak (New York/Oxford) 168–76

Slovic et al. (2002) – Slovic, P., et al., "The affect heuristic," *Heuristics and Biases. The Psychology of Intuitive Judgment*, eds. T. Gilovich et al. (Cambridge UK) 397–420

Smith and Kirby (2001) – Smith, C. A., and L. D. Kirby, "Affect and cognitive appraisal processes," *Handbook of Affect and Social Cognition*, ed. J. P. Forgas (Mahwah NJ) 75–92

Smith et al. (2006) – Smith, P. B., et al., *Understanding Social Psychology Across Cultures. Living and Working in a Changing World* (London/Thousand Oaks CA)

Smock (1971) – Smock, D. R., "A method for predicting success in rural development," *Themes in Culture (Essays in Honor of Morris E. Opler)*, eds. M. D. Zamora et al. (Quezon City, Philippines) 58–72

Southall (1970) – Southall, A. I., "The illusion of tribe," *Journal of Asian and African Studies* 5 (1970) 28–50

Spain (1982) – Spain, D. H., "Configuration and character in American anthropology: a reconsideration," *Crisis in Anthropology. View From Spring Hill*, 1980, eds. E. A. Hoebel et al. (New York) 165–85

Spencer (1872) – Spencer, H., *Social Statics, or, the Conditions Essential to Human Happiness* (New York [London 1850])

Spencer (1892) – Spencer, H., *The Principles of Ethics*, 2 vols. (London)

Sperber (1975) – Sperber, D., *Rethinking Symbolism*, trans. A L. Morton (Cambridge UK [1974])

Spiro (1999) – Spiro, M. E., "Anthropology and human nature," *Ethos* 27 (1999) 7–14

Stanovich (2002) – Stanovich, K. E., "Rationality, intelligence, and levels of analysis in cognitive science. Is dysrational possible?" *Why Smart People Can Be So Stupid*, ed. R. J. Sternberg (New Haven) 124–58

Stanovich and West (2000) – Stanovich, K., and R. West, "Individual differences in reasoning: implications for the rational debate," *Behavioral and Brain Sciences* 23 (2000) 645–65

Stewart (1999) – Stewart, M. A., "Rawls, John A.," *Cambridge Dictionary of Philosophy*, ed. R.Audi, ed. 2 (Cambridge UK) 774–75

Stickney (2009) – Stickney, L. T., "Affect and decision making," *Decision Sciences* 40, 2 (2009) 4–6

Stocking (1986) – Stocking, G. W., "Anthropology and the science of the irrational. Malinowski's encounter with Freudian psychoanalysis," *Malinowski, Rivers, Benedict and Others*, ed. G. W. Stocking (Madison WI) 13–49

Stowe (1911) – Stowe, C. E., *Harriet Beecher Stowe. The Story of Her Life* (Boston/New York)

Strauss (1992) – Strauss, C., "Models and motives," *Human Motives and Cultural Models*, eds. R. Andrade and C. Strauss (Cambridge UK) 1–20

Sullivan (2004) – Sullivan, G., "A four-fold humanity: Margaret Mead and psychological types," *Journal of the History of the Behavioral Sciences* 40 (2004) 183–206

Sullivan (2006) – Sullivan, G., "Culture and personality," *Encyclopedia of Anthropology*, ed. H. J. Birx (Thousand Oaks CA) 641–45

Swatos and Kivisto (2005) – Swatos, W. H., and P. Kivisto, "The contexts of the publication and reception of the *Protestant Ethic*," *The Protestant Ethic Turns 100. Essays on the Centenary of the Weber Thesis*, eds. W. H. Swatos and L. Kaelber (Boulder CO/London) 110–37

Tassinary and Cacioppo (1992) – Tassinary, L. G., and J. T. Cacioppo, "Unobservable facial actions and emotion," *Psychological Science* 3 (1992) 28–33

Taylor (1928) – Taylor, H. O., "A layman's view of history," *American Historical Review* 33 (1928) 247–56

Terraciano et al. (2005) – Terraciano, A., et al., "National character does not reflect mean personality trait levels in 49 cultures," *Science* 310 (2005) 96–100

Theissen (1983) – Theissen, G., *The Miracle Stories of the Early Christian Tradition*, trans. F. McDonagh, ed. J. Riches (Edinburgh; Ger. 1974)

Thompson (1964) – Thompson, E. P., *The Making of the English Working Class* (New York)

Thornton (2008) – Thornton, T. F., *Being and Place Among the Tlingit* (Seattle)

Tierney (2000) – Tierney, P., *Darkness in El Dorado: How Scientists and Journalists Devastated the Amazon* (New York)

Tilly (1981) – Tilly, C., *As Sociology Meets History* (New York/ London)

Tilly (2003) – Tilly, C., "Why read the classics?", Paper for the session on the Value of Classical Social Theory (Annual meeting, American Sociological Association, August 2003) 1–5 in http://professor-murman.info/index.php/weblog/tilly/ (as of Aug. 2012)

Tilly (2006) – Tilly, C., "Afterword: political ethnography as art and science," *Qualitative Sociology* 29 (2006) 409–12

Tomasello (2009) – Tomasello, M., *Why We Cooperate* (Cambridge)

Tomasello (2011) – Tomasello, M., "Human culture in evolutionary perspective," *Advances in Culture and Psychology*, ed. M. Gelfand (Oxford) 1–51

Tooby and Cosmides (1992) – Tooby, J., and L. Cosmides, "The psychological foundations of culture," *The Adapted Mind. Evolutionary Psychology and the Generation of Culture,* eds. J. H. Barkow et al. (Oxford) 19–137

Tov and Diener (2007) – "Culture and subjective well-being," *Handbook of Cultural Psychology*, eds. S. Kitayama and D. Cohen (New York/London) 691–713

Toynbee (1947) – Toynbee, A. J., *A Study of History*, abridged by D. C. Somervell, 2 vols. (Oxford)

Triandis (1989) – Triandis, H. C., "The self and social behavior in differing cultural contexts," *Psychological Review* 96 (1989) 506–20

Triandis (1995) – Triandis, H. C., *Individualism & Collectivism* (Boulder CO)

Triandis (2007) – Triandis, H. C., "Culture and psychology. A history of the study of their relationship," *Handbook of Cultural Psychology*, eds. S. Kitayama and D. Cohen (New York/ London) 59–76

Tribe (1988) – Tribe, K., "Translator's Introduction," *Max Weber. Essays in Reconstruction*, by W. Hennis, trans. K. Tribe (London) 1–17

Tribe (1971) – Tribe, L. H., "Trial by mathematics: precision and ritual in the legal process," *Harvard Law Review* 84 (1971) 1329–93

Trivers (1971) – Trivers, R. L., "The evolution of reciprocal altruism," *Quarterly Review of Biology* 46, 1 (1971) 35–57

Turiel (1977) – Turiel, E., "Distinct conceptual and developmental domains: social convention and morality," *Nebraska Symposium on Motivation* 25: *Social Cognitive Development* (Lincoln NE/ London) 77–116

Turiel (2006) – Turiel, E., "Thoughts, emotions, and social interactional processes in moral development," *Handbook of Moral Development*, eds. M. Killen and J. G. Smetana (Mahwah NJ/ London) 7–35

Turiel and Killen (2010) – Turiel, E., and M. Killen, "Taking emotions seriously: the role of emotions in moral development," *Emotions, Aggression, and Morality in Children: Bridging Development and Psychopathology*, eds. W. F. Arsenio and E. A. Lemerise (Washington DC) 33–52

Turner (1920) – Turner, F. J., "Social forces in American history", *The Frontier in American History* (New York) 311–34 Turner (1920a) – Turner, F. J., "Contributions of the West to American democracy," *The Frontier in American History* (New York) 243–68

Turner (1920b) – Turner, F. J., "The significance of the frontier in American history," *The Frontier in American History* (New York) 1–38

Turner (1961) – Turner, F. J., "The problem of the West," *Frontier and Section. Selected Essays of Frederick Jackson Turner*, ed. R. A. Billington (Englewood Cliffs NJ) 63–76 Turner (2000) – Turner, J. H., *On the Origins of Human Emotions. A Sociological Inquiry into the Evolution of the Human Affect* (Stanford)

Tversky and Kahneman (1988) – Tversky, A., and D. Kahneman, "Rational choice and the framing of decisions," *Decision Making. Descriptive, Normative, and Prescriptive Interactions*, eds. D. E. Bell et al. (Cambridge UK) 167–92

Tversky and Kahneman (2000) – Tversky, A., and D. Kahneman, "Loss aversion in riskless choice. A reference-dependent model," *Choices, Values, and Frames*, eds. D. Kahneman and A. Tversky (Cambridge) 143–58

Uhlmann et al. (2008) – Uhlmann, E. L., et al., "Implicit theism," *Handbook of Motivation and Cognition Across Cultures*, eds. R. M. Sorrentino and S. Yamaguchi (San Diego) 71–94

Vaillant (1983) – Vaillant, G. E., "Childhood environment and maturity of defense mechanisms," *Human Development. An Interactional Perspective*, eds. D. Magnusson and V. L. Allen (New York/London) 343–52

Vayda (1976) – Vayda, A. P., *War in Ecological Perspective. Persistence, Change, and Adaptive Processes in Three Occanian Societies* (New York/London)

Vaillant (1983) – Vaillant, G. E., "Childhood environment and maturity of defense mechanisms," *Human Development. An Interactional Perspective*, eds. D. Magnusson and V. L. Allen (New York/London) 343–52

Verbeek (2006) – Verbeek, P., "Everyone's monkey: primate moral roots," *Handbook of Moral Development*, eds. M. Killen and J. G. Smetana (Mahwah NJ/London) 423–59

Verdery (1995) – Verdery, K., "Introduction," *National Character and National Ideology in Interwar Eastern Europe*, eds. I. Banac and K. Verdery (New Haven) xiii-xxvi

Verdery (1995a) – Verdery, K., "National ideology and national character in interwar Romania," *National Character and National Ideology in Interwar Eastern Europe*, eds. I. Banac and K. Verdery (New Haven) 103–33

Verduyn et al. (2009) – Verduyn, P., et al., "Intensity profiles of emotional experience over time," *Cognition and Emotion* 23 (2009) 1427–43

Versnel (2011) – Versnel, H., *Coping With the Gods. Wayward Readings in Greek Theology* (Leiden)

Veyne (1976) – Veyne, P., *Le pain et le cirque: sociologie historique d'un pluralism politique* (Paris; edited by O. Murray in the translation by B. Pearce, *Bread and Circuses: Sociology and Political Pluralism*, London 1990)

Veyne (1988) – Veyne, P., *Did the Greeks Believe in Their Myths? An Essay on the Constitutive Imagination*, trans. P. Wissing (Chicago/London 1988 [1980])
Vickery (1973) – Vickery, J. B., *The Literary Impact of The Golden Bough* (Princeton)
Voget (1964) – Voget, F. W., "Warfare and the integration of Crow Indian culture," *Explorations in Cultural Anthropology. Essays in Honor of George Peter Murdock*, ed. W. H. Goodenough (New York) 483–509
Vuilleumier (2009) – Vuilleumier, P., "The role of the human amygdala in perception and attention," *The Human Amygdala*, eds. P. J. Whalen and E. A. Phelps (New York/London) 220–49
Waal (1991) – Waal, F. B. M. de, "The chimp's sense of social regularity and its relation to the human sense of justice," *American Behavioral Scientist* 34 (1991) 335–49
Waal (2005) – Waal, F. M. B. de, "Morality and the social instincts: continuity with the other primates," *Tanner Lectures on Human Values* 25, ed. G. B. Peterson (Salt Lake City UT) 1–39
Waal (2008) – Waal, F. M. B., "How selfish an animal? The case of primate cooperation," *Moral Markets. The Critical Role of Values in the Economy* (Princeton) 63–76
Wagner (1940) – Wagner, G., "The political organization of the Bantu of Kavirondo," *African Political Systems*, eds. M. Fortes and E. E. Evans-Pritchard (Oxford) 196–236
Wainryb (2006) – Wainryb, C., "Moral development in culture: diversity, tolerance, and justice," *Handbook of Moral Development*, eds. M. Killen and J. G. Smetana (Mahwah NJ/London) 211–40
Weber (1920) – Weber, M., *Gesammelte Aufsätze zur Religionssoziologie*, 6 vols. (Tübingen)
Weber (1978) – Weber, M., *Economy and Society. An Outline of Interpretive Sociology*, trans. E. Fischoff et al., eds. G. Roth and C. Wittich (Berkeley)
Weber (1991) – Weber, M., *From Max Weber: Essays in Sociology*, trans. H. H. Gerth and C. W. Mills, ed. 2 (London)
Weber (2008) – Weber, M., *The Protestant Ethic and the Spirit of Capitalism*, trans. T. Parsons (Lexington KY)
Weber (2008a) – Weber, M., *Roman Agrarian History in Its Relation to Roman Public & Civil Law*, trans. R. I. Frank (Claremont CA)
Wegner (2002) – Wegner, D. M., *The Illusion of Conscious Will* (Cambridge)
Weiner and Graham (1984) – Weiner, B., and S. Graham, "An attributional approach to emotional development," *Emotions, Cognition, and Behavior*, eds. C. E. Izard et al. (Cambridge UK) 167–91
Westermarck (1906) – Westermarck, E., *The Origin and Development of the Moral Ideas*, 2 vols. (London/New York)
Westermarck (1932) – Westermarck, E., *Ethical Relativity* (New York)
Weyer (1955) – Weyer, E., *Jungle Quest* (New York)
White (1968) – White, L. M., "On the concept of culture," *Theory in Anthropology. A Sourcebook*, eds. R. A. Manners and D. Kaplan (Chicago/New York) 15–20
White et al. (2011) – White, L. T., et al., "What is the meaning of 'on time'? The sociocultural nature of punctuality," *Journal of Cross-Cultural Psychology* 42 (2011) 482–93
Whiting et al. (1956) – Whiting, J. W. M., "The learning of values," *The People of Rimrock. A Study of Values in Five Cultures*, eds. E. Z. Vogt and E. M. Albert (Cambridge) 83–125
Wikan (1989) – Wikan, U., "Managing the heart to brighten face and soul: emotions in Balinese morality and health care," *American Ethnologist* 16 (1989) 294–312
Williams (2000) – Williams, S. J., "Is rational choice theory 'unreasonable'? The neglected emotions," *Rational Choice Theory. Resisting Colonization*, eds. M. S. Archer and J. Q. Tritter (London/New York) 57–72
Wilson (1995) – Wilson, E. O., "The morality of the gene," *Issues in Evolutionary Ethics*, ed. P. Thompson (Albany NY) 153–64
Wilson (1963) – Wilson, M., *Good Company. A Study of Nyakyusa Age-Villages* (Boston)
Wilterdink (1994) – Wilterdink, N., "Images of national character," *Society* 32 (1994) 43–51
Winter et al. (1981) – Winter, D. G., et al., *A New Case for the Liberal Arts* (San Francisco)

Winter et al. (1998) – Winter, D. G., et al., "Traits and motives: toward an integration of two traditions in personality research," *Psychological Review* 105 (1998) 230–50

Wolff (1971) – Wolff, P., "The 1391 pogrom in Spain. Social crisis or not?" *Past & Present* 50 (1971) 4–18

Wong et al. (2011) – Wong, S. W. H., et al., "Integrating fMRI psychophysiological measurements in the study of decision making," *Journal of Neuroscience, Psychology, and Econonomics* 4 (2011) 85–94

Wood (1992) – Wood, G. S., *The Radicalism of the American Revolution* (New York)

Wood (2009) – Wood, G. S., *Empire of Liberty. A History of the Early Republic, 1789–1815* (Oxford)

Wyatt-Brown (1982) – Wyatt-Brown, B., *Southern Honor. Ethics and Behavior in the Old South* (Oxford)

Young (1993) – Young, A. F., "Afterword," *Beyond the American Revolution. Explorations in the History of American Radicalism*, ed. A. F. Young (De Kalb NE) 317–64

Young (1999) – Young, A. F., *The Shoemaker and the Tea Party. Memory and the American Revolution* (Boston)

Young et al. (1991) – Young, C. H., et al., *Inventory of Longitudinal Studies in the Social Sciences* (Newbury Park PA)

Yu and Yang (1994) – Yu, A.-B., and K.-S. Yang, "The nature of achievement motivation in collectivist societies," *Individualism and Collectivism. Theory, Method, and Applications*, eds. U. Kim et al. (Thousand Oaks CA) 239–50

Zabell (1993) – Zabell, S., "A mathematician comments on models of juror decision making," *Inside the Juror. The Psychology of Juror Decision Making*, ed. R. Hastie (Cambridge UK) 262–69

Zajonc (1980) – Zajonc, R., "Feeling and thinking. Preferences need no inferences," *American Psychologist* 35 (1980) 151–75

Zajonc (1984) – Zajonc, R., "On the primacy of affect," *American Psychologist* 39 (1984) 117–23

Zajonc (1998) – Zajonc, R., "Emotions," *Handbook of Social Psychology*, ed. 4, eds. D. T. Gilbert et al. (Boston) 591–632

Zajonc and McIntosh (1992) – Zajonc, R. B., and D. N. McIntosh, "Emotions research: some promising questions and some questionable promises," *Psychological Science* 3 (1992) 70–74

Zak (2008) – Zak, P. J., "Introduction," *Moral Markets. The Critical Role of Values in the Economy*, ed. P. Zak (Princeton) xi-xxii

Zak et al. (2007) – Zak, P. J., et al., "Oxytocin increases generosity in humans," *Public Library of Science One*, Nov. 2007 e1128

Zhou et al. (2009) – Zhou, X., et al., "The factor structure of Chinese personality terms," *Journal of Personality* 77 (2009) 363–400

Index 1: Ideas

A

approximation 12, 22, 98, 106, 122f, 126f, 129
American Revolution 109–15
animals including insects, see social instinct
approval 7, 26, 30f, 94f

C

capitalism 1, 28, 41, 102f
class 5, 8, 84, 107–17, 131
cliometrics, see quantifiable
collectivism 24f, 32, 44, 97, 119ff
Confucianism 118ff
cross-cultural study 13f, 20, 22–28, 97, 99, 101, 126, 129

E

Economic Man 49, 57, 59, 61f, 64, 128
emotion 1f, 32, 46, 54f, 76, 85
– force of 55, 85f, 94, 110, 115, 121f
empathy 10, 12 89, 118, 131f
euergetism 2

F

feelings, see emotion

H

herd instinct 63, 74, 128
historical method 3–9, 85, 106, 115–18, 120ff, 124, 127, 130ff
homo sapiens 38, 57, 59, 67, 72

I

intuition 61, 74, 78, 81, 87, 96

J

jury trial 9–12, 66, 72, 131

K

kula 47f, 50f

L

law 66, 93, 110
laymen 16, 63ff, 66, 71
limbic system 77f, 88

M

mentalities 73

N

national character 1, 23ff, 44, 99, 101f, 106f, 120f
neuroscience 62, 75–81, 83, 90, 97f, 129f
new cultural 3–6, 8
nominalist, see realist

P

personality, individual 15–18, 28f
– modal 45f, 49, 106, 118, 126
– nation/group/ 13, 20, 22, 35, 41, 49, 55f; 99–122 passim; 125f
philosophy:
– see Index 3 (Plato, Aristotle) and Index 4 (Rawls, Spencer, Turiel)
Protestant ethic 102f
proverb(ial) 32, 72f, 99, 125

Q

quantifiable 9, 15, 17, 42, 57f, 64, 98, 123, 127

R

realist philosophy 8, 20, 36, 45, 54, 66f
relativism 19, 69–72, 84ff, 87, 94–97, 129f
religion 2, 39, 67–71, 93, 101ff

S

"science" 6f, 9f, 17, 38f, 98, 121, 123
social instinct (human) 7, 31, 54, 77, 80, 88ff, 96
– (non-human) 30, 88f, 133

species, animal/human 73, 75, 86–90

T

thought-feelings 79f, 128f

U

utility, utilitarian 49, 60, 65, 71, 91

Index 2: Peoples and Places

A

Africa 20, 22, 28, 34, 51f
American Indians 34, 43f
Ashanti 32
Asia 20, 22, 24, 28
Australia 2
Austria 25
Azande 72

B

Bali 79f
Boston 112, 114
Brazil 84
Britain 26, 92, 106f,. 109f

C

Canada 29, 31
China 22, 37
Croatia 22

E

Eskimo 39, 69
Ethiopia 68

F

France 101

G

Gabuku-Gama 53
Germany 20
Ghana 31, 35
Greece 22, 37
Greek (ancient) 37, 68ff, 87, 92

I

Iatmul 50
Iceland 20
Ifaluk 55
India 26, 96f
Indonesia 26, 42
Inuk 69
Iran 40
Ireland 108
Italy 26
Ivory Coast 35

J

Japan 21, 32, 86, 119
Java 34

K

Kedang 42
Kede 47
Kiriwinan Islands 47, 49
!Kung 28
Kwakiutl 35f

L

Latin America 28, 100
LoDagaa 35

M

Maasai 27
Malawi 51
Melanesia 47

N

Navaho 45
Netherlands 20
New Guinea 34, 39, 50, 53, 86
Niger River 47
Nigeria 43
Nuer 34
Nyakyusa 51

P

Papua 80
Paris 3f

Philadelphia 84
Poland 22, 35

S

Samoa 42
Sweden 20

T

Tahiti 47, 68
Tlingit 69
Toulouse 4
Trobriand Islands 38, 48
Truk 47
Turkey 22

Y

Yanomami 34, 43

Z

Zuni 37, 54

Index 3: Historical Individuals

A

Adams, John 111
Adams, John Quincy 100
Alcibiades 42
Aristotle 30, 52, 54, 73

B

Brummel, George "Beau" 42

C

Carlyle, Thomas 127
Cook, Capt. James 40, 68

D

Dostoevski, Fyodor 4
Dwight, Timothy 116f

E

Edwards, Jonathan 107

F

Franklin, Benjamin 104, 107f

G

Gage, Phineas 79
Guerre, Martin 4f

H

Herodotus 96
Hewes, George Robert Twelve 114, 132

J

Jefferson, Thomas 124

L

Lincoln, Abraham 132

M

MacIntosh, Ebenezer 112f
Monroe, James 100

O

Oliver, Andrew 112

P

Paine, Thomas 115, 133
Philip II of Spain 99f
Plato 54, 87, 93
Protagoras 19

R

Revere, Paul 127

S

Shaka 34
Stowe, Harriet Beecher 132f

T

Twain, Mark 4

Y

Yali 68

Index 4: Modern Authorities Discussed

A

Allport, Gordon 16, 21, 29
Aunger, Robert 55

B

Barnouw, Victor 45
Bateson, Gregory 45
Benedict, Ruth 36ff, 45
Bernard, Jessie 41f
Billington, Ray 116
Boas, Franz 35f, 41
Bolyanatz, Alex 72
Bourdieu, Pierre 52
Braudel, Fernand 99f
Briggs, Jean 31f, 39
Brosnan, Sarah 90

C

Cameron, William 17
Chagnon, Napoleon 43
Comte, Auguste 29

D

Damasio, Antonio 31, 77-80, 129
Darnton, Robert 3f
Darwin, Charles 30, 46, 89, 94
Davis, Natalie 3ff
Dülmen, Richard van 104
Durkheim, Emile 36

E

Engermann, Stanley 58f
Epstein, Seymour 16ff, 26, 65

F

Fisher, H. A. L. 6, 8
Fiske, Alan 95f
Fogel, Robert 58f
Frazer, James 67f
Freeman, Derek 42

G

Gammage, Bill 2
Geertz, Clifford 3, 5, 34
Genovese, Eugene 58f
Gilje, Paul 114
Ginzburg, Carlo 3
Gluckman, Max 38
Goody, Esther 31f
Gutman, Herbert 58

H

Haidt, Jonathan 84, 87, 91, 96
Hallowell, Irving 44
Harris, William 131
Hinde, Robert 13, 29
Hoerder, Dirk 111
Hofstede, Geert 24f
Hogan, Robert 30

K

Kahneman, Daniel 61ff, 65, 71, 74f
Keynes, John Maynard 63f
Kitayama, Shinobu 13, 119
Kohlberg, Lawrence 29, 84
Kousser, J. Morgan 10f
Kuper, Adam 54f, 72

L

Lang, Peter 76
Lévy-Bruhl, Lucien 69
Littelton, C. Scott 68f

M

Malinowski, Bronislaw 38, 48f, 57, 59, 68
Markus, Hazel 13, 119
Marx, Karl 57
Mauss, Marcel 39
McSweeney, Brendan 24
Mead, Margaret 36, 42
Mischel, Walter 15-18, 31

N

Nussbaum, Martha 66

O

Oatley, Keith 131f

P

Parsons, Talcott 52, 95
Piaget, Jean 29, 84, 91
Pink, Dan 10
Posner, Richard 66

R

Radcliffe-Brown, Alfred 37
Rawls, John 66, 71, 96
Rosaldo, Michelle 129

S

Sahlins, Marshall 45, 59, 72
Sapir, Edward 120
Saucier, Gerard 22, 27
Schwartz, Shalom 25f
Shiller, Robert 62, 64, 71, 74
Shils, Edward 52, 95
Shweder, Richard 28
Smock, David 43
Spencer, Herbert 37
Spengler, Oswald 37
Strauss, Claudia 52
Sullivan, Maria 28

T

Terman, Lewis 14
Tilly, Charles 102
Triandis, Harry 27
Tribe, Lawrence 9, 12
Turiel, Elliot 83ff
Turner, Frederick Jackson 115-18
Tversky, Amos 61ff

V

Verbeek, Peter 30
Verdery, Katherine 121f
Veyne, Paul 69

W

Waal, Frans de 88ff, 91
Weber, Max 102ff, 106ff
Wegner, Daniel 182f
Westermarck, Edward 90f
Weyer, Edward 39
Wood, Gordon 107, 112ff

Z

Zajonc, Robert 30, 76, 85

Bei Fragen zur Produktsicherheit wenden Sie sich bitte an:
If you have any questions regarding product safety,
please contact:

Walter de Gruyter GmbH
Genthiner Straße 13
10785 Berlin
productsafety@degruyterbrill.com